MORE THAN YOU KNOW

MATT GOSS

More Than You Know

The Autobiography

HarperCollins*Entertainment*
An Imprint of HarperCollins*Publishers*

HarperCollins*Entertainment*
An Imprint of HarperCollins*Publishers*
77–85 Fulham Palace Road,
Hammersmith, London W6 8JB

www.harpercollins.co.uk

Published by HarperCollins*Entertainment* 2005
1 3 5 7 9 8 6 4 2

A catalogue record for this book
is available from the British Library

ISBN 0 00 720145 1

Set in PostScript Linotype Sabon by
Rowland Phototypesetting Ltd, Bury St Edmunds, Suffolk

Printed and bound in Great Britain by
Clays Ltd, St Ives plc

*Dedicated to my grandad, Samuel Matthew Read –
aka Harry – I love you*

Contents

Acknowledgements

Special thanks: to all my family; Richard Smith, Gary Howard, and all at Mission Control; Peter Blomqvist, Max Bloom, Roseann McBride, Aaron Labatte, and all at Concept Music.; Joe Bradley; Stephen Emms, Nadia Khan and all at Emms Publicity; Charlie Lycett; Mick Garbutt; Michael Metcalf; Jackie Brambles; Neil Fox; Schooley; Eva Simpson; Jessica Callan; Nikki Waldegrove; Matt Connolly and all the staff at Fleming Connolly Lander; Barrie Marshall and all the staff at Barrie Marshall Arts; Rick Vaughan; Steve Hulme; Mark Hamilton; Joe T. Vanelli and all at J.T. Company; Rob Ferguson; Annette Barrett; Martin, Kaye & Alfie; Steve Martin; Abigail Magnus; Leyton Bracegirdle; Sheena Mason; Rachel Seagrave; Phil Byrne; David Ravden; my band and all the musicians I have worked with over the years (thank you, guys, you all know who you are); to all my fans . . . you continue to be a source of real strength for me.

Picture Acknowledgements

All photographs supplied by Matt Goss with the exception of the following:

Classic Bros © Hilaneh von Kories/London Features International

Bros winning the Brit award for 'Best Newcomers' in 1989 © Ilpo Musto/London Features International

11,000 fans waited for a signed album at HMV in Oxford St © Ilpo Musto/London Features International

The infamous Brosettes © Eugene Adebari/Rex Features

The power of performance . . . © Frank Griffin/London Features International

A memory I will never forget . . . © Eugene Adebari/Rex Features

Me and Prince Charles © Tim Graham/Corbis

A great moment . . . © Christopher Jackson/Getty Images

Whilst every effort has been made to trace the owners of copyright material reproduced herein, the publishers would like to apologise for any omissions and will be pleased to incorporate missing acknowledgement in any future editions.

ONE

Innocent As Snow

When I was a little boy and had toothache, my grandad would lay his hand on my cheek and the pain would go away. I can still feel the roughness of his builder's hands on my young face. His home, a flat in Crawford Road, Camberwell, south-east London was an emotional anchor for my childhood, one of the few constants in my early life, along with my twin brother Luke and my mum. We moved house so often, nine times in all. That flat was the only place that stayed the same. At that tender age, I knew so little of what lay ahead. No one could have possibly predicted I would lead a life as exciting, traumatic, extreme, painful, loving and rewarding as I have. There would be so many moments of such exhilaration that I felt as if I'd been blessed. There would also be several times when I would wish that Grandad could have laid his hands on me and made the pain go away. Back then, as long as the toothache subsided, I was happy.

For the first five years of my life, everything seemed normal. Mum and Dad had fallen for each other in, of all places, a hospital, when my mum and her sister Ann were visiting their gran. My parents were both very stylish, shared a passion for music and quickly fell madly in love with each other. My dad, Alan Goss, was a bit of a Mod and my mum, Carol Read, liked the way the Mods dressed. They were both barely into their twenties but the relationship was immediately very intense – so much so that less than a year after they first met, Mum accepted Dad's proposal of marriage, at Christmas 1967.

Mum was the middle of three kids and, unusually, was exactly twelve years older than her younger sister, my Aunt Sally. There must be something in the family genes about babies arriving on the same day! Reading between the lines, I think Mum sometimes felt a little bit of a piggy-in-the-middle, with Ann being the first-born and Sally being the apple of her parents' eye, the baby. But Mum never complained, ever. It's just not her way. Besides, she was very close to both her parents. When her mum died, on Bonfire Night, 1971, my mum was devastated.

Grandad was bereft. His wife Win was everything to him. She was a very spiritual lady and their hearts were seamlessly dovetailed. Grandad's full name is Samuel Matthew Read (which is where I get my Christian name) but most people know him as Harry. He was a gunner in the Second World War and his trade throughout most of his life was as a builder's foreman. He'd planned on studying to become a surveyor but the army interrupted that; on his return from war, he found work in a trade desperate for labour to help rebuild the capital. Consequently, he worked on the construction of some of London's many important buildings.

When he lost his wife, rather than disown his faith, Grandad leaned towards it. Although he was a bit of a ruffian, Grandad found that he had a gift and subsequently became a faith healer. Obviously, many people are sceptical of this whole subject, but I have seen what he is capable of with my own eyes. I could choose from scores of incidents to illustrate this. For example, many years ago, a man who'd heard about Grandad's gift came to Crawford Road, explained that he had been diagnosed with brain cancer and given only three months to live. He asked only that Grandad help him to prepare for what was coming. Along with a friend, Grandad gave this man intense healing. One month passed, then two, then three and still there were no signs of this man's physical or mental deterioration. Then the cancer started to regress. Eventually, the disease was just a single, small tumour which surgeons were able to remove successfully. That man is still alive to this day.

You can call that the power of the mind enhanced by positive energy if you like, but in essence that is what healing is. The fact is, this actually happened. It is also true that my toothache would miraculously dissipate when Grandad placed his hand on my cheek. But I don't know how he brought my goldfish back to life one day! This fish was as dead as can be, completely still and I was crying my eyes out. Grandad went upstairs and gave it a little rub and next thing I knew, it was alive again. My cynical side might think he replaced it with a new one, the sleight-of-hand approach to faith healing! But it meant the world to me regardless.

Grandad can also do psychometry, whereby you give him an item – a necklace, ring, or a coin for example – and he will give you a reading from it. I believe that both my twin brother Luke and I have inherited some of these abilities. We can both do healing to a degree, and I definitely have psychic tendencies. Yet, if I had foreseen the life I was about to lead, I would not have believed it.

My father's family situation was altogether different to my mother's. His own father left the family home when Dad was just a little boy and his mum later remarried. His family lived in a council house in Dulwich but he never knew his father growing up (although he eventually went looking for him, more of which later). Unfortunately, once I reached the age of five, there were certain parallels in my own childhood with what my father went through.

Luke and I arrived on 29 September 1968 at Lewisham Hospital. It hadn't been an easy pregnancy for my mum – at twelve weeks there was a concern about a possible miscarriage which required her to be hospitalized. We were born eight weeks prematurely and even after Luke was delivered from my mother's womb, no one knew that she was carrying twins. In fact, they cut the umbilical cord after Luke was born, thinking that was that, but that meant I was inside my mum being starved of oxygen. Doctors later said that Luke and I had been curled up back-to-back and thus our heartbeats had been exactly synchronized. As my lungs did not inflate properly, I was a 'blue baby' so along with my brother I was rushed straight into an incubator and fed intravenously. The early arrival meant that we had no eyelashes or nails and were both worryingly underweight, coming in at just over four pounds each – I was slightly heavier than Luke even though I was born eleven minutes later. Mum spent only ten days in hospital, despite it being a distressing birth, but she and Dad had to visit us in our little plastic hospital cocoons for some time – Luke for a month, myself for six weeks – before they could take us home.

Mum and Dad were living at 94 Tressillian Road, a one-bedroom flat in Brockley at the time, with Mum working as a hairdresser and telephonist and Dad working long hours within the souvenir supply trade. They had very little money and with Dad away working so much, Mum was faced with most of the day-to-day demands of looking after twins. Perhaps inevitably, the stresses and strains on this young couple gradually began to take their toll and erode that idealistic and exhilarating love they had felt when they first met. Dad left briefly when we were less than three years old, but he and Mum soon reconciled.

I'm not going to pretend that I have vivid memories of every house we lived in and every street on which I wandered as a child: I don't. My mind is a scramble of different addresses, friends made then lost, countless new school gates and the repeated realization that we were moving once more and it was going to start all over again. What I do recall are certain events, particular moments of extreme clarity in that transient haze, like stark rays of sun piercing a mist. When I think of these moments, they are absolutely crystal-clear, as if I had lived them only yesterday.

One of my earliest memories is of a house in Bramdean Crescent in Lee, before I was even of school age. It was a three-bedroom terraced house with an extra feature – it was haunted. Mum hated it there because of this presence – a very dark spiritual energy – and eventually we left. We weren't going to be one of those families in the horror movies where they check out the cellar and make friends with ghosts. It was very unsettling indeed.

In 1973, when Luke and I were heading towards our fifth birthday, we all went on holiday to Majorca. Put simply, this was the last time in my childhood that I remember feeling part of a family. My mum and dad just looked *so* good together. I thought my dad was incredibly handsome (and still do), with his dark hair and piercing blue eyes; Mum was beautiful, so fair-haired and with beautiful green eyes. Of course, during the holiday they acquired lovely sun-tans – the weather was amazing – so I have this overriding memory of them being very brown, healthy and just so good-looking. They were wearing

Seventies gear that was the height of fashion and they looked extremely cool. I was bursting with pride.

I cherish so many good memories of that holiday. My parents would go out for dinner looking fantastic and come back full of chatter, having had a great night. I can still see myself running through the streets of Majorca with Luke, both of us holding Dad's hands as he said, 'You've got to see the bull in this shop! You've got to see this!' When we got there, breathless and laughing, there was a huge stuffed bull from a local bullfight. It was quite scary, but it was so exciting as well for Dad to run with us all that way to make sure we saw it. That's what dads do.

We stayed in a lovely villa. One night when Mum and Dad were out having a meal, there was a violent thunderstorm. I was upstairs, walking around in the dark looking out of the windows at the black clouds and torrential rain. Next thing I knew, I was lying winded on a bed *downstairs*. Luke was shouting out, 'Matt! Where are you?'

'I'm downstairs!' I replied, totally confused. I hadn't noticed the edge of a balcony and walked straight off, falling down a floor and on to a bed. We laughed so much.

I also squashed a cockroach with my bare feet, a big black cockroach, which was fairly unpleasant. Luke and I would play in the pool for hours – I had a Dumbo inflatable and Luke had a Mickey Mouse; I can still smell those rubber rings to this day. Silly memories, important memories. Family memories.

Reminiscing about that holiday, I can still sense the sun-tan oil in my nose, I can still picture Mum and Dad looking so bronzed and stunning, I can still feel the excitement and emotion of being a proper family welling up inside me. In my adult life, I have been fortunate enough to travel the world many times and enjoy some wonderful holidays, but that time in Majorca was easily one of the best holidays of my life.

Unfortunately, it was also to be my last happy memory of childhood for a while. Three weeks after we came back, my dad left home – for good.

Who knows what undercurrents had been bubbling between Mum and Dad in Majorca. They certainly did not allow any problems between them to spoil that fabulous holiday. In retrospect, that must have been very difficult for both of them and I am grateful that we were shielded in that way, even though it made what was about to happen back at home a very sharp shock.

I have a vivid memory of the night when my dad actually left. Mum sat Luke and me on the windowsill, and said, 'Dad won't be coming home, me and your dad aren't going to be living together any more, he loves you deeply but . . .' That was the beginning of a feeling of strangeness in my life.

From then on, my childhood felt somewhat transient, emotionally and physically. It was very disjointed and hard to feel connected to one place. To feel *safe*. That's never changed, particularly with what I do for a living. I have such a need to feel safe in my life – but I don't feel safe. I think this undercurrent started that night on the windowsill.

While we were in Majorca, I thought, *This is so fantastic, I hope we can do this all again next year.* That's how you view things when you are so young. But it wasn't to be. With Mum and Dad separated, there would never be enough money to take us away to such glorious places again. Even if there had been, that sense of family would not have been there anyway. It just wouldn't have been the same.

I am so conscious of talking about these events, but I must preface it by pointing out it's just one of those situations that happens in life; it's nobody's fault. Separation is not easy on anyone. Dads go through loss, mums go through loss, and husbands and wives go through loss. But purely on the level of being a child, the starkest realization was that we were not going to go back to Majorca next year after all. It's also strange how after Mum and Dad separated, I became so much more aware of certain elements that I'd previously been blissfully ignorant of. Suddenly, school was full of other kids from broken homes, little people with secret histories.

By the time my parents separated, my father had been a policeman in the City of London force for over two years. He'd trained when Luke and I were two and a half, and even back then there were tensions between him and Mum. When we went to Majorca, we were living in a police house at 17 Priestley Road, Mitcham; that provided our family with a level of security that was very welcome. Unfortunately, the crumbling edifice of my parents' marriage never matched the solidity of a safe, secure police house.

Separation and divorce were not looked upon in a very good light within the force, so it was an especially difficult time for both Mum and Dad. One unsettling memory I do have of the police house in Mitcham is that for a couple of weeks, a man stood outside our home. We were never sure of what was going on but it might possibly have been someone watching to see if Mum was living with anyone, because there are obviously rules about who lives in a police house. We reported this to the police, as did several neighbours. Sometimes this man would be sitting in a car and other times he would stand by our hedge reading a newspaper. We were only kids and it scared the hell out of us but it was especially disturbing for Mum.

My early childhood was painful, constantly seeing my mother in tears, genuinely aching. Every night she would come in to our bedroom and give us a kiss, then sing us to sleep, songs like 'American Pie' and 'Fly, Fly Superbird' – I can hear her singing them now. But then she would leave the room and we would wait for her to start crying. Many years later, I wrote a song which my mum doesn't know about called 'Ms Read', her maiden name; 'I can hear you crying Ms Read'. It was very sad to see her like that.

Mum always did her crying in private, and tried to shield us from as much as she could. We knew she was upset but we were only little and we didn't always know how to approach her; all we really wanted to do was give her a cuddle and make her feel better.

The break-up of my parents' marriage hit us very hard. Its effects manifested themselves in many ways. One night my mum went out of the front door to go to the phone box. It was dark, being around nine o'clock, and Luke and I flew into a blind panic. We screamed and screamed, tears pouring down our cheeks, and ran out of the house. Mum was really startled and said, 'What's wrong? What on earth is wrong?' We'd thought she was going to leave us.

I can still feel the chill of the fear that I had, thinking she was not going to come back. It's an awful memory. 'Of course I was coming back, my loves. I'm just popping to the phone box.' Mum was brilliant, she went back inside and zipped us up in our parka coats over our pyjamas and held our hands down to the phone box. She was smiling and being so lovely with us to cheer us up, but inside that must have been a terrible thing for her to see.

I don't know how we got by. One afternoon, Luke and I wanted to do something but we had no money. We asked Mum but she said, 'Look, I've got nothing,' and she opened her purse to show us a single twopence coin. Then she went to the phone box and, as we followed her, it started raining heavily. We stood outside and watched Mum put the coin in to phone her dad – that was what calls cost in those days. We had to wait outside and watch Mum hunched over the phone, absolutely sobbing to her father. It was pouring down with rain by now and it was an awful moment. I just felt so useless.

But then, we looked down at the ground and there was a one-pound note, just lying there in front of us. That was a lot of money, a week's food at least. A crumpled, green, old one-pound note. I picked it up and started banging on the phone box window. No answer from Mum. Again, Bang! Bang! Bang! Mum was still crying and shouted, 'Hold on!'

So I did it again.

Bang! Bang! Bang! Finally, she looked round and there we were, standing in the teeming rain, proudly holding up this note. We didn't say anything, just held it up. Mum looked at the money and then at our beaming faces and said, 'I've gotta go, Dad!'

We ran home holding her hands, sprinted upstairs and put the note on the boiler, then just sat there, the three of us, waiting for it to dry. And as the dampness evaporated, the edges of the note started to curl up and there was another one stuck to it. It was one of the most insanely amazing moments ever. I just kept thinking, 'You could buy two hundred Black Jacks with that,' but in my heart of hearts, I knew that putting food on the table was more important.

Another time, my mum slipped a disc and my brother and I kept her alive on jam sandwiches for a week. She could not move out of bed, so we made her cups of tea and jam sandwiches. We were really proud of ourselves, looking after her when she was always so doting on us. Luke and I are her life, always have been, sometimes to the point where I feel guilty, she has put so much into us. She is my angel.

One time when I was eight, I really needed my angel. For some reason, my knee had swollen up to quite a size, it looked very odd. They took me in for a check-up and said they would have to investigate further as it wasn't clear what the problem was. I was taken to the local hospital and all sorts of doctors and people in white coats busied themselves around me. Eventually, they inserted a huge needle into my leg to scrape cultures off the kneecap. Unfortunately, it is very difficult to anaesthetize the kneecap because of the lack of muscle and the proximity of the bone to the skin, so I had no painkillers. I was in agony. To this day I have a very strong phobia about needles and I don't think you have to be a psychologist to work out why.

Tests were done and I was told I'd have to stay in for ten days. One day, Mum came to visit and was talking to a doctor by my bedside when he asked her to go outside. Once they were out of the room, he talked to her in somewhat hushed tones. Mum came back in all teary, although desperately trying to look cheerful. I later found out that they suspected I had septic arthritis and among all the sheaves of paperwork Mum had had to sign and agree to, one had asked for her consent to amputate my leg. That's a dreadful position for any parent to be placed in.

Fortunately, the swelling began to subside and it turned out that there was no lasting damage. Nonetheless, I had to sit there for ten days which, to an eight-year-old boy, seemed like for ever. My dad bought me a little wooden box that had a maze and some ball-bearings in it. It was like some Stone Age Gameboy, it predated hand-held computer games, but I bloody loved it, it was such a good present. I spent hours every day trying to get the little silver balls to tumble their way through the maze to the finish. That simple little toy got me through those ten endless days. I wish it had been as easy for Mum and Dad. Eventually I was sent home with a clean bill of health (a bout of measles had also sent me to hospital so I should have been used to it!).

There was still the fear within me though, a constant sleeping partner. One result of this was that I wet the bed up until I was in my early teens. I used to put three felt-tip pens vertically under my wet sheet to lift it off the mattress so it could dry, then I would try to sleep on the floor. When I heard Mum coming to my room in the morning, I would knock the pens away quickly so that when Mum felt the sheet it would be dry. There was so much fear. As trivial as it sounds, I truly believe in talking about this unwelcome habit – kids go through hell, the fear of not wanting to wet the bed so badly it makes them do it anyway.

Eventually, my dad took all the pressure off me and his intervention really helped. He told me to hit the pillow with my fist the number of times that coincided with what time I wanted to wake up and go to the toilet. I did exactly that, I woke up and went to the toilet when I wanted to and the next morning I hadn't wet the bed. It took me a further two years to believe I had finally stopped.

When I try to claw back memories of that time, it all feels very musty to me, not lived in, painfully desolate. I don't like remembering back then and I don't get a nice feeling when I think of those early years. The house in Mitcham holds very little but cold memories for me. I didn't wake up looking forward to the day, I genuinely didn't. That's a sad way for a young chap to feel.

I always used to like lying under things, tables, chairs, hiding. Always hiding. There was one particular table made out of a solid piece of wood and that was my favourite hiding-place, my sanctuary.

One Saturday, my mum's sister got married and Lukie and me were asked to be pageboys. We were both so excited; we were given tuxedos and were even bought new shoes from

Clark's – they were expensive and it felt like we'd won the football pools because we were shopping there. It was a great day but when we came back to the police house, the back window was smashed and there was blood smeared on the remaining shards. Bloody fingerprints were on the window and the door handle. It was very frightening. We didn't know if an intruder was still in the house and Mum was on her own with six-year-old twins. We anxiously walked in through the damaged door to find that every stick of furniture had gone. Everything – even my little table.

TWO

This Lonely River

Luke and I were eight years old when my mum met her future husband, Tony Phillips. Prior to that, she had been very considerate to us, she hadn't really had any boyfriends, even though times had been very difficult for her and she must have craved adult company and support.

We were still living at the police house in Mitcham when we first started noticing the man who was making our mum smile again. For the initial few times, we only saw Tony briefly to say 'Hello'. Over a few weeks, he started seeing Mum more often, and then one night we heard our dog Tiny barking frantically and realized that Tony was coming up the stairs. He calmly walked into our bedroom, introduced himself to us and – rather brilliantly – told us a story. Looking back, it must have taken some courage for him to do that and likewise for Mum to let him, but it was a lovely gesture and I can remember the tale as if he had only told it yesterday.

It was about a magnificent bird in a forest, the fastest and most beautiful bird of all, which for some reason had lost its feathers. The bird was very sad but all the other animals in the forest saw this and decided to collect together bits of their own feathers and fur for him. Tony told the story so well; I remember lying there entranced, desperately wanting to know the ending. Then, Tony explained, using honey from the bees the animals stuck this collection of feathers and fur on to the bird, which once more became the fastest and most beautiful creature living in the forest. It was a happy ending for the bird and I remember that moment, it was very peaceful.

It was such a simple and lovely story. It was a long time since we'd had a man come in and say goodnight to us. Tony is a peaceful and calm person, he doesn't get fazed easily and it was the first moment for as long as I could remember where there was an element of order and peace in our life.

There was one aspect of Tony that was out of order, however, and that was the dodgy tartan trousers he used to wear (he knows I have to reveal that). At first he also drove a rather nice 7 Series BMW and then an E-Type (he owned a garage at the time), both of which were dream cars to us two boys, given how little money we had at home. One day Tony explained that regretfully he was short of money as well and would be swapping the BMW for a Morris Minor. That's quite some leap backwards. So, after a brief flirtation with leather seats and sports trims, it was back to Skintsville in the Goss household.

Although Tony brought a sense of peace and calm to our house, I didn't really feel any more secure. Unfortunately, he was going through a divorce, like Mum, so he had no money either. However, what he also brought into the house was Carolyn and Adam, his two children and, with their entry into my life, I have at times felt like the richest boy in the world.

When I first met Adam, he looked like a gargoyle: he had the biggest mouth. I used to think that he could swallow an apple whole. Over the years, his mouth has stayed pretty much the same size, but the rest of his body has caught up.

He was really only a baby when we first met, six years old. I don't know how I can accurately explain my initial feelings towards them but he and Carolyn just *fitted*. We seemed tailor-made for each other. We never *ever* had any problems connecting. Two families colliding like that can produce a source of great tension, but with Adam and Carolyn there was only ever a tangible sense of gain when they came into my life. I thought 'Wow! We have a bigger family now!' It felt like we were a little bit less destructible.

With Adam, we felt very connected. He would always be pulling funny faces, keeping us laughing. Actually, back then he was very frail, he had really severe asthma, wheezing all the time and his health suffered terribly. However, this didn't stop him playing around and being a lot of fun to be with.

There was also a swift emotional connection with Adam's sister Carolyn. I'm quite a tactile person, Carolyn was too and she was very kind with it. She was such a beautiful person, even at the tender age of seven she wanted to do more for the world. She was very clever too – she went on to pass ten 'O' levels and three 'A' levels before lining up a university degree. They both reminded me of Tony. It might sound an obvious statement to make, but Carolyn was like a girl-version of Tony and Adam was simply a boy-version of Tony.

Previously, I'd felt quite vulnerable. We all did at times, me and Mum and Dukus, as I often called my twin brother (he would call me Maffy). When I say I felt vulnerable, that is not because of my dad not being there, it is just the way I felt. Then Adam and Carolyn arrived and I suddenly felt that there were a few more people in the gang, a bigger team, we were a little bit less vulnerable. I also sensed that Adam and Carolyn were, like me and Luke, rather weary. They had gone with their mother when she and Tony had split up and there had been much pain on both sides. Of course we were only young so we would still lark about, but there was definitely an unspoken acknowledgement of being a little bit bruised from the break-ups.

Divorce is just something that happens in life, you can't say who's right and who's wrong. What you can say is it's a fact that when parents split up, emotional upheaval is the inevitable result. Whether parents like it or not, such events do affect kids. It hurts them. They are not stupid, they want to do the right thing for their parents, be there for them and not whinge, but this also means that they have quite evolved feelings of pain and confusion.

When you put a couple of new kids into the mix, it can often polarize emotions and cause even more friction. However, for me at least, it created this strange reassurance that I wasn't the only one feeling a little battered. Within a matter of a few weeks, whenever I knew Tony's two kids were visiting I would be shouting, 'Oh wow! Adam and Carolyn are coming round!'

And yet, for all the pain that Adam and Carolyn had obviously gone through, part of me was oddly glad that their parents had split, at least in the sense that it brought Tony to my mum. I couldn't love Tony more. As a boy Tony was in a cast for two years from the waist down – the doctors didn't know if he was even going to be able to walk again. He's since had two hip replacements but has never moaned about his pain; that's not his style. Tony is not the tallest man in the world but he has not a shred of a Napoleon complex about him. Although he is quite a small guy, mentally he is a rock. I am so lucky, he's a great step-dad.

When my dad came to see us, I do remember some good times. We went down to the local swamp one afternoon and caught a load of frogs. We triumphantly took them back to the house and made a rock pool for them out of a plastic container, some stones and tap water. It was the summer of 1976, which was the hottest English summer for over two hundred years. There was something about that summer that seems to have stuck in the minds of many, many people. It wasn't a good summer for my frogs, though. I went out to play one day and innocently forgot to top up their water. When I came back there were just these raisins with legs stuck to the rocks! There wasn't a drop of water left, it had all evaporated, leaving behind this sorry collection of green Californian raisins with legs. I was gutted.

Like most young boys, we got up to lots of typically cheeky behaviour that warms my heart when I recall it. Just silly, innocent childhood stuff like kids do. I remember having a look at Jennifer-who-lives-opposite-the-corner-shop's bum and front bum. She had one of each, we were amazed to learn. Me and Dukus hid in a wardrobe which had no doors, at the back of our garage, with Jen in the middle, and we showed her our bums and she showed us both of hers. Jen had her knickers down when my mum walked into the garage. All three of us stood stiff as a board, terrified that Mum would find us with Jen showing us her bits. Luckily, Mum left and we had got away with it.

There were two girls next door with whom we had a little bit of a schoolboy feel, but I wasn't too keen because they had noses like rabbits. Worse still, they actually constantly twitched their noses *like* rabbits, it was very disconcerting for a little boy. Even now, when I think of them, I can't remember what they actually looked like, I just remember thinking of them as rabbits. Proper rabbits.

Dukus and I would often throw darts the length of the playing field but one time I didn't get out of the way quickly enough and it stuck in my rib. I went indoors and showed Mum. She just calmly pulled it out of me and said, 'Go on then, carry on playing.'

We finally moved from Mitcham to a house in Herongate Road in Cheshunt, which Tony and Mum had managed to buy. Yet again Luke and I had to start another school, this time St Clement's Church School. By then I enjoyed sports and particularly excelled at athletics, specifically the long jump, triple jump, high jump, javelin, discus, 800 m, 1500 m and the relay! I also played rugby (Luke and I were both second row) and a little bit of football. I went to gymnastics a couple of times but only to see the girls in their leotards. We both liked to trampoline into the pits but that was about the extent of our gymnastics career. I was very useful at rounders and that provided me with my biggest single sporting highlight of my schooldays. One sports day, my team was way behind when I came up to strike. I amazed myself and all my team by hitting eight consecutive rounders, one after the other. I just kept belting the ball for miles. As a result, we came from behind and won and the rest of the team carried me round the school playing field in celebration, chanting 'Two, four, six, eight, who do we appreciate? Matt!!!' When you are just a kid, moments like that stay with you, it was really special.

They are particularly special when you are constantly struggling to lay down some foundations, to make friends and to settle in. St Clement's was my third primary school so by then I was getting used to the stigma of being the 'new boy' all the time.

I think Mum has a bit of gypsy in her, she's got that bug – her Granny Rampton was a Romany gypsy. I've never been one to complain to my parents, 'Why did you do this? Why did you do that?' I adore the ground my mum walks on. But I don't think, given the choice, I would travel around so much if I had kids. Don't get me wrong, we had an *amazing* upbringing, but I never had the chance to really connect anywhere, I never felt that anywhere was my home. I never felt particularly safe, there was an underlying sense of being afraid.

It wasn't a physical fear of being bullied. Luke and I could look after ourselves in any schoolyard and we were never pushed about, it just didn't happen. We both have that streak in us to be able to look after ourselves, and I am sure Luke felt that he looked out for me, and I felt that I did the same for him. I definitely had quite a few fights at school, but I also knew the law of the playground jungle and chose my fights with care, careful to realign my 'rep' every now and then with a choice new opponent! So, no, we were never bullied.

Yet I remember always being petrified walking into another new school. It was just so unsettling. I never had the same friends for very long, I would work at it and make some great friends and then we would move again – yet another new address. That was hard. It's funny how you can crave what you don't have. People often talk about travelling as the Holy Grail of a lifestyle. But for me, it's really lovely when I hear people talk about their childhood home, the place where they grew up with a big garden and their friends round the corner. I can't even fathom what that would be like as a kid, we just didn't have that. It sounds idyllic.

Like millions of people who watched the hit TV show *The Good Life*, Mum and Tony wanted some of the same. It was very common where I was brought up in London for people to want to get out, to seek that cherished escape to the country. In addition to that impulse, Tony and Mum weren't too happy with the schooling available to us in Cheshunt, so after a few months considering their options, they decided to up sticks and head for Cheddar in Somerset. They found a home with the delightful name of Jasmine Cottage in Tuttors Hill and that was where we set up home next. We would live there for one day short of a year, when we were eleven.

I hated it. Cheddar is not a great memory for me. We were both caught up in fighting a lot because we were from 'The Smoke'. It was such a clash, us turning up with our Sta-Prest trousers, Doc Martens and waffle cardigans in this sleepy Somerset tourist destination; and it wasn't just the kids down there who were worlds apart from us. I remember one day talking to the school games teacher:

'Sir, you got any trainers, sir?'

'Trainers?' he replied. 'What are trainers? We call 'em daps down 'ere.'

We might as well have been in a different country.

Starting Fairlands Middle School would have been difficult enough for any child, but having just moved to the area from a city exacerbated that ordeal a hundredfold. Much of the time, Luke, Adam and I hung out together, often nicking fudge from the local shop. I think it says a lot about a town that a shoplifter's main bounty is fudge. One day we thought we'd up the ante a little bit so Adam nicked a Rubik's cube, only to be caught almost immediately by Tony, who was distinctly not impressed. Tony marched Adam straight back to the shop and made him apologize on the spot. So now the outsiders had a serious lack of street cred. We still laugh about that today, although Carolyn was not very amused!

We did a bit of poaching for trout as well. We didn't have proper fishing rods, just this solitary basic reel. We told our few mates to meet up one day and the five of us headed down to the river to take it in turns dangling the line over a bridge. The first boy quickly got a bite and began to pull the line out of the water when SNAP! it broke. The second guy stepped up to the plate and not ten minutes later the same happened again, he got a bite, he pulled on the line and SNAP! it broke. By now, being five young lads, we were thinking there was some kind of freshwater Jaws down there, we just had to catch it, the excitement was mounting. So I went and got the strongest fishing line I could find, thicker than a guitar string; I was thinking to myself, *This stuff could lift a car, it is not going to snap on me.* Sure enough, a few minutes after I gingerly dangled the line in the water, I got a bite. I am not joking when I say it was almost like cheese-wire cutting through my fingers. After a titanic struggle, I finally pulled this fish out of the water and it was a huge catch. To this pre-teen blond London boy, it looked like the mother of all trout. I was beside myself with pride and excitement and immediately started sprinting home – I knew that Tony loved trout and I was desperate for him to see it. On the way back, an American tourist stopped me in my tracks and said, 'Hey man, I'll give you fifty bucks for that,' and I blurted out, 'Oh no! I'm taking it back to Tony!' and just carried on running without even breaking my stride.

It took at least ten minutes to run all the way back home. I burst into the kitchen and put this beast of a fish in the sink ... and it was still alive! This thing just would not die. My grandad was there so he started smacking it over the head and still it wriggled around. I'm ashamed to say that in the end we just whacked it in the freezer. That did it. I still feel a bit guilty about that. We kind of murdered it, accidentally on purpose.

We had some bad luck with animals in Cheddar too. We had a goat called Mary. The back garden of Jasmine Cottage was about an acre, and was totally overgrown and covered in nettles and weeds. We brought in some electric ploughs and rotovators to remove it all but they just weren't strong enough. Then we sent in Mary. Within a fortnight it was all gone. She would eat a mountain of nettles or weeds and look up as if to say, 'Next!'

Tony loved Mary. Every morning he would go out to feed her, disappear for a good few minutes and he would have love in his eyes when he came back! I reckon there was a bit of a crush going on there, both ways! We would have goat's milk on our cornflakes, too.

One day we came back from school to find a vet trying to save Mary's life. She was pregnant and there had been complications which required a caesarean. The intervention was not a success and both Mary and the kid goat died. It was really gruesome and we were all devastated. Tony was gutted at the time but laughs now when he remembers trying to work out if you should bury a goat 'horns up' or not!

We also had a cat called Jessica, as well as two dogs, Bill and Ben, who would actually pull Luke and me along on our bikes and skateboards. Those dogs were gorgeous, and absolutely mad. We also had a beautiful Yorkshire terrier called James, the love of my mum's life, but he was run over and poor Mum found him on a wall, just lying there dead, where someone had placed him after the accident. Mum was distraught. So for many reasons, Cheddar was not a beacon of happy memories for me.

It wasn't all bad there, but the fleeting brighter moments were suffocated by missing London and not liking our peers. I pretty much kept myself to myself. Life there just didn't feel right – it was a beautiful place, but the kids were just wankers to us because we were from London! However, one pool of happiness within the muddy water of life in Cheddar was Bridget, the prettiest girl in the school. One day I was leaving school for home when a girl came running up to me and said, 'Matt! Matt! Bridget really likes you,' and I said, 'Who's Bridget?' At that moment, the school coach drove past and as it headed off slowly up the lane, I could see the whole back row were looking out of the window at me and this girl.

'Bridget's the girl in the middle,' she said.

'Bloody 'ell! That's Bridget?!' I was stunned. Everyone fancied this girl, she was gorgeous.

Bridget's messenger friend immediately gave two thumbs up to the back of the coach and the entire row of girls just exploded. It was a surreal moment, because up until then I had just felt invisible, I didn't think anyone had even noticed me. I was delighted.

Within a week, we were snogging in Farmer Giles's barn (complete with my teeth-brace, which I had until I was sixteen). Luke was snogging some bird in there as well. To this day, there's nothing like snogging when you are a young teenager, it was the best thing, and you'd snog like ten girls in an afternoon. Anyway, Farmer Giles was pretty notorious in the narrow streets of Cheddar for having a Morris Minor pickup with a man-eating German Shepherd dog prowling in the back. This animal would actually reach out and try to nip you as his owner drove past. Pretty quickly you'd learn to dive into a shop doorway if you heard the stuttering rumble of Farmer Giles's Morris engine. This dog was the stuff of legend – I once saw half a Jack Russell that had been part-eaten by this dog.

We knew that we were in the lion's den by snogging away in this barn, but we figured it was unlikely he'd come back while we were actually there. Wrong. Like startled rabbits, we all jumped to our feet in unison when we heard Farmer Giles's van trundling into the yard and towards the barn. There was only one course of action – we scarpered. I vividly recall running at full pelt across a field, lips numbed from hours of snogging and legs chafed from hours of dry humping through jeans, with the giant German Shepherd rampaging after us, drooling at the prospect of a kill. Eventually, after what

24

seemed like an interminable and enduring panic, Farmer Giles finally called his dog off the chase. It was one of the scariest moments ever, like some twisted horror-version of *Last of the Summer Wine.*

Luke and I weren't the only ones who didn't settle in Cheddar, Tony really disliked it too. Before a year was out, the decision was made to sell up and move out. I can't say I was disappointed, even though the prospect of starting at yet another school wasn't a bright one. I was just glad to be leaving. So we packed our suitcases, left Jasmine Cottage and headed back to London.

A few days after arriving back in the capital, I said to a kid, 'You got any daps?'

'What the fak are daps, mate?' he said. 'They're called trainers up 'ere . . .'

THREE

Some Roses In My Cheeks

We'd sold Jasmine Cottage when we left Cheddar, but hadn't yet bought a house back in London, so for about two months we lived in a caravan. I was just about to start secondary school, which is such a formative period of childhood, and here we were living in a caravan. I hated living on that site with its cold, concrete communal shower stalls and cramped spaces. Yet, even though I wasn't a fan, I knew that we were only there because of circumstances, a moment in time, and my mum's continued dedication to Lukie and me far out-weighed any dislike I had of my temporary home. I could have lived anywhere as long as I was with Mum and Luke.

Looking back, knowing how hard life was for her at times, my mum was just a tower of strength. She would drive us ninety minutes to school in Camberley every day then just after lunch get back in the car to pick us up again. It was such an effort for her but she never batted an eyelid.

Unfortunately, my dad's perception of the situation was different. He decided then that these were not the ideal circumstances for two children to be in and announced that he wanted custody of us. It was a heavy moment for my mum.

Dad was elusive at times when I was younger, or that's what some of my memories tell me. I didn't quite understand him then. It is hard for me to talk about these things because I love him so much and as adults we are great friends. He is sensitive to those difficult times, understandably, but I am often put in a position when I am asked questions about such things, so I will try to be as respectful as I can whilst still recounting the history.

As an adult, I can probably understand Dad's perception of our temporary caravan lifestyle, his feelings came from the right place. But life's not always about perception, it's about finding out the facts, and certain situations are not always exactly how they appear. Despite how it might have looked, I loved my mum desperately, so I was essentially happy at the site and, although I didn't like it on the surface, I didn't feel any less safe because I was in a caravan. When the custody issue was raised, it was an intensely fearful moment for my mum, I know that now, but I don't have explicit memories because I was only a kid. All I knew was that I was very happy as long as my mum was with me. So, when I heard I had to go to court, it was no problem. I just thought to myself, *I will go and tell the judge how I feel, which is that I am not going anywhere. I love Dad but I do not want to leave Mum.*

So that was what I did. Luke was exactly the same and there didn't seem anything else to discuss. That's as simple as it felt to me at the time. We were old enough at that point to say to the judge, 'No, I want to live with my mum,' and as I recall it, our frankness resolved the issue.

What I will say from that experience and having seen the effects of such predicaments on children and parents, is that if it is at all possible for couples who have separated to keep a line of communication open, even if it is formal rather than friendly, then please try to do so. After that issue was settled and we stayed with Mum, communications between her and Dad opened up a little bit – prior to that they had sometimes been quite constricted (it is strange as an adult to think they were once so deeply in love). Better communications in these circumstances will eventually benefit the children, no question.

As I've mentioned, while we were living in all these different places, the one constant that never wavered was my grandparents' flat in Crawford Road, Camberwell, the one place that felt like 'home' to me as a kid. When I remember Crawford Road I think of white pepper. My grandad used to put stacks of white pepper on his roast dinner.

In that flat I saw my mum happy, her mood would change when she got there and so that was uplifting for us too. I would love going round to find my Aunt Sally at home. Even though Sally was a gardener at Buckingham Palace, she used to dress a bit like a hippy and always had an afro comb which she would be pulling through her hair. She would buy a new pair of gleaming white plimsolls, come straight home and bury them in the garden for an hour. As a little kid, I was absolutely bemused, but now I understand that she wanted them to look worn-in.

Grandad's neighbour Rita had a daughter, Dawn, whom I fancied. I have to admit, though, I had an even bigger crush on her mum! I really used to fantasize about her – all I wanted to do was have my wicked way, even though at that age I am not sure I knew what that was! Dawn had been the first girl to let me put my hand down her knickers but Tony caught me doing it on the steps and made me come in and tell the whole family.

It was in Camberwell that a man tried to snatch me into a car. I can still see his face vividly, dark-haired and with a moustache. I often used to sit on a wall by the old people's home at the top of Crawford Road. One day I was on there, just hanging out and being a seven-year-old kid really, when I heard a noise behind me. I looked round and saw this man reaching for me. Over his shoulder I could see his car parked by the grass verge with the back door open. I jumped off the wall – which was about ten feet above the pavement on that side – and ran all the way home. I won't say it haunts me to this day, because it doesn't, but at the time it scared the hell out of me.

I bought my first record at Crawford Road in 1978. It was Ian Dury and the Blockheads' 'Hit Me With Your Rhythm Stick'. I listened to it over and over and over again, until my brother started pleading with me not to play it any more. I loved that single. I was really intrigued by Ian Dury too, this man on the telly who, to a young boy with no knowledge of such things, looked like a cripple. I was fascinated by him, he just looked as if he was in pain. I heard people saying he had polio, which sounded like the bubonic plague or something to me – guaranteeing that I was always first in the queue to take the little cube of sugar dipped in polio vaccine. It sounds simplistic I know, but I was only a child. I didn't stay a fan of the Blockheads for long, it was just that one moment, but your very first record is an important snapshot in your life.

The diversity of my mum's and Aunt Sally's taste in music rubbed off on me. There was a lot of rock in there, Cream, Free, AC/DC and so on, but Mum also loved artists like Roberta Flack. When The Fugees later covered 'Killing Me Softly', a definitive cover version if there could be such a thing, the memories came flooding back for me when I first heard it on radio. It was like a time warp. Sally would always be singing, as would my mum. Sally used to tell us all about the concerts she went to see. She had a lovely voice and it was great to hear Stones and Beatles songs when she belted them out. Whenever we'd visit Sally at her flat on the Peabody Estate on the Old Kent Road, I used to love singing with her. After a while, I began to try to out-sing her, that's when I started to get that sensation that I could do anything with my voice.

I was heavily into Stevie Wonder, and Michael Jackson was a big favourite too. Like forty million other album-buyers, I was into *Thriller*, how could you not be? But for me *Off The Wall* was something special too. The songs were just monumental, and knowing that Rod Temperton, an Englishman from Cleethorpes, could write tracks like 'Rock With You' and 'Off The Wall' makes it even more incredible to me.

By the end of the Seventies, like so many other British kids, I was massively into ska. I was never really into punk, not least because I was just too young, but Two Tone fascinated me. In the space of two years it seemed bands like The Specials, The Selecter, Madness and The Beat dominated the school playgrounds of Britain. I was in one of those playgrounds and couldn't help but be infected. It's funny how adults theorize about genres of music – in the case of Two Tone they talk about how it perfectly captured the social tensions of Thatcher's Britain, how it fused Jamaican ska with inner-city desolation and so on. I am aware of that now. Back then, it was so much more personal. It was a style of music and a sartorial choice that, for this eleven-year-old at least, was far more pragmatic than the pages of a broadsheet feature.

I had the full ska uniform: the pork-pie hat, Fred Perrys, Doc Martens, Sta-Prest shirts. We all did. Then there was the music. I adored The Specials, it was obvious Jerry Dammers was a genius. I had every Madness album. The Specials' 'Ghost Town' is still one of my favourite songs ever. That song is always feted by critics for soundtracking the whole social polarization of Thatcher's Britain, but for me and my mates, it was more about the death of ska – ironic since it was their most successful song and a Number 1 hit. We simply felt like saying,

'No! Don't say the clubs are closing down, because we are still dancing . . .'

The music was so deft too, so clever and that has stayed with me. It can be quite hard to splice elements of ska into my albums themselves, but if you go to one of my shows, you will find parts of the gig are drenched in ska and the crowd will be skanking away! Playing live allows you to do that, to break out of any pigeonholes that your records might be placed in. I think it surprises many people that my live set can include ska and Stevie Wonder but to me that is as natural as putting on 'Superstition' straight after 'Ghost Town'. They are both phenomenal songs, that's all there is to it.

While life in Crawford Road was heavenly to me, the time I spent with my dad was a little less straightforward. Not because of Dad, as we were always so excited to be going to see him, even though it wasn't as often as we all would perhaps have liked. It was because he had remarried back in 1976, to a woman called Margaret and, inevitably, that complicated matters for everybody.

I wasn't particularly fond of Margaret, to say the least. She never made me or Luke feel welcome, never made me feel at ease around my own dad. It was often the smallest things, like rationing how much ketchup we could have on our food, or how many biscuits we were allowed to eat. It was weird because Dad was always the one who would dunk two biscuits in his tea at the same time. We would look forward to having a cup of tea and biccies with Dad so this was all very suffocating. Margaret was really formal. She wasn't off with us in front of Dad, but the most credit I would give her is to say she was polite. I always used to look forward to seeing Dad, of course, but I genuinely did not look forward to seeing Margaret.

Luke and I were never rude to her. In fact, we tried hard

with her but Margaret never made us feel loved or wanted. Nonetheless, I promise you, we were very well-behaved children. Dad insisted on that and Mum had raised us that way as well. Speak when you are spoken to or, if you have something you feel really strongly about, then you can speak up. Adults had the right of way in our house, and rightly so. I believe that is the best method with kids. So we were never rude to Margaret, but that didn't change the chilly atmosphere.

One time, my dad pulled up at a petrol station to fill up the car and while he was paying at the counter, Margaret leant over the seat and said to us, 'I'll give you a pound if you tell me whether your mum is with anyone.' We basically told her to stuff her pound, as politely as we could. When my dad got back in the car we said nothing. Neither did Margaret.

It wasn't just us that were affected, my dad's time with his boys was affected too. I remember being made to sit in the dining-room one night when all I really wanted to do was sit on the couch with my dad, my dinner on a tray, and watch TV with him. We weren't allowed to, but you know what? I think Dad wanted to do that too.

I feel for my dad in a way on that level because if Margaret had made him happy then that would have been cool with us, but I never really had the feeling that she did. There was always an underlying atmosphere, it was really tiring. Then, one day when we were all on a day-trip to Blackpool, while visiting family in Preston, Dad suddenly stopped the car by the sea and said to Margaret, 'You know what, Margaret? If you don't want to spend time with my kids, if you don't want to see the boys, then you're not welcome when I bring my kids out. When are they ever rude to you?'

At that exact moment, I felt incredibly awkward because I feared Margaret would become even worse and really hate us in the future. But then – and I'm not going to lie – once I was over that initial spasm of fear, I was so happy inside that Dad had stuck up for us, his boys. I think that was pretty much one of the last times we hung out with Margaret.

A line of sorts had been drawn, but Margaret was obviously still there whenever we visited Dad. Every visit was tiring, we were drained by it all. We just wanted to see our dad and have a nice time. Even to the day that my dad and Margaret split up (they eventually divorced), we never had the feeling that she really liked us.

When they did separate, my dad was obviously feeling a lot of pain which wasn't nice to see for two young boys. I'd seen Mum so desperately troubled by her marriage break-up but I'd never seen Dad upset like that and I really felt for him. Yet, to be brutally honest, part of me was quite relieved. We had, at best, a tense relationship with Margaret, and at such a young age there isn't yet room for being gracious or magnanimous. You just want your dad.

My father leaving the family home paralleled what had happened to him when he was a boy. His own dad had left but, unlike my father, had not kept in touch with his growing son at all. Before he had split up with Margaret, my father's mother died and Dad started to look into where his own dad lived, to try to reconnect with him and that estranged side of the family. In my book, that was a very brave thing to do. I admire him very much for making such an effort in very difficult circumstances. He managed to re-establish contact and for a few short years we were graced with a whole new strand to the family. Suddenly we had a new grandad, a new grandma, new cousins and aunties, we'd gained a whole new family seemingly overnight, it was just the most exciting thing. And this wasn't like a fifth cousin four-times-removed – this was a legitimate, direct bloodline through my father.

However, so much of my life has pivoted around gain and

loss, gain and loss, and this was to prove no different. When Dad and Margaret broke up – Margaret was having an affair – my father's own dad, my newly discovered grandfather, took Margaret's side. Yes, he sided with a woman he wasn't related to and hadn't known for very long against his own son. To me that was absolutely disgusting. Even if Dad had been mainly in the wrong (which as I understand it he wasn't), you can't take sides against your own. That's his own son. I was incensed.

I don't see that side of the family any more, their own actions have wrenched them back out of my life. I do see Dad's sister and her family at gigs and on other occasions and they are all absolutely lovely, Janet, Sara and Mark. They supported my dad during that time. Janet sided with him, her brother – I have a lot of time for Janet. I have no negative feelings for my dad's family. I would have loved nothing more than to have had a healthy, loving relationship with my new-found family but, as I am sure anyone would agree, my loyalty lies with my father. As for my dad's dad? He can kiss my arse, I have no time or respect for him after what he did.

I know that episode broke my dad's heart. To realize that he had grown so far apart from his dad that they could no longer even reach each other must have really hurt. What's more, I know that it hurt my dad's step-father, who in my mind and as my dad also realizes, *is* his real father. My dad now regrets searching for his biological father, but even more regrets the hurt it caused his step-father. I know my dad only considers himself to have one father and that's Grandad Weston.

I have no time for what happened and probably remain more angry about it even than my dad does. He is quite philosophical when he thinks about it and seems to have been able to move on. It remains incomprehensible to me. You lose your son for many, many years, somehow that son plucks up the courage to come and find you and kick-start a relationship that time and circumstances threatened to have destroyed for ever, then you take the side of someone who is not even part of your direct family! The way that families behave sometimes is unbelievable to me.

Fortunately for Dad, there was a fantastic new wife around the corner. Her name is Helen and Dad married her in 1996. I honestly think that at that time in my dad's life, she was the best thing that could have happened to him. She is the same age as me (so well done Dad!) but she has an old soul, and I mean that as a great compliment. She has not only made my dad younger, but conversely she has made him older as well, made him more peaceful. She is a very gentle person and that has definitely rubbed off on my father. Helen is very considerate, very loving, she makes my dad happy. She is a tiny, petite woman who looks even younger than she is and, being the same age as Luke and I, we have great fun calling her step-mum! She cringes but it is hilarious. She'll return the fun by putting her arm around me and saying, 'You're my step-son!' I am really glad that Helen is in my dad's life, she is a lovely lady.

FOUR

Redirected

Luke and I were as one back then. When you are floundering for foundations, you look to the constants in your life. I had my mum, there was Crawford Road and there was my beautiful twin brother. Luke was my saving grace, he was one of the reasons I could feel safe. We were young twins with strong personalities, so of course we would fight but we would always have a good time together. When I think of Luke back then, my face just cracks into a big smile, and I end up laughing. He was a hilarious physical comedian as a kid, always mucking around, a typical drummer I guess! I used to love how he made me chuckle, I'd be crying and aching on my sides, breathless from laughing. We did have other friends though, which was healthy. I like having best mates; I know hundreds of people, but I only have a couple of best mates. At Collingwood, I would befriend a boy who was my best mate through all of secondary school and on through the madness of the Bros years, a great guy called Lloyd Cornwall.

We went to Collingwood Secondary School in Camberley, south London, a year later than everyone else because of our stay in Cheddar, so not only was it yet another new school but by the time we arrived, most kids had gravitated towards certain friends and cliques had already been formed. However, we were into cool music and quickly became popular at the new school, which was a nice feeling. One of our new mates in that first year at Collingwood was a quite academic boy whom we met in the school dinner queue. His name was Craig Logan.

As for other teenage boys, one of the most important things in life was girls. Lukie and I have never done badly with girls. Luke dated prettier girls than me but I was more shy in that area. As we grew up, he went for a different type of girl, ones that would drive cars and stuff like that, which when you are a teenager is a defining element of your personality to other kids. I still had plenty of little romances though. There was a girl called Caroline whom I really liked when I was fourteen, but she moved to America and I was heartbroken. Caz was lovely, she wasn't the prettiest girl in the school but to me she had the sweetest way about her (her best friend was Luke's girlfriend, that's how it was in those days!). Then I dated a girl called Cindy who still to this day is one of the loveliest girls I've ever met. She was my first love. Her parents worked for an oil firm and they had a lovely house on the Wentworth estate by the golf course. She was American and unfortunately she too moved back to the States. She was just so gentle, an earth angel.

I lost my virginity to Cindy. I was sixteen, quite late for a guy I guess. That first experience of making love was quite amazing for me. We'd heard all these stories that you had to use lubrication, so I covered my knob in after-sun lotion. From that shaky start, it was actually wonderful, not the horror story that many people experience! Afterwards, we both just smiled and smiled for hours. That is a great memory, although one that inevitably comes with a certain whiff of after-sun.

Those secondary school and teenage years can be so in-fluential on your personality. For example, I have a real fear of sirens. If I hear a motorbike rev in a certain way, it will give me an absolute chill. Part of me sometimes wonders if I grew up during air raids in a past life. More specifically, while I was at Collingwood, we had a couple of incidents with sirens that, looking back, must have had quite a lasting effect on me. The school was near to Broadmoor hospital which over the years has housed notorious individuals such as the Yorkshire Ripper. Every Monday escape sirens would go off to test the system – this unnerving sound was strangely reassuring to locals because it meant that everything was working. Religiously, every Monday, this siren would howl across the area.

However, at the back of your mind, next to the face-at-the-window and the bogey-man-under-the-bed, you knew that if a siren went off *on any other day* then there could be someone out there that you really didn't want to meet.

On one particular day, I was out on a school cross-country run, trekking through the woods near to Broadmoor. I was on my own thinking of nothing much when I heard the siren. The sound registered in my ear and a split second later I thought to myself, *It isn't a Monday*. I shit myself. I started thinking, *Maybe they have just found him, or has he been gone for half an hour on the run . . .* ? By the time I'd run another mile, I was convinced I was about to stumble across some mass murderer. Obviously I didn't, but I felt a panic that stays with me to this day.

Another time while I was at Collingwood School the four-minute nuclear warning went off. It sounds bizarre but it is true. Camberley was one of the few places in Britain where the nuclear warning signal actually went off accidentally. This blaring siren was absolutely everywhere, yet you couldn't tell exactly where it was coming from. It was almost as if it was inside your brain rather than coming in through your ears. After four minutes of that, I was ready to explode myself!

We were in school at the time and it was such an extraordinary circumstance to find yourself in. We were in woodwork and the teacher, Mr Linnell, was usually a grumpy old bastard. However, when the siren went off, he had this really peaceful look on his face. Mr Euston was the same – he had a cool swagger about him like Lee Majors from *The Six Million Dollar Man* and he also seemed strangely serene that day. Even now I think they knew more than we did.

The headlines on the local papers the next day said, 'Camberley Plays It Cool With Four-Minute Warning.' Funnily enough, we still have the tray that Luke was making in that very woodwork class. Mum still uses it for tea. This tray is indestructible. If a nuclear bomb had obliterated Camberley that day, I am certain that in among the fall-out and hinterland of atomic waste, Lukie's tray would have been on the floor, right at the centre of the explosion, unscathed. Ten out of ten, Goss.

To any secondary-school pupil, teachers can provide both the best and worst moments of your time in class. I think it was our English teacher Ms Funnel who wore fishnets, that was fantastic. One time she climbed on my desk to open a window with her fishnets on, I remember that very clearly! But the best teacher was Ms Sinkovich who, for some reason, used to play an accordion while wearing very short skirts, which to a hormonally-charged teenage boy was definitely a nice bonus.

Mr Brooks was a great biology teacher, phenomenal. To this day, I still remember every valve in the human heart and how it all works, solely because of him teaching us so well. He was cool with it too. One day, a mate of mine dropped a condom on the floor. I don't really know why we had them at that age because we'd have only lasted ten seconds had we caught sight of a naked woman anyway. This condom went 'SPLAT!' on the classroom floor. A hushed nervousness fell over the room, you could almost hear people thinking, *Oh my God! Mr Brooks is going to go mad!* Sure enough, Mr Brooks saw the condom, but simply crouched down, picked it up, said, 'I'll save this for later' and promptly put it in his pocket and carried on teaching.

Another nice memory (albeit earlier at St Clement's) is that of Mr Bromley and the eclipse. He had a really great way about him, he was a very knowledgeable, gentle but very firm teacher. While he was teaching us, there was a solar eclipse which we all watched; rather than just make an afternoon of it and then forget about it the next day, Mr Bromley said, 'When there is another eclipse, let's meet on the top of Box Hill.' I thought that was an amazingly thoughtful thing for a teacher to say to his class. It would be lovely if that sentiment could be in all classrooms, that kind of foresight.

I don't know if Mr Bromley would even remember saying that, but when it came to the eclipse in 2002, I was in LA and I thought about him all day, wondering if he was sitting on Box Hill all those thousands of miles away, and indeed if anyone else was sitting with him.

Without doubt the person I have the fondest memories of is Jane Roberts, my drama teacher and someone I still hold dear to my heart. I would love to get back in touch with her. She was so different to your normal drama teacher, and absolutely brilliant at her job. Jane gave me a lot of confidence in myself as a performer. She used to say, 'You have something special about you, you've got what it takes,' and constantly encouraged me. In fact, I would say that she is the reason that I was able to pursue my career as I did, she gave me that confidence.

40

I absolutely trusted her judgement one hundred per cent so when she said I had what it takes, I believed her and my confidence surged.

Despite what people may think, I have never been a confident person. As I have grown older, I have become a more self-assured man, but on a vanity level I am not confident. I don't want that to change. I have always had an absolute dislike for arrogance. In the Bros years, the press would often say we were 'brats' or 'arrogant' and those words really stung. I would be devastated if someone said that about me. I find arrogance so boring, so uninteresting. I love kindness, respectful people; life is too bloody short to be around arrogance. Jane knew the difference between arrogance and confidence and she instilled some of the latter in me, for which I will be eternally grateful.

I should point out that at secondary-school age, I absolutely loved drama. Acting was my bug, not music. I desperately wanted to be an actor, even my work experience was at Windsor Theatre. For some reason, one of my first assignments from Windsor was to go into central London, by myself, and buy some blank bullets. That was pretty daunting!

It was always acting and, later, music for me. I just wasn't interested in anything else, especially the sciences (although I loved biology). I hated physics. When I did the exam for physics I just put my name at the top of the paper and walked out. I knew I didn't want to put myself through an hour and a half of stress – I wasn't going to build rockets. The teacher actually shook my hand, he seemed to admire the fact that I knew what I wanted not to do.

Jane was always very encouraging and I was a good pupil – I suppose because I wanted to learn more and more and more. My application paid off when I won the lead role in a 1984 production of *Cabaret*. It was a big show, beautiful costumes, expert sets, you would never have known it was a school effort, Jane made such a perfect job of it. I was in my element on stage playing the German Master of Ceremonies at a pre-war Berlin nightclub. I won a standing ovation and loved every minute of it – I am still very proud of that performance. It was the first time I really felt appreciated in that environment. It would have been odd to think that less than a decade later, I would be sitting in a hotel suite with Liza Minnelli herself, who had won an Oscar in 1972 with that very same musical . . . but more of that later.

It was my show-stopping performance in Jane Roberts's production of *Cabaret* that brought me very directly to a crucial crossroads in my young life. Jane later took me to one side and said that there had been a scout from RADA at the show and if I wanted to, I could get invited to attend that very famous drama school (the following year I was in *Sweeney Todd*). Yet, while on the one hand that was everything I ever wanted to hear, one aspect of the *Cabaret* show had really stuck in my mind, and that was how natural and comfortable it had felt being on stage singing. The way singing made me feel, the way it physically felt in my throat, I knew that was the way forward. It was a really stark contrast to anything I had ever done before – I loved acting and was good at it for my age, but the singing was on another level altogether. It just felt so comfortable, so natural.

It's funny how your childhood can be such a mish-mash of memories and it is very telling which specific moments stand out. In view of our future careers, one moment in Collingwood was very significant. In the early Eighties, Two Tone had started to fade and several new bands were coming through. The Thompson Twins were really big news all over school and, indeed, the country as a whole. We'd all started buying music magazines and really getting into bands in a big way, so imagine the buzz when my mate won a competition in *Smash Hits* to go and actually meet the Thompson Twins . . . in New York!

I thought he was pulling my leg when he first told me. To secondary-school kids, it just didn't compute, it was so fantastic. But sure enough he had won and was duly despatched on a Jumbo to spend time with the band. Then, as if that wasn't startlingly brilliant enough, they ran a feature in *Smash Hits* showing him hanging out with the Thompson Twins in New York, inside limos, at the gig, backstage . . . we couldn't believe our teenage eyes. We were saying, 'It doesn't get bigger than that, that's it, he's made it . . . we know him.'

What I didn't know then, as I flicked through the pages of that magazine looking at the Big Apple, the music-biz glamour and the faces of this band that we all followed, was that only a handful of years later, Bros would be on the cover of the then-biggest-selling edition of *Smash Hits* ever.

FIVE

The More I See The More I Want It

The primal attraction I felt to singing during the performance of *Cabaret* wasn't the first time I had ever thought of being in a band. In fact, Lukie and I had been in bands already. It was just that moment was when it became very clear that music was at my core, rather than acting.

By then, I'd been in and out of several bands, none of them particularly any more sophisticated than a thousand schoolboy groups. Luke had been playing drums for a while. He had an MPC kit, which was like a briefcase full of pads that you plugged in, it was a brilliant piece of gear. All credit to Tony, despite money not being exactly plentiful, he somehow managed to save £400 to buy Luke this first drum kit outright. I'd briefly dabbled with a saxophone but was never really very interested.

My very first band was when Dukus and I were twelve, with our mate Peter Kirtley. At that age you can be a bit of a wanker, and I'll be honest, we only asked Peter to be in the band because his dad had some equipment. It was a decision of convenience, we needed instruments, he had them. I played monophonic keyboards – one finger – and sang. Luke played drums and we asked our new friend Craig Logan to join, because he had a bass guitar. We called ourselves Caviar. What a dodgy soul name! We didn't have a clue what caviar was but we knew it was expensive, so we thought 'job's done!' Then we found out it was fish eggs.

Caviar mutated through various combinations, and we joined other bands including one with two other brothers on guitars who were brilliant for their age. Luke was becoming well-known locally for his drumming so he was already in the band and had done a couple of gigs with them, but they didn't have a singer. With my enjoyment of singing on stage in mind, I was keen to get involved, so I asked Luke if he could get me an audition. I turned up and started singing Paul Young's big cover hit, 'Wherever I Lay My Hat' and after about three lines they said, 'Fucking hell! You're in!' They were called Hypnosis. They gave me my first experience of singing live on stage in a band, and Luke was the one who arranged the audition, it was down to him. Hypnosis was destined not to last either. I really hope those brothers ended up in the music business because they were such good guitarists.

Then Luke and I left and started our own band called Epitoma. We'd picked up a Latin dictionary and found the word for abstract which was 'epitoma', but that sounded like some terrible disease. You can just picture a doctor saying, 'I'm sorry to have to tell you this, but you've got epitoma.' Eventually, we ended up settling on the name Ice. That was supposed to be an improvement.

God only knows how but we got a gig at some old working-class club where we were basically asked to play in front of a load of old grannies. We were on the same bill as a number of cabaret acts, but we were 'the band' and were really excited regardless. We rehearsed and talked about it for weeks. Ice's live debut! We'd even got George Michael's 'Careless Whisper' rehearsed perfectly. At the time, a local guy was 'managing' us, but when he went on stage to introduce us he said, 'Ladies and gentlemen, please let me introduce you to . . . Pulse 2!'

He'd changed our bloody name without telling us, right before we went on stage!

We were fuming! I defiantly walked out on stage to a ripple of apathetic applause that would have barely registered on the massed hearing aids in the smoke-filled room. Resplendent in my long soul-boy hair, Duran Duran-esque suit and over-sized earrings, I could barely contain my anger when I said, 'We're not Pulse 2, we're Ice!'

Like anybody gave a fuck.

Shortly after the debacle of Ice/Pulse 2, Craig, Lukie and I broke away and formed our own band as a trio. We heard about a band called Breathe who were really popular locally around Camberley. I loved the guy's voice and they were doing quite well, then they actually had a hit, called 'Hands To Heaven'. When that happened, we thought *Shit! How many successful bands come out of the same small area like Camberley?* They had changed managers and we found out about the one they had started off with, a chap called Tony. He lived on the Old Dean Estate so we bunked off school one day and went down there to see him. He was totally up for it. One of the first things he said was, 'I am going to rent Concorde for you lads, fill it with record company executives, while you guys play in the aisle. It's going to be massive!' We were *so* excited.

For about two days.

Then we did our research and found out that the aisle on Concorde was barely wide enough to fit a snare drum in, let alone a complete band. The sheer joy of walking around school thinking, *Yeah! We're going to play Concorde! Yeah!* only lasted forty-eight hours. That statement and idea was his crowning glory and his downfall all in one. That was one of our first experiences of managers.

One day we were practising and I'd just got my copy of Michael Jackson's *Thriller*. When my mate Neil arrived to watch the rehearsal, I said, 'Hey, listen Neil, I've written this new track, what do you think...?' and I started singing, 'Looking out...' reciting the words to what I knew was the classic Jackson track 'Human Nature'. Neil's eyebrows shot up and he was enthusing, 'Fucking hell, Matt, that's fucking wicked mate!' We were actually writing material as early as then, but I must admit it wasn't up to that standard!

One thing about being in a successful band is that it makes you pretty much unemployable. In my opinion, once you've topped the charts or, indeed, even been in the charts at all, you see things through such a specific, extreme lens. Afterwards, it's like your retinae have been distorted and there's no way of reverting to a more orthodox way of looking at life.

Before Bros, however, I did have aspirations for 'normal' jobs as well as being in a band. I thought about being a hairdresser as my mum had been. I'd read Vidal Sassoon's life story about how he'd been discovered and made his mark, and I thought it was an amazing tale.

So I found myself a Saturday job in a local hairdresser's. As a kid, you are always looking to get some money in – by now I was obsessed with fashion, and clothes were expensive. But, boy, did I have to earn my money at that salon. I will never forget the feeling of washing really thin, spindly, hairspray-drenched, granny's hair. It was like trying to undo a knot in a really fine chain covered in sticky oil, it just felt wrong!

It was quite comical really what those old women used to do to their hair. I used to think about how they were going out with their formal blue rinses, feeling all spruced up and smart, but actually looking like ancient punk rockers.

I fancied my boss, she was really cute, but unfortunately there were other women with designs on my green gills. My nemesis at the salon was a German lady with a very strong Bavarian accent. She really took a shine to me and would storm into the salon saying, 'Vere iz Matt? I like Matt. I vant Matt to vash my hair!' As soon as I heard the door open and that commandeering voice say, 'Matt! I vant Matt!', I would cringe inside and no amount of pretending to clear up out the back would keep me out of her clutches. She insisted that I wash her hair every time and she would lie back in the chair and mumble, 'Oooo, yah, yah, yah, ooo!' It used to totally give me the creeps.

One Christmas the salon held a raffle to win – of course – a state-of-the-art hairdryer. As the young buck, I was chosen to pick the winning ticket and guess whose name I pulled out of that hat? Yes, the bloody German. I was horrified.

She came in for a haircut and was told that she had won the star prize. My boss said to her, 'We have to tell you, Matt picked the winning ticket . . .'

'OOOhhhhhh!!! Matt, I like Matt, I vant Matt, Maaatttt! I luv Matt!'

So that pretty much killed any remaining desire I had to be a hairdresser.

I also did a paper round, which might just be the worst job in the world. As any schoolboy or girl with the scars to show for it would know, you had to get up at the crack of dawn, trudge down to the newsagent's and sling a bag of papers on your shoulder which felt like twice your own bodyweight. Before you left the shop the strap would be cutting into your shoulder so painfully it hurt even to move. Then you'd start the round and find that no matter which route you'd been given, there was always one house that was two miles out in the sticks which wanted just one bloody paper! By the time I got to school, I would desperately need to fall asleep. It was awful, I hated it.

I had a brief ambition to be a vet because, like many people, I love animals. I love being around them – my two dogs mean the world to me, but more of them later – and find cruelty towards animals deeply harrowing. I sometimes see those adverts on TV when they show abused 'circus' animals and it makes me want to be sick. For a while when I was a kid, I thought I wanted to be a vet, but then I found out you needed to study for many years which was not something I was prepared to do. People who do that and become vets are astounding.

Next up for me was some really hard graft at a car-valeting business run by my brother's girlfriend's brother. Luke worked there as well for a while. Who says nepotism doesn't benefit people? Well, it didn't do me any favours . . . I was paid fuck all, just over ten pounds a day I think it was, to clean five cars. The business would make well over eighty pounds for those same vehicles. It wasn't easy work either; one day I fainted in the back of a car from the fumes of the cleaning products. Valeting firms use a spray paint to make the wiry carpets in car boots crisply black again, but it is so unhealthy. I remember working away with this veil of fumes around my head, then waking up and it being half an hour later.

The sole highlight was when a beautiful Ferrari came in one day. I jumped in and drove it past my old school, thinking, 'I gotta get one of these!' But that was scant relief from what was a pretty horrid job. Shortly after the drive in the prancing horse, I said I thought I deserved a pay rise, suggesting maybe if I did six cars a day my boss could pay me what he made on the last car. I did get a pay rise . . . by two pounds a day. I left soon after.

In a way, that was probably the best thing he could have done, because after that I realized the band was the only way forward for me and we really cracked on.

We all agreed to leave school so that we could pursue the band with more focus and energy. The day came and Luke and I left school, excited at the prospect of effectively being in the band 'full time' with no distractions (I'd passed a few 'O' levels). That was quite a risk in a way but we had the courage of our convictions. However – eventually – Craig admitted to us that he hadn't left school after all, that his parents insisted he had to stay on for another year before he could work on the band (he was a year younger than us). I think in a way they thought that would probably be the end of the band.

Instead of replacing him immediately, as most kids with grand aspirations would have done, we chose to wait for him – for a year. During those fifty-two weeks, Lukie and I rehearsed and played, organized band practices around Craig's school schedule and essentially put our life on hold so that we could stay loyal to him and keep him in the band. We never batted an eyelid, he was our best mate, he was in the band and we were going to wait for him.

He was virtually living around our house anyway. Mum looked after him as if he was one of her own. We would often go into London clubbing and Mum would always help all of us dress, Craig included.

At the time and certainly in the light of later events, people have often asked me, 'Why wait for him?' The best analogy I can offer is this. If you imagine two people walking down a country lane and it's frightening and dark and there isn't a light for miles. If you are with your brother, it's a bit creepy, you're a bit scared. You put your best mate in the middle of it, and it becomes an adventure, a laugh. That's what Craig was, he was that implant that we needed as brothers. So we waited for him.

Luke's girlfriend at the time, Lorraine, had a nice big house and was quite wealthy. This was useful because her mum, Norma, was very cool and said we could use her living-room for band practice, which on reflection was very generous. She fed and watered us in this lovely house, which was very kind. My brother's girlfriend was pretty tasty and had cute friends, her mum was tasty as well, so it was a good period of band practice, of which I have very fond memories.

Bass, drums and vocals was an unusual format for a band so young as us. We rehearsed very hard, working whenever we could. We were an odd blend of ska and soul; I was heavily into The Specials but also loved performers like Frankie Beverly and Maze – the song 'Joy And Pain' still sends me straight back in time to snogging girls at the school disco.

Things took a promising turn when we started rehearsing at the house of a man called Bob Herbert, who was the father of Luke's latest girlfriend. He looked very young for his age, was cool, fun and full of ideas. He later went on to manage The Spice Girls for a while and his son Chris is also a very successful band manager. He was in the accountancy business and had had some dealings with the Three Degrees. At the time, however, he was just starting out in management, so we were the guys on whom he was testing his ideas – not in any manipulative way at all, he was always very gracious and genuinely enthusiastic about what we were doing. He had a summerhouse in the back of his garden by the pool and that's where we used to rehearse.

We bought a Breville toaster and a large amount of cheese and bacon sandwich spread, the sort that comes in tubes with the most peculiar taste combinations imaginable. That was our ready-made sustenance for weeks while we rehearsed furiously, five hours a day and more. There was something about that time that felt safe to me, it was a secure environment. Pretty quickly we changed our name to Summerhouse.

I wrote one of my first songs in that summerhouse – it was called 'Pyramids'. How incredibly Eighties to write a song about the pyramids! It was all about the mists of time and God knows what else, heaven knows why I chose to write about that. There was also a song called 'Mystery Lady' which actually wasn't too bad, but unfortunately we brought that relatively promising track down a level or two in quality by recording what can only be described as probably the worst video of all time. It was just one shot of us in a big room, wearing really dodgy suits and long mullet haircuts, with plumes gushing out of a smoke machine that was being operated by Bob who, unbeknown to him at the time, was just about visible pushing the button on this contraption in the corner of the shot. It was just hilarious.

Our rehearsal space took a turn for the worse when Bob bought an old house for development and said we could have free rein to practise in there. On the surface this sounded great, but when we got there it was like something run by Norman Bates. The abandoned house had no windows in most rooms, was soaking with damp and was so cold we all huddled up in huge jackets and Lukie had to play the drum pedals in thick socks. My mum went mad when she learned we were spending a lot of time in there. Still, it was as close as we ever got to playing the working men's club next door, which resolutely refused to book us. Maybe it was when we changed our name to Gloss, and they were worried about introducing 'Matt from Gloss!' So it was back to the summerhouse for more bacon-spread sandwiches.

It was actually a really lovely time and I have to say Bob was instrumental in that final stage of the band before we were dis-covered. If I am honest, in terms of feeling like you were making serious progress towards a record contract, there were un-deniably times when you couldn't help but feel we were just the band at the end of the garden. But Bob was vital, no doubt.

Perhaps the most significant thing Bob did was introduce us to Nicky Graham, a record producer who had worked with Barbara Dickson, The Nolans and Andy Williams. Nicky came down to see us play a show in April 1986 in Lightwater, just off the M3, liked us and thought there was something to work with. That was, essentially, the moment we started to go overground.

Unlike a lot of bands of that age, we were 'discovered' and that's the way I think it should be done. We did not audition for the parts in front of a panel. We were a bona fide gigging band, albeit a little inexperienced and rough around the edges, writing songs and practising like crazy. A known producer came to see us play and it was in a live environment, raw as you like, and we impressed him. After a few conversations, Nicky asked us if we would like to meet a manager he knew of in London, a chap called Tom Watkins, who happened to manage the Pet Shop Boys. We were seventeen.

We left Bob Herbert's management after about a year but not necessarily because it wasn't happening fast enough – we didn't know what 'fast' was. We just felt we needed to move on. Then when we were told we were going to meet Tom Watkins, it was such a culture shock. Literally, on the way to the meeting we were thinking, *Fuck! This is the manager of the Pet Shop Boys!* The first time we met him was at his own very lovely flat in Blackheath. That initial discussion went well and further meetings were arranged.

Even knowing what I know now, and however difficult the later days of Bros proved to be, I still maintain that going to meet Tom, talking about the band and possible record deals and all that flurry of activity that kicked off shortly after Nicky spotted us was a fantastic, exciting, *unbelievable* time. We were so young and here was one of the industry's biggest managers talking to us across a desk in a swanky West End lawyer's office. It was hard not to be dazzled.

I genuinely have amazing memories of those times, even though they happen to be the days that would mould certain future events. However, I can't sit here and write my autobiography and feel negative and weird about experiences that, at the time, were nothing but exhilarating. Maybe I'm too philosophical. I don't know, maybe I'm naïve. Whatever the cause, that's how I see those events, it was the stuff of dreams.

SIX

If I Was A Wishful Thinker . . .

Once Tom was involved, through his Massive Management company along with his partner Mick Newton, events moved *very* quickly indeed. It was December 1986 and within a very short space of time, our band would be all over the papers. For now, however, we didn't even have a record deal, yet that seemed an insignificant obstacle. Suddenly, demo tapes were recorded – there had already been a false start when Arista pulled out of a deal at the last second. It was disappointing at the time, but with Tom on board anything seemed possible. We were having meetings to discuss which record company would be best, CBS/Sony or EMI, the people behind Michael Jackson or the ones who looked after The Beatles. A few weeks earlier we'd been wiping bacon spread off our guitars in the summerhouse.

Tom was a very big character, physically and in terms of his presence. He would bundle into meetings full of ideas and it sounded like the world was ours for the taking. And you know what? Tom was right.

The name Bros came about from one of these highly-charged meetings and it seemed to fit perfectly. Tom even had his designer Mark Farrow create that famous logo which all seemed very ambitious yet totally natural at the same time. The strategy worked and the music business was soon talking about Tom's latest act.

Eventually, we signed to CBS/Sony for an advance of £260,000 for the debut album. What that actually equated to for us in hard cash terms was a wage of fifty pounds a week. In a way, I have to be honest, I was more excited by the fact that someone was going to pay for us to go into a studio to make a record and then, amazingly, it would get released. It was a period when even the air I breathed seemed to be rich with dreams. When I arrived home one day after yet another exciting meet, this fantasy life turned to a horrific nightmare when Mum broke the news that she had been diagnosed with cancer.

Every day for weeks, my Aunt Sally had pestered my mum to have a check-up, for no other reason than she had a feeling she should get looked at. Thank God Sally did because eventually Mum did go in and they found something. The surgeons removed what they thought was everything but placed Mum on a strict routine of further check-ups to monitor the situation. Fortunately, three years later she was given the all clear.

The pace of the band was relentless. A girl called Tula, who was working with Tom, took us to the Cuts salon in Soho where we had all our hair chopped off really nicely. Prior to that our hair had been long, very Eighties, very Duran-esque (we also played around with a lot of different styles, even the Buffalo Boy look). I knew in my heart of hearts that the hair had to come off, I'd been thinking about it for some time anyway. When I was about fourteen, I went on holiday with my grandad and Aunt Sally, because I was Nobby No Mates and my brother had gone off sunning himself with some tasty bird, like you should be doing at that age! So what's the next best thing for a pubescent, hormonally-challenged teenage boy? Go to Greece with your grandad and aunty.

Neither of them were great sun-worshippers, so I found myself on the beach alone most days. On one particular afternoon, I was lying down on the golden sand, with my beautiful long blond hair, slim body, very few hairs on my legs. The next thing I know, five guys start putting their towels down around me. I thought, *Oh my God, they think I'm a fucking bird!* So in the deepest voice I could muster, I said to the guy next to me, 'Can you pass me the oil please?' I've never seen five lads scarper so bloody fast!

When the day came to get the hair cut, it was a relief. What was strange was that prior to having the short cut, both Lukie and I did very well with girlfriends, we never had a problem. However, when we had that James Dean cut, it was like flicking a switch, it all started kicking off. Not long after, I was standing in a phone box when a girl who didn't normally give me the time of day drove by in her car – and did a blatant double-take. She stopped the car and clearly didn't know who it was, then as she got closer she said, 'Matt?' That felt good! My mum still has the ponytails, the string of hair that we had chopped off.

Our look – chunky Doc Martens, ripped Levi 501s, white T-shirts, Harrington jackets and James Dean-esque haircuts might seem quite tame, but at the time it was very striking. A lot of our gear was bought from American Classics and Red Or Dead and both shops did a roaring trade with Brosettes. Duran Duran and Wham! had both enjoyed massive success in the Eighties but their younger fans were starting to look elsewhere. New Romanticism was still very popular with all its flamboyance and melodrama, Goths were always skulking around (a look I have always liked when it is done well), soul boys were besuited and very smooth, casuals were in the mix too, but our look was very different. It just seemed to hit a chord with people. I think it was a time when a new generation was up and coming and wanted their own uniform.

I have often heard people suggest that we were 'dressed' by our management and PR team. Let me say now for the record, that is absolute nonsense. I have never, *ever* been dressed. I am the one who loved James Dean, I was a massive fan, hence the red Harrington. I loved James Dean's hair. That's where it came from and I don't care what anyone says. The ripped jeans were just a case of the trousers we had on having worn out. Simple as that. Next thing you know, everyone is ripping brand-new jeans to simulate the 'look'. I have never been the sort of person who will sit down with a stylist and say, 'Do what you want with me.' I firmly believe that you can't be in bands and not have opinions. Our look might not have been considered state-of-the-art West End fashion, but people loved it.

When our management team said, 'Okay, we're ready, let's go in and make the album,' it was so exciting. We were recording at Hot Night Studio in Farm Lane, Fulham, on the top floor of a building in a trading estate. I went in on the first day with a lucky T-shirt that I was determined to wear to record all my lead vocals. Even though it was our debut album, to this day it was one of the few times that we really cracked on with the whole record from start to finish. We didn't rush anything, it was just that the pace was blistering and yet so productive.

We weren't studio virgins. In fact, we'd done quite a lot of recording for our age. Before things kicked off with Bros, we'd met a fireman called Ray Hedges – he went on to have success and work with Take That – who owned a sixteen-track, two-inch recording studio. It was pretty impressive, proper gear, and we recorded quite a bit of material with him, so being in the studio with Bros was nothing new.

Nevertheless, we couldn't wait. Each morning we would make our way to the studio, full of energy and ideas for the day's work ahead. We were delighted to discover that our producer was Nicky Graham – I think we needed to bring Nicky in, it was quite formulated and organized as a result. He had charts on the studio wall which listed all the component parts of each track and we would diligently work through each one day by day, ticking off lead vocals, bass, guitar, drums and so on as we went, like an advent calendar. It was just the most amazing feeling.

I remember looking at my reflection in the vocal booth thinking, *I cannot believe I am making a record!* I just sang my heart out on all those tracks, 'I Owe You Nothing', 'When Will I Be Famous?', 'Drop The Boy', 'Cat Among The Pigeons', really giving it my all. When I had finished the vocals, I was more reflective and I distinctly recall saying to myself, *I wonder if anyone will actually get to hear these songs?*

We were fortunate to be using very experienced musicians, which was a great education for us, to be in there for a couple of months working in that environment. But we were far from puppets, as some of our harsher critics would later suggest. We would work with Nicky on songs in the loft of his house in Wimbledon, then they would be taken into the studio to be recorded. It was never a case of songs being given to us on a platter – 'Here's a tape with the songs on, learn them.' Far from it. On reflection, I really did enjoy those moments with Nicky in Wimbledon.

My advice to any artist working on their debut album is to savour it. Get on with having a good time because that pure, naïve 'Shit! I'm making an album' moment lasts for only a brief time. Once the first song is out and you've got a hit, it *all* changes. Before that, you don't know if anyone will ever hear it, so just enjoy making that music. It is one of the purest moments you can have in the music business and, for me anyway, the recording of Bros's debut album was delightful.

Both 'When Will I Be Famous?' and 'I Owe You Nothing' are credited on the Bros albums as written by Watkins/Graham, so neither Luke nor I receive any money from the publishing of those songs. However, 'Famous' was essentially a spoken-word song when I first heard it, but by the time I had sung my lead vocals, I had added a lot. I think that there are moments in those songs you just couldn't write, it's just my style of singing. I've always been forward in simply opening my mouth in the studio and going for it, it's impossible to have that kind of character and that kind of sound without the lead singer. The famous 'oh-ah' and other ad-libs are not something that you could write down, but as a singer you are naturally inclined to come up with melody. If you listen carefully to 'I Owe You Nothing', you will realize that it is a very difficult song to sing; 'Famous' has a four-bar section in half-speed waltz time and when people heard we wanted to put 3/4 timing in a dance record they said it wouldn't work. We stuck with it and we were right, but it was very demanding to sing, naturally. I would say that I added a lot but at the time I didn't know anything about publishing splits and how money was generated. You think you are involved in making a record, so I was putting my ideas forward and singing, as was Luke.

To Tom's great credit, he had a famous line that he used to apply to us all the time: 'You can't make chicken soup out of chicken shit.' Nonetheless, we did not get publishing credits on those two songs.

That's one of the key reasons why I soon wanted to get involved in the writing of the songs I sing, because it was all so disappointing when we realized later that even though we'd put so much effort and work into those songs we would not be entitled to any publishing monies. Having said that, I harbour no bitterness whatsoever about that situation, I don't have the energy to focus on that, it's just not wise – I will discuss my feelings towards Tom and Mick in more depth later on in my tale.

With the benefit of hindsight, what I will say to anyone going into a studio for the first time is if you are adding *anything*, then you are entitled to some of the publishing. At such an early stage in your career when you are around more experienced people, it's a hard conversation to have, but you have to make your point. It also sets a precedent for future work – usually I will not go into a studio as a writer unless there is fifty per cent for me. I do lyric and melody, all the arrangements, some programming, harmonies and so on, elements which are never going to be worth less. If you have three people in a room, then it's split three equal ways, but I would also say, to go beyond three people writing in a studio . . . it might work in Nashville, but be careful. Whichever line-up you have, get it understood what the splits are; it cuts out the disappointment. Believe me, I know.

By the time we were recording that debut album, the word on the street about Bros was already reaching epic proportions. We were increasingly being asked to do photo shoots and interviews and on some days it was as if everyone knew about us already. We were starting to be mobbed before we'd even had a hit.

We did some PAs to fan the flames, although not exactly hundreds like some young bands do. Nonetheless, something intangible was happening and we were already getting a following. Girls were beginning to go mad when they saw us. That was quite a shock, I can tell you. One of the first times it began to dawn on me that something was happening, was outside my mum's house in Peckham (this would be the location of some of the most insane moments of Brosmania over the coming years). I came home one afternoon after doing some recording and there was a girl hyperventilating outside Mum's house. I instinctively thought it was a passer-by in distress, so I ran in and anxiously said, 'Mum, quick! There's a girl outside and she's obviously not well, she's hyperventilating. Look! Look!'

My mum followed me out of the front door and looked down the street. There was no one there. I was completely bemused. We went back inside, puzzled, but I was not happy, there had definitely been a girl out there in discomfort, so I had to look out of the window to check again. This time there were four girls and they were all hyperventilating. I dragged Mum out to see if we could help. When they saw me, they freaked out and their condition escalated to what can only be described as hysteria.

'I think that's because of you, Matty,' said Mum, a cheeky and proud little smile spreading across her face.

Within what felt like a month of that day, we were being mobbed by hundreds of screaming girls every day without fail.

We hadn't even released a record yet.

SEVEN

A Righteous Way Of Getting Paid

August 1987 saw the release of our debut single, 'I Owe You Nothing'. The song was already being played repeatedly in certain cool clubs so hopes were high for the actual chart.

It peaked at Number 74.

It seemed to matter very little. In the post-Millennial pop climate, many labels might have abandoned ship at that point, but fortunately for us – and Sony in the end – our record company was undeterred. Our second single was pencilled in for October.

Even after the disappointing chart placing for our debut single, the fever swelling around Bros seemed to increase. When our follow-up single was issued, 'When Will I Be Famous?', everything changed. Normal was a word I would no longer be able to use in my life. We were told we might go in at Number 40.

'Maybe, Matt.'

'When Will I Be Famous?' mid-weeked at 41 so we knew we had a chance. Back then you had to sell thousands of records just to get into 'the Forty'. To me, Number 40 would have been an incredible achievement; after all, we were a completely new band. I remember lying in my bedroom on a Sunday night with my mate Lloyd – Luke was downstairs – listening to the chart countdown, as we had done for most of our lives. Before, we'd have been listening to see if The Specials or Police had charted and where. Now we were waiting for Bros, it was the most extraordinary feeling of disbelief and anticipation.

'And at Number 40 . . .'

. . . it wasn't us.

It was Simply Red with 'Ev'ry Time You Say Goodbye'.

It was just the most awful feeling.

They played that record and we were barely listening, we were so deflated. Then the DJ said, 'Number 39, they've done it, it's Bros!'

We all just went nuts, Luke ran in and we were going crazy. All I remember was jumping up and down in a frenzy, swearing in excitement, hugging each other. We were inside the UK Top Forty! It didn't make sense, it was amazing. We'd charted. It was a quite phenomenal moment.

And it just got better. As Brosmania started to break on the unsuspecting shores of British pop, the single stayed in the Top Forty for nearly four months. Eventually, it reached the giddy heights of Number 2.

In one sense, when 'Famous' hit Number 2, we were dumbfounded. By then, however, Brosmania was in full flow (an alternative name, 'Brosteria', was less popular). When I try to analyse why the hysteria surrounding Bros was so intense and so sudden, I still can't put my finger on it. Yes, we were good-looking boys, we'd had a Number 2 single, we had a great album coming out and we were working very, very hard promoting the band. But there were certainly plenty of good bands who were getting far more press than us – at that stage anyway

– who were much less fawned upon. When the mania first exploded, we'd only really had one published piece of high-profile press, a brief interview in *Smash Hits*. People often ask me why it took off like it did and I can truly say I don't know. Bros had a natural, massive momentum, which is quite rare I think. There was just something magical about what was going on.

There were a couple of watershed moments when you could visibly see the hysteria cranked up a gear. One of those was playing a PA at Busby's in Tottenham Court Road, but perhaps the biggest single event that seemed to have a massive effect on our popularity and profile was when a gentleman called Michael Metcalf gave us a slot on the TV show *The Roxy*. We were waiting anxiously to get *The Roxy* and then finally it came in. That programme and Michael in particular took a gamble when Tyne Tees announced they would be doing a special on us. I remember being at a Sony/CBS conference doing some meet-and-greets when someone took me to one side and said, 'You have to go *now*, you've got *The Roxy*!' We were absolutely mobbed just trying to walk into the TV studios and looking back at the video footage, you can see we are beaming. It was a pivotal moment and we knew it. Yet even that hysteria was nothing compared to the frenzy that erupted after our performance of three songs was broadcast, along with some interviews. After *The Roxy*, there was no stopping it.

To this day one of the cameramen from *The Roxy* tells the story that when he thinks of that show, the hairs on the back of his neck stand up. He was stunned by the hysteria and likened it to the mass adoration he had also witnessed when he filmed The Beatles back in the Sixties. He wasn't comparing us to The Beatles – of course not – but he said that our fans' behaviour was identically, inexplicably insane. It wasn't just the fans screaming at the limo or at the stage door. Within what seemed like a few weeks, we began to notice blatant manifestations of our popularity. It was a steep learning curve for us and it never plateaued.

When you are being feted to such a degree, you realize very swiftly that you have a very immediate and powerful influence over your fan base and beyond. Needless to say, that is why we were always so anti-drugs. On a more superficial level, the strangest things can remind you that you are being watched every second of every day. I soon learnt to be careful what I said in interviews. Thousands of fans are waiting on your every word and casual comments in front of a journalist can have repercussions for years. For example, I used to love Caramac and I made the mistake of saying that in one magazine. A much bigger belly and a few hundred spots later and I'm praying, 'No more Caramac guys! Please!' To this day, one girl will still bring me a few Caramacs whenever I do a show. It's delicious, don't get me wrong, but it's a bit like the first drink you get drunk on – if I smell Pernod-and-black I gag, and Caramac is starting to have that effect.

The famous Bros Grolsch bottle tops on the shoes was a funny example of that. I was bored one day and was playing about with some bottle tops that were lying around, and for some reason I whacked them on my shoe. It wasn't premeditated in any way, just something to do really.

Three days later, I was driving down Kensington High Street when I saw a girl walking past with Grolsch bottle tops on her shoes. I blinked and shook my head, almost cartoon-like, to make sure I had seen correctly.

I had.

Putting it down to some one-in-a-million coincidence, I carried on driving. Fifty yards further on, I saw another girl wearing them, then another and another. It was just crazy, and quite a shock to see the impact my supposedly insignificant fashion decision had made.

Even today, not a twenty-four-hour period goes by without someone mentioning those Grolsch bottle tops. But do you know what? Grolsch never even sent me so much as a single bottle. They never phoned, wrote or got in touch! I was later told their sales had gone up by a third. Cheers!

It wasn't just the bottle tops that these kids copied. Suddenly, everywhere you looked there were ripped jeans, Harrington jackets, cropped haircuts, Doc Martens decorated with watches or playing cards, you name it, if we wore something, within hours it was on the street. A new breed had arrived: Brosettes.

And there were millions of them . . .

I used to drive over Hammersmith flyover frequently, and as I sped into London, I would always look down from my concrete vantage point and take in the sight of what was then known as the Hammersmith Odeon. It was such a huge venue, just under 4000 people and only the really big bands could fill it. I had been to my first-ever concert there, to see Depeche Mode, one of the biggest bands on the planet. To me, in a new band only just signed, the prospect of playing there seemed an unattainable dream.

Then our management phoned us with news of the schedule for our first tour. They reeled off a list of venues which didn't really register that much to me, to be honest. Then they said . . .

'In London you will be doing Hammersmith Odeon . . .'

'What? You're kidding me?'

'Er, twice.'

It was just hard to believe the words I was hearing . . . two nights at the Odeon!

67

A day later they phoned back. 'Matt, hi, listen, both Odeons have sold out. You're now doing four nights.'

By now I was in seventh heaven.

The phone rang again. 'Sorry, Matt, I forgot to mention, we've added a Wembley Arena date too.'

I knew things would never be the same again.

Arriving for that first Wembley Arena performance and seeing the empty venue, just contemplating how many people would have to leave their homes to fill it, was a phenomenal feeling. Doing that show with my brother made it extra special. It was such a milestone, but the speed of Bros's rise to major fame was so rapid that there were so many milestones. They came so thick and fast that it was hard to actually see them as landmark moments. Signing with Tom. Signing with Sony. The first Top Forty. Our first big show. Five Hammersmiths. That Wembley Arena. Our first *Top of the Pops*. Being on the front cover of *NME*. Our first TV interview, switching Radio 1 on to the FM frequency . . . it was endless.

Every time we played a gig or released a record, the hysteria we witnessed was more extreme than the last time, even though we'd thought it had peaked back then. It hadn't. It was hard to believe, but we were in the process of becoming chart regulars. Eventually we would go on to notch up eleven Top Thirty singles and three Top Twenty albums.

The debut album *Push* was released in April of 1988. By mid-afternoon on the Monday of release, we were told the record was on target to sell 150,000 copies on that first day alone. That was gold in less than twenty-four hours, halfway to platinum. When the sales figures were tallied up on Saturday evening, we'd shifted over 300,000 copies, that's platinum in less than a week. Only a new instalment of the mega-hit compilation album *Now That's What I Call Music* managed to keep us from debuting at Number 1. *Push* went on to spend fifty-four weeks in the UK Top Forty – more than a year – and notched up over 5.5 million sales worldwide.

Calm is not a word you could use to describe the scenes on Oxford Street when we agreed to do a store signing to promote our hit single, 'Drop The Boy'. For a start, 11,000 fans turned up. Central London was gridlocked and it made the evening news. They showed clips of snaking lines of police, two or three deep, arms locked, straining to hold back the massed ranks of Bros fans. It felt like a once-in-a-lifetime, insane moment, but Bros was already becoming a byword for generating such frenetic behaviour.

When we came to leave the shop, it was a security nightmare, so my press officer Jo put my by-now-famous red jacket on and a towel over her head, then plunged out into the hysteria, diving into the limo through a sea of grabbing hands. While the fans were distracted, we were bundled into a black police riot van which headed off the wrong way down Oxford Street at what felt like 80 mph. As we looked back at the swarming hordes, we saw four teenage girls who had rumbled our escape plot. They were wide-eyed and racing after the riot van, unable to run as fast as they obviously wanted to because they were carrying something large and black.

It was the door to our limo – they had ripped it clean off its hinges.

We were used to getting hefty bills for dents in limos, that went with the territory, but this was something else. You quickly learn to take certain precautions when you know fans will be somewhere on any given day. We would remove our jewellery or loose clothing, tuck everything away, otherwise it would just be shredded off us – after all, if these fans could rip a door off a car . . . so there was often a real sense of personal danger. Of course, I loved it, although I always found it frightening leaving a venue, not for myself but because I felt a genuine fear that kids might be knocked over by the car or the crowds.

Many times you'd feel a searing pain on your head just as you heard a girl screaming, 'I've got it! I've got it! I've got his hair!' and you'd be thinking, *Yes, and half my bloody scalp as well!* It was funny, Brosettes were like a bloody army, they were proper hardcore, a force to be reckoned with! When you had three or four thousand of them turn up . . . you were in trouble!

Did I find it oppressive or claustrophobic? Not one bit. What's not to love about doing a job that is so different to what is considered 'normal'? What's not to love about your life being absolutely barmy?

Inevitably, a few fans crossed the line into rather more unsettling areas. We had our share of death threats. Plenty in fact – that's not some perverse pop star bragging, just an observation that this sort of behaviour goes with the job. We had a few letters from jealous boyfriends and over-obsessive fans, every band I know gets that, but it can still be a bit freaky. However, one series of letters was particularly chilling. I received four death threats in four separate letters, each mailed from the four most extreme points of the compass in the UK. These letters told me how the writer was going to kill me and when they were going to do it. We'd had threats before but there was something about the way these letters had been written – and the elusive nature of the premeditated mailing from four distant postcodes – that made it all seem a little too *thorough*. I said to my dad, 'Look, I wouldn't normally bother you with this but . . .' so he had a look at what had been going on. He became concerned when it transpired there were no fingerprints on any of the four letters – nothing.

A Righteous Way Of Getting Paid

There was an interval of about two months from the letters being sent to when they said I would be killed. It turned out that on this particular day we were due to fly out of Heathrow, not an ideal location in which to keep a low profile. We arrived at the airport encircled by ten bobbies, with a further inner cordon made up of ten of our own security. I knew it was serious when they insisted I wear a bullet-proof vest. That was a very uneasy experience. Until you put a bullet-proof vest on in genuine fearful circumstances, you don't think of such things, but I can tell you that your arms immediately start to feel big and your head seems enormous (and your balls feel massive!). Everything is exaggerated, you are like some cumbersome, over-sized target. Then your mind starts to interfere, making you think, *What about my throat? What about my eyes?* But the considered approach is that you protect the 'vital organs' and hope they don't put a bullet in the brain.

Eventually after many stressful minutes being hustled through Heathrow's multitude of gangways and endless corridors, we arrived on the other side of security in a cordoned area that was safe. I was just so relieved. I sat down heavily under the weight of the bullet-proof vest and exhaled in pure relief. They found the letter-writer, and it was a fanatical fan. A simple case of 'If I can't have you, then nobody can.'

On more than one occasion I have received entrails in the post. I've had both of what I would class as 'good' and 'bad' entrails. I've had good, basically a raw animal's heart, that says 'This represents my love for you.' You think, *Well, at least it's coming from a good place,* but it's still pretty bloody creepy!

Then you get 'bad' entrails. These essentially say 'I am going to rip your heart out, 'cos you've ripped my heart out, if I can't have you, no one can . . .' etc. The first time you receive such a 'delivery' is obviously pretty weird, like something out

71

of a horror movie, but after a while you do get more used to it and just whack it in with the boiling bunny in the soup pot.

Fortunately, it wasn't usually so threatening. There was one fan who used to send me tinned food, more often than not meatballs. Believe it or not, that used to freak me out more than the entrails, because with a pig's heart and the like, you could probably spot that person coming a mile away. There's no denying their thought process is odd: *I am obsessed with this certain person so what I will do as a token of that deep love and to show that I care for them, I'll send them a dead animal's heart in the post.* Strange, absolutely bonkers perhaps, but I can just about follow that. But tinned food? There's a saying that in New York you can spot a crazy person coming two blocks away; but in LA they could be standing right next to you and you wouldn't know. Likewise, there is a deep, underlying yet unfathomable philosophy to sending somebody tinned food. I found it so bizarre.

This person stepped it up a gear once. I was coming out of a venue after preparations for the Royal Variety Show. We'd done the dress rehearsal and I was wearing my very beautifully tailored stage clothes. We had an hour to get ready so there was no time to change. As we started to pull away from the stage door, I spotted a fan, whom I knew to be the girl who sent me tinned food. She was holding a large gift-wrapped present and looking very anxious that she might not be able to give me this parcel. As the limo started to move past her, she became very, very agitated, so much so that I actually thought she was going to have a seizure. I asked the driver to pull over and I opened the car door so she could give me her present. Relief swamped her face once she had delivered the gift. As we started to drive off I took the exquisite wrapping paper off the present, intrigued by what she'd so desperately wanted me to see.

A Righteous Way Of Getting Paid

It was a half-thawed turkey.

I have to admit that I sat there, half-defrosted turkey juices seeping out all over my exorbitantly expensive stage trousers, and I pissed myself laughing. Thanks a lot! In sixty minutes I am on stage in front of thousands of fans and I'm sitting here with a turkey on my lap – with giblets.

Maybe you have never received such a gift so perhaps you've never thought this one through, but the gift of the turkey was one thing; what actually disturbed me the most was the persistence she showed in getting the present to me. Looking back, it has to be one of the funniest gifts I ever received, I've been chuckling about it for fifteen years since.

Why did she do it? To be honest with you, I never really wanted to have that conversation with her . . .

EIGHT

A Pocket Full Of Green

In the UK, 1987 and 1988 were incredible years for Bros. Our singles were puncturing the Top Five with ease ('I Quit' and 'Cat Among The Pigeons/Silent Night' rounded off the year of hits), entire tours were selling out in forty minutes and the fan hysteria reached such proportions that the police force had to have meetings with our road managers to coordinate motorway roadblocks. We were all over the tabloids on a daily basis. Columnists were running features on 'Brosette uniforms', sociologists were analysing why these girls were so unconditionally obsessed. Our fan club 'The Bros Front' was voted the best and most popular in the country with tens of thousands of members, our debut album soared past the million-sales mark, we had our own comic book published and even Pepsi had got in on the act, with a lucrative six-figure sponsorship deal. Brosmania was everywhere.

I think perhaps a lot of people don't realize this, but Brosmania was *global*. Literally within a year of first breaking in the UK, there wasn't a country we could go to where it wasn't crazy. Every country in the world was truly, absolutely bloody mad for Bros, except for one. Only the United States did not

74

fall under the spell (more of which later). Every landmark moment in the UK was repeated all over the world, and in certain cases, the hysteria was even more rabid. I was at the centre of the storm with Dukus and Craig and I absolutely loved it.

Our first European tour was at the very start of 1988, quite early on in our career, but you have to remember we were a gigging band before we were discovered, so spending weeks out on the road was the stuff of dreams to us. Unlike many British acts, we weren't flying off as conquering heroes to land in a country where you played third on the bill in a truckers' café. We played each country's biggest venues every night, such as the cavernous Buddha Khan in Japan. We rammed them all full to the brim. We never became used to that either. I remember constantly pulling up to venues that seemed to tower into the clouds and saying to Lukie, 'Oh my God, is that where we are playing?'

One of the best feelings about being on the road with Bros was that people always knew you were in town. When you tour with a band like that, with an operation that massive, people know you've arrived. The band would go out with their Access-All-Areas laminates and always bring back two or three guests. It didn't matter what city we went to, everyone knew, the venues would have been running ads for weeks, the magazines and TV would have been featuring us for months, it was blanket coverage everywhere. That gave you a real presence when the tour bus finally pulled up, that was a good feeling.

Physically as well, the Bros touring party was quite a sight. We'd have multiple juggernauts, thousands of fans, floors of hotels, miles of cables, everything was done on a vast scale. The best kind of venues are those known as a 'multiple' – where you are playing more than one night at the same gig. When you are constantly touring and living out of suitcases, hotel rooms (however plush) and eating food stolen on the go, it was a delight to pull up outside a multiple and say to yourself, 'Okay, this is going to be my home for the next few nights.' That's one of the few occasions on the road when you can slow down a little bit. But as soon as those multiples are over, it's back on the bus, off on the road and onwards and upwards.

You hear so many musicians moaning about the rigours of the road. I can't understand that, I really can't. I love it, it makes the blood course through my veins. Of course you get tired, you have little squabbles with your touring party over silly things, you miss home and your loved ones, it's relentless, etc, etc. All of the above and then some. But every night you get to perform for an hour, maybe ninety minutes, more if you are lucky, and that makes all the stuff between leaving the stage one night and walking back out the next a price well worth paying.

I'm not just saying this about my time in Bros when we were feted wherever we turned. I love playing live, period. It is addictive, it creates such a high, making that music and feeling like a unit with your band. It's incredible. What being in Bros meant was that, literally, we could tour whenever we wanted. The money was there to back it up and we could sell-out as many venues as we could physically play. I know that logistics have made this more difficult for me later in my career, so I do miss being able to tour wherever I want, I miss touring terribly. I know that contradicts everything I have said in this book about feeling transient, but I am just telling it as I feel it. Touring is the currency of my life and I wish I had more.

There hasn't been one hour of writing this book and there isn't a single second of any given day when I don't feel like getting on stage and doing a gig. I feel very honoured and very blessed that I am still in a position of touring after all these years and I pray with all my heart that I will be able to tour until the day I leave this mortal coil.

Bros were so prolific with touring that the number of countries we had visited almost became something we prided ourselves on; not in so facile a way as collecting stamps on a passport, it felt good to know we'd taken our show to a certain country. Unfortunately, that never happened in Austria. Why? Because of a hilarious experience that was straight out of *The Pink Panther*. During one of our European jaunts for *Push*, we pulled up at a venue in Vienna ready to prepare for the show. Our tour manager was very unhappy with the size of the stage – not for any egotistical reason, but simply because he thought that the stage could not safely accommodate our production, which was huge. He was convinced that the stage would not even be able to support our lighting rig.

'What do you mean, it will probably be okay or it's a bit of a risk?' I asked.

'Listen,' he replied, 'there is a possibility that the lighting rig will fall into the crowd and if that happens, people could get injured or worse.'

'Look, we don't understand about structural issues, load-bearing values and suchlike, what is the bottom line here?'

'You could kill people.'

We cancelled the gig on the spot, headed back to the bus and made our way to Italy to continue the tour. That was that. Or so we thought.

We returned to Austria some time later to do extensive promotion for our second album, *The Time*. There we were met by the usual assembled mass, about 150 journalists waiting to do a press conference. Except this time there were three uninvited guests, who had slithered in unannounced – a lawyer belligerently flanked by two 6' 4" policemen. Without any warning, they said, 'We are here to seize your British passports.' They explained that the promoter represented by this lawyer was suing us for a large sum of money for failing to perform and leaving him out of pocket. Again, they demanded to seize our passports.

'Like fuck you will, seize my arse!'

'Er, boys,' said our tour manager, leaning over conspiratorially. 'Get back into the van and let's go.'

What followed was a classic car chase lifted straight from the movies. We sped off into the Viennese afternoon, hastily followed by this weedy little lawyer woman and her two hulking policemen. We managed to put enough distance between the two vehicles to allow us to screech up to the British Embassy gates, pile out and walk – fairly briskly but not without a certain well-dressed panache – into reception.

'We need to see the Consul straight away please.' A phone call was made and the message came back, 'You'd better come in.' We were so well-known at that point that our names and faces seemed to be everywhere.

So we sat in the Embassy all day, no refreshments to speak of, just a few cans of Coke, while the whole precarious situation was analysed. At the time this all felt very threatening. We contacted Sony/Epic in America, who offered to fly over their top legal eagle that night. By this point, I am not kidding you, there must have been eight police cars and countless news trucks outside the Embassy. We were looking out of the window in utter bemusement; after all, we'd only gone to do some promotion! We were saying, 'What is it with this bloody place?' Ironically, we'd genuinely missed not having played there as it was one of those countries we didn't have under our belt.

Fortunately, we were dealing with the coolest British Consul I've ever met in my life. 'Okay, chaps,' he explained after much deliberation. 'I've looked into this, made a few phonecalls and I have assembled a masterplan of devilish brilliance. This is what we are going to do . . .' We looked at him in eager James-Bond-esque anticipation. 'We're going to leg it.'

He further explained, 'We need to get you back to the hotel. We are going to pull up your van outside the front of the Embassy, get some of my staff to open the doors and say, "Ready! Okay! Here they come!" as if to usher you out. While they are doing this, you, me and two more of my staff will run to the hotel!'

It might sound simplistic but we had to leave the Embassy somehow and we could hardly be helicoptered out! So there we were, whisked out of the rear exit of the British Embassy, sprinting through the streets of Vienna, with the equally breathless Consul showing us the back route to the hotel. When we got there and ran into the lobby, it dawned on us that the whole farce had actually made the evening's news. Despite our valiant escape plan, the police quickly caught up with us at the hotel and we were immediately put under house arrest. Our passports were, indeed, seized.

Next thing I knew, I was being grilled by numerous stern-faced suits who asked me all sorts of questions about the cancelled gig and the size of the production and so on. I didn't have answers to what they needed to know, so I said, 'Just call our tour manager, I'm in the band and this sort of information isn't anything to do with us.'

When Epic's US lawyer arrived, he immediately plunged into lengthy discussions with the promoter's representatives and other authority figures who had gathered, vulture-like. Somehow, he managed to get our passports back, before walking calmly over to us and saying quietly, 'I would recommend that you leave right NOW!'

And that's exactly what we did. We boarded a plane and

I've not been back to Austria since. All we wanted to do was play Austria and to this day I still want to, but this one aggrieved promoter prevented it. As comical as it was, I stand by the central issue – if a tour manager tells me not to do a gig because there is the possibility that people could be injured, I'm not going to do it.

Our first dates in Australia were an intensely exciting time. Just the concept of flying to the other side of the globe with our band was exhilarating. In the UK and Europe, the hysteria was permeating every minute of our day, but with the prospect of flying at hundreds of miles an hour for nearly a day to another continent, we had no idea what to expect. We left 3000 fans behind us at Heathrow but weren't sure what would face us down under. I thought there might be a few hundred fans waiting for us, maybe a thousand if things had got really out of hand.

How wrong can you be?

With the Jumbo safely nestled into its bay, the plane's captain came on the intercom and said, 'Would everyone except Bros and their party please leave the plane.' Cue several hundred intrigued passengers disembarking. Then the same voice came over again and repeated, 'Would everyone except Bros and their immediate circle please leave the plane.' So we sat still some more, a rising tide of anticipation welling up in my stomach. We were informed there were one hundred airport staff waiting to escort us through what is known in the business as a 'tarmac transfer'. As soon as we exited the plane, I knew why. There were 11,000 fans roosting below the mezzanine gantry at Sydney airport. I just turned to Luke and said, 'What the fuck?'

Our hotel offered scant respite from the madness. We checked into our rooms and I started to collect myself for a gruelling schedule of promotional work that was lined up for that very first day. I switched on the news and was distracted by what appeared to be a clip of The Beatles, soundtracked by their classic 'She Loves You' single. For a few seconds I didn't realize that, rather than the Fab Four, the grainy, black-and-white footage was actually of our own arrival . . . then the soundtrack went into 'Famous'. It was truly mad.

All our gigs were a sell-out and had been for weeks – it was just one sold-out arena after another. We did a seven-night run at the cavernous Sydney Entertainment Centre. Bon Jovi held pretty much every box-office record for merchandise sales in Australia but as our tour scooted around that vast country, we were breaking every single one of them. So much so that it became something we wanted to do, something we all became interested in, breaking Bon Jovi's records. We were doing £100,000 a night in T-shirts and programmes, usually shifting more than a thousand of the latter at every single show. I vividly recall our tour manager walking into our dressing-room one night and saying, 'Here you are lads, this is what we've taken in merch tonight,' as he emptied a bin-liner bursting with money, wads and wads of notes, on to the floor. You look at that and you think, 'Okay, I can afford a new jacket!'

People often ask me if these sort of experiences felt uncomfortable or peculiar. I can tell you now it feels absolutely amazing. I am certainly not going to theorize over it and suggest it is anything *but* amazing. Being in a band is an incredible way of life. Getting off a plane after almost a day and a night to find thousands of screaming fans who had been waiting for you for hours is, for me, as rock and roll as it gets, and utterly soul-stirring.

Going back to the hotel after each night in Sydney and seeing the very beautiful Whitney Houston having a drink at the bar only increased the sense of bewilderment. It wasn't just the gigs or the transfers or the sacks full of cash ... even record-store signings were just another way for the hysteria to manifest itself. A signing at a large HMV in Australia was organized and we had thousands of fans turn up, absolute pandemonium. Considering the population of Australia is only twenty million, that was proportionately like having over 30,000 turn up that day in Oxford Street. Later, we would have both the Number 1 and Number 2 singles in Australia, the first act to do that since Elvis.

NINE

Dreams Cannot Rescue Me

Bros was becoming the biggest band in the country and, indeed, across most of the world. All our hopes and aspirations for the band were coming true almost by the day. In the middle of March 1988, our third single 'Drop The Boy' had hit Number 2, and would eventually spend nearly three months in the Forty. We thought things were just getting better and better.

Then my sister Carolyn was killed by a drink-driver.

I was due to go out to Europe on a promotional tour and the night before I started arguing with Carolyn. She was finding it frustrating sometimes to be known only as 'Bros's sister' or 'Matt's and Luke's sister', rather than Carolyn Phillips. I became really angry with her and she did with me. We must have argued for a good hour or so but, fortunately, we eventually got to a good place and things calmed down.

'Look, if someone says "This is Bros's sister", say "Hello, my name is Carolyn". Is that too difficult?'

She looked at me and said, 'You bastard!' and broke out into one of her beautiful smiles and gave me a big hug.

I said, 'I love you and you love me, right? Then be proud of me.'

That was that, and we ended up having a really good night.

So then I went to Europe for a few days' promotion. Whenever we came back from abroad, there would be four limos waiting for us: one for me, one for Luke, one for Craig and one for the management. This time though, there was just one solitary limo. I got in and we immediately started driving in the wrong direction.

I said to Mark, one of our managers at the time, 'What's wrong?'

'Oh, nothing,' he said. 'We're going to your mum's.'

'Why the fuck are you lot coming? What's wrong?'

He said nothing.

'What the fuck is wrong?' I repeated, but he wouldn't say anything. I wanted to be sick.

'Who's died?' I said. I wanted to be sick, to crap myself. 'Mark, tell me it's not my mum.'

He still didn't say anything so I grabbed him by his collar and said, 'Fucking tell me it's not my mum.'

'It's not your mum,' he finally said.

I knew then that someone had died.

I got back to Mum's house in Peckham and there were hundreds of fans outside as normal, only on this day they were standing in silence. I ran into the house and saw my mum and my heart was somewhat appeased. But she was crying. Then Tony, my step-dad said, 'Carolyn died last night.'

It was just the most painful, disgusting, awful moment. It is impossible to put a finger on the pain.

Carolyn was killed by a drunken driver. She was only eighteen. Her friend Emma Harvard had been in the Vauxhall Cavalier with her at the time and was also killed. The day was Good Friday, 1988. The man who killed them also lost his life.

The hardest thing for me is the thought of Tony, God bless

his beautiful little heart, following his daughter down the motorway behind the ambulance, praying that she was going to make it. She died on the operating table. The pain that I feel for Tony and his lovely ex-wife Pauline is unbearable sometimes. What must have been going through their heads? The stillness and the fear in that car following their daughter who was mangled up in an ambulance, I just . . . cannot comprehend. My heart goes out to any parent who has lost a daughter or son.

I understand that the family of the driver responsible have never apologized to Carolyn's mum Pauline or sent her a letter or flowers. I know they lost somebody and that is hard, but I don't understand why they have never said anything. But loss is loss to me. As a man that has faith, I mourn their loss too; I really mourn the loss of Carolyn's best friend; and I painfully mourn Carolyn. I have empathy for the family that lost the driver of the car but he had been drinking so there is inevitably some anger there.

Yet time is an incredible healer and I feel for everyone involved. If you want to trudge through life, wear boots of hatred, because they will weigh you down. To fill your life with hatred or blame will make those negative emotions responsible for what happens *next* in your life, which will only perpetuate an endless cycle. Having said that, I fully recognize that I can only step back and say some of these things because it is many years since that dreadful night when my sister was killed. At the time, there was a great deal of anger and a seemingly infinite burden of grief. I thought I would crumple at any second.

Then it started again; I felt unsafe, and guilty. What happened created much guilt within my brother and me. I know I felt incredibly guilty about going to collect a gold disc on *Wogan* the day after, even though everyone – Carolyn's mum,

Tony, Adam, my mum – all said that's what she would have wanted. Tony actually said, 'You are doing this and you are going to do it for Carolyn.' I remember doing the show which, in theory, should have been a big moment for us. *Wogan* was a huge draw at the time and we were the highlight of the evening, but it didn't mean anything to me, I was a shell, robotically doing my job. Wogan came on and gave us the disc, the audience clapped, Terry was very complimentary, it was so weird. I just felt nothing except guilt. Even talking about it now feels surreal.

It was so hard during that period. Bros was just taking off and there was consequently a constant underlying feeling of guilt afterwards. Carolyn never saw us reach Number 1, and we were never able to shower her with gifts and life experiences that, as successful pop stars, we would have loved doing. She was killed when we were at Number 2 in the charts with 'Drop The Boy' and so we were not able to see as much of our family in the months leading up to the tragedy as we would ideally have liked, we were working so hard. Then she was gone.

I just couldn't get Carolyn out of my head for ages. The funeral did not help me mourn at all. I felt rather embarrassed because there were so many photographers at the church. Despite our pleas for privacy, a major tabloid revealed the location. I spoke to them personally and said it would mortify me if there were thousands of fans at the church, but they ignored my request – remember, we'd only recently done that insane signing in Oxford Street.

Yet, when we pulled up for the service, only one fan was there with a single flower. She didn't say anything to us and just put the flower through the car window. Apart from the single respectful girl, not one fan had turned up, out of respect for our privacy. At that time, Bros hysteria was manic, I saw so many incidents where I really thought the fans couldn't help

Left My favourite picture of my dear and handsome grandad

Above Grandad Read and Grandad Weston

Mum and Dad on their wedding day

Mum and Dad proudly looking at their sons

Above Us and our beautiful mum

Right A brotherly moment

Above A peaceful moment

Right Luke looking over me

One of my favourite memories . . . water fights in the back garden

Above The beginning of a new family . . . me, Luke, Adam, Carolyn, and my dear stepfather Tony

Above Me, Mum and Luke in Cheddar with our dogs Bill and Ben and our cat Jessy

Above Mum and Tony on their wedding day

Right Dad putting on a brave face visiting me in hospital (this was pre-Game Boy) during my septic arthritis scare

Left Even I don't know who I am in this photo

Below Luke snogging his girlfriend Julie and me just about to with Kaz . . . still in school uniform (check out the skinny tie)

Left Me at fifteen years old, master of ceremonies in the production of *Cabaret.*

Above My first girlfriend
Cindy

Right New Romantic

Below Mulletts rule . . .
that's my story and I'm
sticking to it.

The first Bros photo shoot

Right Somebody I miss everyday of my life . . . my sister Carolyn

Below I love to work a crowd

themselves, so when they stayed away from the church that was a very beautiful surprise for me.

Don't misunderstand – I know why the photographers were there, that's what happens, but I still felt embarrassed walking to the church. I wanted to say out loud, 'I am here for Carolyn, I didn't ask the cameras to come.' It was a very strange experience for me, not a moment when I mourned personally.

Unfortunately, there was also one truly sickening incident. When we came out of the service in tears, we heard a chuckle from the line of photographers. Hard to believe I know, but let me tell you one of the photographers laughed. Luke was already distraught and this callous chuckle was too much, so he made a V-sign and swore. It was the instinctive reaction of a man who was ravaged by grief, rightfully so.

The next day, a tabloid ran a photograph showing Luke making that gesture with the headline 'Bros Star's 4-Letter Fury At Funeral'. What's more, they said Luke had sworn at 'on-lookers'. It was hard to comprehend that this photographer had gone to that funeral, watched a family bury a daughter and sister, then laughed in such an offensive manner, gone back to his office, shown an editor his picture – and they ran the story. They'd had their moment, and it was nothing to do with the death of my sister. Words fail me. It showed me that some tabloids had no due process, there was no safety-valve whatsoever for what was appropriate. It was poor judgement on their part, to say the least.

As I've said, the funeral was a strange experience and not one that helped me come to terms with my loss at all. I cried at the time, of course I did, but for a while there was just this ache inside me. I didn't mourn for Carolyn until about six months later. I went to Barbados with a PA, John Buckland, just to get away from things. I remember thinking how still everything was, really still. I didn't have to do promotion, perform, talk, interview, do photo shoots – nothing, just stillness. It was a rare chance to catch my breath.

By actually stopping for a moment, events suddenly caught up with me. One afternoon I was lying on my bed on my belly. Although it was daytime, it was really dim because I had the shutters down. There were two beds in the room, with a gap between them. I looked across and that's when I saw her.

Carolyn.

Looking up at me. Smiling at me.

I *saw* her.

I was petrified of seeing her all cut up and mangled from the accident but she didn't have a scratch on her. That was so nice to see, she wasn't bruised and she had a gorgeous smile on her face. I was afraid a little, it startled me, but at the same time I have such tremendous faith, and here she was, glowing, smiling at me.

I cried for six hours straight.

I finally mourned for Carolyn, my beautiful sister.

John eventually came round for me and said, 'Are you okay, Matt?' To his credit, he took me to a place called Cobbler's Cove for a drink. I got drunk as a skunk, really properly drunk, on the house cocktail called Cobbler's Coolers. The bar rule said if you can drink this rum punch and walk round the pool once without falling in, you can have free drinks. We had two of these drinks, stood up to walk round the pool and . . . well, let's just say we didn't get free drinks. It might sound trivial given what had just happened in my room, but the whole experience was immensely cathartic. It was something that I needed to do.

Unfortunately, I was alone. I've always felt really comfortable with my own company, I've often been a loner and it makes my mum sad to think of the amount of time I spend alone. But I've felt safer on my own sometimes. I don't know if that's a good or bad thing. At least, on this occasion, my loneliness for once had allowed something good to happen – had I travelled with a partner, then maybe I might never have lain down that afternoon, never have seen Carolyn's angelic face smiling at me, never truly mourned for her. And yet, by way of contradiction, I felt desperately lonely. I was away on holiday in a gorgeous resort, I didn't have any work to do and yet I was emotionally on my own. I just felt desperately lonely.

In the autumn of 2004, someone was fixing my old friend Simon's car and it came up that he knew me. The guy working on the car stopped what he was doing and said, 'Oh my God, my sister was in the car with Carolyn when she died.' He saw the whole thing. That weird twist of fate all those years later reaffirms how many lives that crash affected.

There is a lyric in my song 'Goodbye' from my 2004 album *Early Side Of Later* which says, 'I understand that there must be pain, it's designed to illuminate the joy.' Life is a comparison. You don't know that you are truly happy unless you've had pain, and I don't think you know genuine pain unless you've been happy. I like the idea of learning how I feel and comparisons play an important part in that. Carolyn being killed at the very moment when our pop careers and all our music dreams were coming to fruition is probably as stark a comparison as you can get.

Of course, some moments of contrast and comparison are more intense than others. I think that we tend to seek perfection, and as a general rule, human beings associate perfection with joyous occasions. When Carolyn died it was one of the most excruciatingly painful and frightening moments, but it was also one of the purest moments in my life.

I had no choice. If I could not learn from that, if I could not realign certain things in my life because of that moment, then what was the point? Joy can provide perfection, but that is usually a somewhat fleeting perfection; pain can very often produce permanent perfection. Why? Because it will constantly remind you of things and constantly teach you. I don't think joy can do that so much. Nearly every painful moment teaches you something and it is your duty to learn from that.

TEN

Even Angels Have A Past

It's hard to picture what my day-to-day life was like at this point, the peak of Bros's success. I could not move, I could not go anywhere. I would go to the supermarket down the road only to find two hundred fans coming with me. When I went to the tills, they would all be standing there, watching, so I would always ask for my stuff to be put in three carrier bags to prevent people seeing what I had bought. It was such a struggle at times to retain any shred of privacy at all. Yet that was always counter-balanced by the fact that I *loved* what was happening, I loved the fans for being so supportive and I was thoroughly enjoying myself!

When they first called it 'Brosmania', I was very worried that it would be misconstrued as us comparing ourselves to The Beatles, because we did not come up with that name and would, of course, never make that comparison. We would always say in interviews, 'Please don't compare us in any way with The Beatles.' I'm more relaxed about it now and I do think some of the mania, the hysteria was similar to what they must have experienced but you still have to be very respectful when you put yourself in the same sentence as that band.

People mistakenly think you are talking about the band when actually we were talking about the fans.

I was in Soho one time when the mania was reaching a new peak. I was getting absolutely mobbed, chased by paparazzi, screamed at by some fans, it was really wild and I was thinking to myself, *Bloody hell this is mad!* Then, out of the corner of my eye, I saw Yasmin Le Bon and her husband Simon open a door and gesture over to me, saying 'Come in here!' Without thinking how surreal it all was – after all, I was a massive Duran Duran fan – I just ran over to them and walked straight in.

Once inside, I looked around me and then it sank in a little more. Nick Rhodes was having a birthday party. They were all there having a great time. 'Are you okay? That was a bit mad out there, eh?' said Simon and smiled at me, knowingly. It was one of the first instances when I felt safer and more comfortable around other performers. Duran Duran had, after all, been through what we were going through and had moved on to the next level. There was an understanding in Simon's voice – and indeed in the room – of what was happening to me and it felt very nice to be understood so completely for a brief moment.

They sat me down for this lovely dinner in this top restaurant and took me under their wing. Yasmin just seemed so caring and in control. That was a time when two people acted really selflessly and spotted that I was in a bit of a situation outside, then invited me in to a very private party. I was very grateful for that.

I have stayed in touch, I wouldn't say we were best mates, but I've bumped into Simon in so many parts of the world, hotels and restaurants, LA, New York, London and we always have a drink and a toast. I love seeing they're still around, they've broken up and re-formed and fans love them because they have an affinity with so many people's past. It was a very special little island of calm in the raging sea of insanity that was Brosmania.

I knew once I walked out of that restaurant that the madness would begin again. Even when you'd been followed all the way home then walked past another two hundred fans on your lawn, you would hope to find some sanctuary between your own four walls. Not always so. On several occasions I dialled directory enquiries to get a number only to find the woman on the other end recognized my voice and said, 'Is that . . . is that Matt Goss? Oh my God!' recognition was on a level that is hard to explain.

The fame can surprise you at the oddest moments too. One Christmas when Brosmania was at its peak, my whole family was sitting down to a turkey dinner. After the food, we were all pulling crackers which had trivia questions in them, when Grandad chuckled and said, 'I know the answer to this one!' It was a question about Luke and me.

We all slumped on the sofas afterwards to watch the festive special of *Only Fools and Horses* like the rest of the country, an annual ritual almost. It was the episode where Rodney has to pretend to be a twelve-year-old boy in order to qualify for a free holiday which Del Boy had won under false pretences. As a result of spending time with a bunch of pubescent kids, Rodney finds himself fancied by a young girl whose favourite band was . . . who else? Bros.

We were in another episode of that show too, when Rodney was trying to sell 'Free Nelson Mandela' T-shirts – after he'd been let out of prison, as well as Bros T-shirts – after we had split! *Spitting Image* also featured us in a hilarious spoof song called, 'When Will I Start Shaving?', which to my mind was genius. You've watched these programmes as a kid and then to find yourself actually in them is a very strange but fantastic feeling.

Mum's and Tony's home at 314 Commercial Way in Peckham was always besieged by fans. During the Bros heyday, there would never be less than a few hundred girls outside. Tony and Mum would sometimes say 'goodnight' to them at the end of the day, then pull the curtains back the next morning and they'd still be there. They both started to receive 'fan' letters themselves and Mum even took to posting our itinerary on the door to help the fans out. Even our dogs, two miniature Yorkshire terriers called Thomas and Geoffrey, were famous. Tony's business suffered because his answer-machine was full of fans saying 'I love Matt, I love Luke' – our phone number was for sale for two pounds a pop at the local school. The address of the house was graffitied on a nearby wall.

Sometimes, as when Carolyn died, it was the last thing that you'd want to see outside your house, but generally those fans were just being . . . fans. They were a little army, as I have said. Our lives were so surreal by then that a few hundred girls outside your door was just another element that you got used to. On one occasion, we had just landed back from some overseas work and were due to fly out again within a matter of a few hours to another European country to start once more. I asked the driver to take me to Mum's house first. I called ahead and asked Mum if she would be kind enough to cook me a roast dinner. We were on the road so often that hotel meals and touring diets really did start to grind you down. I craved normality in many ways and one of them was food.

It might sound gross but I asked Mum to stick the roast dinner in a plastic bag so I could take it with me in the limo, as I didn't really have enough time to stay and eat. That's how busy our schedules were. When I arrived at her house, there were the usual few hundred girls outside. I spoke to as many as I could in the time I had, ran inside, kissed Mum and said

'Hi!' then ran back outside, said goodbye to the fans and jumped back in the limo, complete with a freezer bag of roast dinner in my hand. I have to tell you it was delicious, a feast of home-cooking, served in a plastic bag.

As we drove off, I saw a tiny fan carrying what was the last remaining piece of Mum's fence that hadn't already been taken away by Brosettes as a memento. The abiding image I have of this particular girl was of a miniature elf walking along the road with a tree under her arm, that's what she looked like to me.

On one occasion, I couldn't resist playing a joke from inside Mum's house. My best mate Lloyd from school was with me through all those Bros years and we always had such a laugh. He eventually moved to South Africa and we have lost touch a little, but for the longest time we were the best of friends. The congregations outside Mum's house had got so out of control that we resorted to putting up one-way mirrored film on the windows so that they couldn't see in. We needed some privacy after all. One day when Lloyd and I were feeling particularly prankish, we both got our knobs out and banged them on the window, we were laughing so much we could hardly breathe. We knew that these girls would scream into unconsciousness if they so much as saw my finger so it was just hilarious. It was a very funny moment in among all the madness.

Not everyone found those fans so amusing. I felt we were actually harassed by the police at times, who on numerous nights threatened to have me or Luke arrested for 'incitement to riot', because of the huge number of excitable people block-ing our street. The girls would often write poems to us or messages on fences. The graffiti was a problem for our neigh-bours and my mum. To this day, there is still some graffiti in Commercial Way.

I was always perplexed that the police could not see that I was an innocent party in all this. I would say, 'Look, mate, this is my home, I am just coming home from work, I am not doing anything to be arrested for.' I understand that it was frustrating for them, frustrating for me, frustrating for the fans and the neighbours but it wasn't our fault. In the East End, we even paid for repairs to a tower block as a gesture of goodwill to the neighbours.

When we first went to Number 1 in the charts in June 1988 with 'I Owe You Nothing', Pepsi sent down a juggernaut with hundreds of cans of soft drinks for the fans and they all sat there in the street, singing our songs and having a great time, it was like an alternative Jubilee! It was only a mere ten months since that song's initial release had flopped, but when we re-released it, that gap of less than a year, 300 days or so, was the difference between only just piercing the Top 75 and . . . going to Number 1. We were at the top of the chart, our first single to be in that slot. I was in an almost dream-like state. I went to Hyde Park with a group of fans and over the course of a few hours we chatted and basked in the knowledge that Bros was at Number 1. We all sat there and shared that moment. I was later told there were 1000 fans there by the end of the afternoon. I said, 'Let's stay calm and share this,' and they did, we all had a great time. I knew there was very little chance that we would be allowed to celebrate this achievement in peace and quiet! I didn't mind at all.

The paparazzi interest in us was so intense. At one point, it was rumoured the press had bought a flat opposite my apartment in Maida Vale. We were never able to confirm or dismiss that definitively, but what I do know is that there were many times when I saw bucket lenses in the windows opposite. Our management always used to tell us to be careful opening curtains and stuff like that. And sure enough, whenever I went out on to my balcony for a coffee or some fresh air, there would be pictures of me in the tabloids the very next day.

The Maida Vale flat was interior-designed for us as a band (by our management) while we were away on tour. We did need a place to stay, but this was really not to my taste. It was all very state-of-the-art minimalism and modernist in style. It had little remote control cars on wires that would fly round the room and put the light on wherever you wanted it. All the wardrobe doors were immaculate Venetian blinds, it was all very sleek. My preference is for more palatial fixtures and fittings, with which I have filled my home in the Hollywood Hills. I am into heavy fabrics, beautiful textiles, and am more old school than new, I love decadent materials, warm environments, I love to feel enveloped and warm and cosy. I would rather stay in a hotel with a good thread count in the linen than somewhere modern and trendy. Back then, when a safe haven of comfort would have felt like a magic pill of security, that cold, hard interior design just didn't do it for me.

The funny thing with this minimalist flat was that there was a suggestion – which was very quickly dismissed – that the three of us should all live there together, like the bloody Young Ones. It's an approach that has been used by managers over the years, perhaps most recently with The Spice Girls, so it can obviously work, but it was not a viable option for Bros. We grew up together, went to school together, formed a band together, toured together and now we were supposed to live together. No, it would have been the catalyst that made the disaster happen earlier. Luke ended up getting a place in Frimley in the country, Craig also bought a home and I bought them out of the flat in Maida Vale.

Having said all that, behind the stark décor, it was actually a lovely mansion apartment, with about five windows across the front aspect. In all but one of the rooms I installed really soft blue lighting. But there was one final room where I didn't have those lights. The reason for that was simple. The photographers only looked at the windows where the blue lights were on. They thought the 'hidden' room was next door, so that became my room where I would sometimes just go in and watch them. You could follow their eyes as they scanned my windows and the blue lights would be the cut-off point for their visual search. It was a good way of having your own room in your own home all to yourself.

We were aware of the power of the media and we gave them plenty of material to write about. Of course, you can't feed stories to the press every day of your life. Very often, there is just nothing happening that is genuinely newsworthy. If that is the case, then yes, they make it up. On the cover artwork of 'When Will I Be Famous?' the lighting on the photo made us look like we had massive dicks. Within hours of the record's release, someone in the press said we'd put kidney beans down our pants to make our wedding tackle look bigger. Apart from being obviously not true, I found it hilarious that they chose kidney beans. When have you ever seen a kidney bean that looks like a very large penis?

It became even more surreal than that. One tabloid ran a story saying that we were not actually twins. What's more, they said that in order to make us look identical, we'd had cheek implants. Another newspaper said I'd temperamentally insisted on a first-class plane ticket to America for a teddy bear I had bought for a girlfriend – complete nonsense, of course. I could write an entire book on the ludicrous things they said about us. It was all so bizarre.

I once half-joked that I fancied having my hair in dreads, it was really just a throwaway comment. Next thing I know, there are mock-up photographs of me in the tabloids with a full head of dreadlocked hair, and headlines calling me 'Wacko Matto'. I love Michael Jackson's music hugely, but that was one comparison I could have done without!

You learned to take most of it on the chin, at least the stuff that was relatively harmless anyway. But there were some things that were appalling. One German newspaper ran a story saying my mum had cancer and that we were completely ignoring her. It was so offensive. Even then we didn't sue (it was complicated, being overseas and so on) although I did try to punch the journalist who wrote the story. Trust me, that was one of a hundred stories that were so wrong, just blatant lies.

It takes so much strength not to lose your mind in that situation. The media as an entity is so powerful but you are just one solitary person. There's no way you can actually physically correct a story unless you can get every one of those newspapers to print a retraction. You can't sue all those people unless you have a spare five million just lying around, and nothing better to do than spend all your days in the High Court.

One thing we always acted on, and to this day I will always act on if possible, is defamation. I feel strongly about drugs, I always have done. Remember, my sister was killed by a drunken driver. I am not a judgemental person, but that is a clear-cut case of right and wrong. We were always vehemently anti-drugs and said so in the press. So imagine my horror when I am driving down a London street in November 1989, getting on with my day and I see a news-stand with one of those headlines in thick, black pen, deliberately styled to look even more dramatic. It said, quite bluntly:

'EXPOSED! HEROIN DEALER IN BROS HOUSE.'

I nearly crashed the car. I phoned Luke and said, 'Have you seen this story?' We had such a young fan base, these sorts of lies could have been deeply damaging to them. We'd also worked very hard on our reputation and here was a paper that seemed to be implying we were involved in heroin. It was stomach-churning. Only three months earlier we'd been at Number 1 in the charts.

There was another story headlined 'Bros And Heroin Henry' which was accompanied by a picture of Luke greeting fans by a car outside the luxury Brompton Park Crescent Estate where he had an apartment. A second photo had been placed next to it with the alleged drug dealer on a cell phone. At first glance, it looked as if Luke and this man were only a few steps apart but actually they were two separate photos. We felt that the clear implication was that we were somehow involved, even though the article said 'the chart-topping star [Luke] knows nothing at all'.

What the story went on to say was that somewhere in the gated community of around 150 very expensive apartments – where Luke lived – a heroin dealer was alleged to be operating. Obviously it wasn't Luke, it had nothing to do with us, but it made a great headline. It was ludicrous but this time we had recourse to the law.

Enough was enough; it was becoming a free-for-all. You can explain away those words however you like, but that headline, printed on thousands of news-stands and in millions of news-papers sold that day, clearly implied that someone, me, Luke, my mum even, someone within our private circle was involved with heroin. Apart from the not insignificant personal distress, from a professional point of view those five words could have a catastrophic effect on our hard-earned fan base. We had to react to this, a line had been crossed.

We sued for libel.

Very-high-profile barristers were employed, court dates were set and meetings held. It was embarrassing to see the journalist in question squirming and blushing profusely, beetroot-red, at the story they had published. When we got to court to begin proceedings, the jury were winking at us and giving us a thumbs-up in front of the defence. There was no credible justification and after three days of testimony, they settled out of court for a substantial six-figure sum, much of which we immediately donated to a drug rehabilitation charity. This was one time when we actually beat the press. I would do the same in an instant. On defamation I would go all the way, I would make it my life's business if someone did that again.

Even though we won that battle, there were so many others that we chose not to fight. If we had, we would have become obsessed, spending far more time in court than in a studio and the bitterness and anger would have eaten away at us until we were just hollow shells. We had no choice but to take much of it on the chin and that was a very, very hard thing to do.

Eventually you stopped buying the papers. You had to, it was a matter of survival. Yet at the same time, it was hard to walk past a newsagent's knowing that you were on the front page that day. I've since been told that during the height of Bros fame, we were the most written-about people in the British press, but for the Royal Family.

ELEVEN

This Crazy Life

One fascinating aspect of being a famous singer is the way that celebrity is viewed; more specifically, how every tiny element of your life is forced through the publicity blender until it comes out the other end exaggerated beyond all recognition. Sometimes, as I've explained, it's hurtful, but often it is hilarious.

If most people took out twenty-five pounds too much from a cash machine and unwittingly went overdrawn, they probably wouldn't notice until they got a letter from their bank or the next time they checked their balance – if I'd have done that, the *Sun* would have run a front-page exclusive saying, 'Pop Loser In Bank Flop'; if you have a row with your partner, you have the chance to make it up the next morning; my quarrel would be on the Internet, word for word, within an hour as a downloadable file. That's how it is, everything is so exaggerated, it is almost impossible to lead a normal life.

And do you know what? I don't actually want to lead a 'normal' life. By that, I am not being condescending to the millions of people who work very hard for a living, I am merely saying I love doing what I do, which is not a normal job by most people's parameters.

But that leaves me with something of a paradox. I love being a musician and performer, I accept the lunacy that goes with that but I still want to keep normality in my life, without diluting what is a fabulous job to have. How do I do that? Comparisons.

The endless proliferation of polar opposites that can confront a pop star often kept me going through the worst days and entertained me during the good times. I might be on stage at 9 p.m. singing in front of 3000 people, buzzing with adrenaline, but when the show is over, I am usually to be found watching the box or mucking around with my PlayStation within an hour or so. Too many bands strive to live the rock-and-roll life – sometimes they get away with it and have a blast, sometimes casualties are unfortunately taken. In my time with Bros, I have certainly ticked many of the boxes that make up that religion. But to me, there is nothing more rock-and-roll than having the screams of thousands of fans still ringing in my ears, like some aural hangover, while I am sitting down having a cup of tea. I need to have some normality. I want to have a life as well. There is no other way for me.

By contrast, pop stardom might make you crave the simpler things in life, but Lukie and I also always loved the celebrity madness that came with being in Bros. We loved pushing both opposites to extremes – Bros rarely did anything by halves. One summer we were playing the huge Montreux rock festival alongside some of the biggest names in the business, including Elton John. We landed at the airport and our transfer to the site consisted of six police outriders on bikes, two police cars in front of them and several limos. Then we saw Elton's motorcade and he had seven outriders! So we said 'We've got to beat that, we gotta get more police bikes!' Each time we were on the same bill as Elton somewhere, we would try to gauge what the scale of his motorcade would be and top it, which with

Elton was always pretty hard but we came close! It was all a bit of fun, you'd have a word with the local nick and add another car to your escort. Then this cacophony of sirens would drive you towards the festival for your slot. It was brilliant. We knew it was all a bit *Spinal Tap* (a film which any self-respecting band should be constantly referencing as they travel around the world) but that was part of the enjoyment, it really can be as insane and ludicrous as that at times.

For the Montreux festival, as is the norm, most bands used the designated hall to hold their press conference. Not Bros. That was never going to happen. We rented an enormous yacht, invited hordes of journalists on board and offered them all a plentiful supply of expensive drinks. Let's face it, if you were a journalist, where are you going to go? The cold conference hall where you've been all week for a vending-machine coffee or a luxury yacht with a free bar? Naturally, we had every journalist covering the festival on this boat on the afternoon of our press conference.

Only we weren't there.

All these battle-hardened journos are standing there, sipping on expensive champagne and thinking, 'Bros've fucking stiffed us here haven't they . . . bastards. Still, might as well have another glass while I'm here . . .' Just then, our helicopter swung into view and we touched down on the helipad at the rear of the yacht. The photographers all went barmy and the lenses were snapping away frantically. What happened? Everyone had a fantastic day, they got the pictures and the story they wanted and Bros made the front pages of all the newspapers the next day – with style.

Some might say that was decadent. They'd be right, it was, but what is the point of being a pop star if you can't give it large and have a laugh? Trust me, it's an amazing feeling to arrive at a press conference in a helicopter on the back of a yacht, have a couple of glasses of champagne and then you are off, 'See you guys later!' Why wouldn't I want to do that and enjoy it?

Freddie Mercury once said, 'People *want* art. They want showbiz. They want to see you rush off in your limousine.' He was right.

Within less than eighteen months of our first single, the Bros machine was effectively a mobile mini-corporation. Behind all the headlines, TV reports, magazine soundbites and radio play, there was a huge amount of work to be done. We were tireless in our work ethic and that is something I am very proud of. We toured that band and we toured it *hard*. Our 'Global Push Tour' in October 1988 cost one million pounds to stage and was a relentless trek around the world. I was in my element.

We didn't skimp backstage either. We were working hard and apparently making money so we felt able to indulge ourselves. I always used to watch *Blue Silver*, which was Duran Duran's tour video, and they had arcade-size video games in their dressing-rooms, it seemed like such a rock-star thing to do. So when we got to the point where we could do the same . . . we did. It might sound a bit superficial but actually it was quite a defining moment. You have a little internal chuckle to yourself when you walk into your dressing-room at some big arena and you see your mates playing video games – a nice little moment.

In most countries we would only be able to go out shopping if certain stores let us in alone after closing time. This might seem a little excessive but we quickly learned it was often a necessity. While touring Japan, we momentarily forgot our faces were well-known out there – being so far from home, thousands of miles away from family, dropped into such an alien culture, it all seemed so improbable. We'd been told we were 'doing really well' in Japan but didn't think twice about going out to sample the local shops. We went into one particular clothes store and were noticed immediately by quite a few people. Five hours later, we were pinned in the back room of the shop by 3500 fans who had heard the whisper and raced there to see us. We had to be escorted out by the police.

At every bullet-train station we pulled up to – Osaka, Nagoya, Hiroshima – you could literally see nothing but faces squashed up against the windows. We didn't get to see the stations themselves, we saw the journey beforehand and then thousands of Japanese nostrils and lips.

During those Far-Eastern dates we stayed at many extremely plush Japanese hotels. Our sax player, Jim Turner, was the joker in the pack on the Bros tour bus. He would always be playing pranks and making us laugh. One night we decided to sort him out so we all jumped him in his room and stripped him stark bollock-naked. We hoisted him aloft, carried him to the lift and pressed the button for the foyer. We were all pissing ourselves and Jim was crying with laughter, shouting, 'You bastards!'

The hotels in Japan are huge corporate affairs and this particular lobby was half the size of a football pitch, marble everywhere with hundreds of Japanese rushing around looking very busy. When the door pinged open, we pushed Jim out as far as we could into the lobby and quickly shut the lift door behind him. Most people would have been mortified and tried to preserve their modesty, but Jim just stood there with his hands on his hips, in a defiant, laddish, football stance. Then, cool as you like, he pressed the 'Lift Up' button. While he waited, he kept nodding to passers-by, 'Evening . . . evening . . . Hi . . . hello . . . evening . . .'

On one of the endless journeys across the USA, we decided to light one of Jim's farts. We got the video camera ready and turned off all the lights on the bus. The whole tour party was crowded around staring at the pitch-black dark spot where we knew Jim's exposed buttocks were. Then he flicked a cigarette lighter and the video screen showed the faintest glimmer of the flame and the hand holding it. We all hushed in anticipation. Then, suddenly, with a rasping noise there was an explosion as Jim farted loudly, then the flame was gone. The entire bus erupted into hysterics. It was side-splitting. It was silly little moments like that that actually helped you stay sane on the road.

One favourite game on tour was laser tag. We each had a laser gun with a headstrap which vibrated your temples quite painfully if you were hit by someone else. About forty of us would take over three floors of a hotel while we rampaged around playing these ever-more-complicated battle scenarios. Sometimes the game would spill out on to the highways and we would be shooting lasers across the fast lane trying to outwit each other. Other times, the bus itself would be the attraction. One time in Ireland we all went bus-surfing around town on the roof. Many tour managers would be reading the small print in the band's insurance policy but our man Kusklik was too busy up on the roof with us.

Although we always steered clear of drugs, I saw enough of them around on tour. It is inevitable, it's everywhere. I saw it every day, bands, roadies, executives, all sorts. You would occasionally see one of our roadies doing a line of coke, but what are the press going to say? 'Veteran roadie seen taking drugs!' I can't tell him what to do, roadies work harder on tour than anyone else (along with catering they are the first up and last to bed) and who am I to dictate what someone wants to do with their life? I used to think to myself, *However hard*

More Than You Know

I feel I am working and however shattered I might be, I always know that roadies and catering are working harder.

My vice on the road was a drinking game called Cardinal. I would get absolutely smashed on tour. You have to understand that the single aim in life for a gaggle of seasoned roadies working with a young band like Bros is to get the lead singer completely hammered as often as possible.

Drinking has always made me feel too grey to consider just escaping by necking one bottle after another. However, I am always up for a session of Cardinal. It was a tough game at first but after a while I became a Cardinal, which was a bloody hard thing to do. Around 2004, I became a Pope, a rare thing indeed. When one of my backing singers Brett was made a Cardinal, he looked like it was one of the defining moments in his life. I've certainly had some of my best times on tour playing that game.

The fact is not lost on me that the performer whom I most admired, the man whose every word I would hang on, both on record and in person, namely Stevie Wonder, wrote the song 'Superstition', one of the most pivotal records in my entire life. That song on the surface might appear to be about superstition, but dig deeper and you will see it is saying *disregard* superstition, you can only rely on God. Yet, by contrast, throughout Bros, the rituals and superstitions were dreadful, I was consumed by them. I'm not sure it was compulsive, but it was a constant feature of my life back then. I'd think, *If only I can get to that lamp-post before that car does.* I'd see a lone magpie and think, *Fuck*, or I'd hear an ambulance go by and hold the back of my collar. Don't put your shoes on the table, don't open umbrellas indoors. I never felt safe in Bros. I felt super-famous, yes, but not safe. As I grew through my twenties, I managed to reel that in quite a lot. It was partly listening to words of songs that helped me change. At the time of writing, I think rituals are very dangerous.

To add to the mix was my grandfather's faith healing and the fact that my family have always been very spiritual – my great-grandmother was, after all, a Romany gypsy. You may be a sceptic, but as I have mentioned, I believe I can give healing, because Grandad has given me so many things. Same goes for Luke. I would like to get into that more as I get older, expanding on that would be amazing.

Being so well-known can make you paranoid. On a super-ficial level, you check in to hotels under a pseudonym. Mine was Richard Hertz. The problem was, we got so many people wanting to phone up to speak to Dick Hertz that I ended up reverting to Matt Goss! However, the intensity of the spotlight can exaggerate your perception and make you paranoid. You would constantly see the tiniest of details in the press and think, *How on earth did you know that?* That, mixed with the fans' attention, would eventually make you worry about the most bizarre things. I once read a story about a guy in America who was filming women through the back of mirrors in hotel rooms. This was discovered when a woman was in a bathroom and switched off the light only to notice a tiny white dot in the mirror, which was actually coming from a room behind the wall. Once I'd read that, I used to go into my hotel rooms with the lights switched off and peer into all the mirrors as a precaution.

TWELVE

Regret Ain't Meant To Last

When you are hailed as a 'sex symbol' in the press, you know that people will be fascinated by the relationships you choose to have. I was with Melanie Sykes for half of the Bros era and we lived together during much of it. I basically kidnapped her from Manchester in my Lotus Esprit SE Turbo and we were inseparable for five years.

We met on a blind date. My fart-lighting sax player Jim Turner said, 'I've got someone you'll like. I think you should meet her.' So I drove up to Manchester to meet Mel. Apparently, she had a picture of me on a pinboard by her bed and her ex-boyfriend hated it. 'What you got a picture of him there for?' I would imagine that when he found out we were actually dating he was pretty screwed up about that! Mel and I used to have a joke that she couldn't have posters of any other singers on her wall.

She arrived at the blind date and was bright red. I was too, so we gave each other a huge hug and went for dinner. She was so nervous she spilt wine in my food, which was fine, but then she got up to go to the bathroom and walked straight into the men's room! Later, I showed her my Lotus and said,

'Do you like it?' and she cheekily replied, 'It's a bit flash, isn't it?' She was really fun, straight away, I genuinely haven't got a bad word to say about Mel.

I came back down to London to work but after three days she called me late at night, very upset, saying 'I miss you'. I drove up to Manchester there and then to 'kidnap' her. She was the first girl I'd ever lived with, so it was serious stuff. She was a model at the time and quite quickly I think she started to get a little bit more known because we did get a lot of press together. Sometimes my PA, Shaun, would even drive Mel to her jobs.

One thing that managers often do when their charges are supported by a fan base of predominantly young girls, is insist that no one in the band has girlfriends. I think this was implied to Luke at some point but he was having none of it either – he had met singer Shirley Lewis when we were in the studio for our first album and they have been inseparable since. Luke definitely put the management straight to say the least, as indeed he did with anything they had to say about Shirley. We never lived our lives like that. It just wasn't an acceptable option.

So my relationship with Mel was very public and, I have to be honest, I don't think it affected our popularity one iota, and the same applies to Luke and Shirley. Of course, that didn't mean there weren't complications. Fans would some-times get jealous and so Mel and I would have little rules. For example, whenever I came back to the house there would be two or three hundred girls outside. We used to make sure that I didn't kiss any of those girls until I had said 'Hello' and kissed Mel first. It seems perhaps insignificant but little things like that were important in keeping our relationship special and grounded in reality.

It was quite comical to see that if I didn't have a girlfriend for any length of time, the press would start to speculate that

I was gay. I remember my mum, bless her, saying, 'Matthew, don't ever get a girlfriend just because of what the press say.' The funny thing is, I am the most heterosexual man but I have to tell you if I was gay I'd be *flaming*! I wouldn't just be gay, I would be on fire . . . but I happen to be very straight.

There were actually very few times when I was young, free and single. So, despite what you might think, I did not have a girl in every (air)port. However, this wasn't for lack of opportunity as you can imagine. Sampling different cultures on the road doesn't just mean tasting unfamiliar foods or immersing yourself in a country's history. It also means the fans might have an Oriental twist or a South American slant. We were on the fifteenth floor of a plush Japanese hotel one time when the dumb waiter in the room opened and two petite fans flopped out on to the floor in a heap. They stood up and started chattering nervously, barely pausing for breath. For some reason, Japanese fans always cover their mouths when they talk to each other about you. We gave them a photograph and signed a few things for them, of course. After all, they'd just crammed themselves, with no apparent regard for their own safety, into a three-foot-square dumb waiter and then been propelled up fifteen storeys, just to try to meet us. It wasn't exactly a cute or sexy look, flopping out and smelling of old sashimi, though I couldn't help but find it endearing.

What wasn't endearing was coming back alone to my hotel one night after a show and having a hand loop up from under the bed and grab my ankle as I got under the sheets. As a kid, your night-time fears revolve around things lurking in dark corners, under the bed and suchlike, so there was a certain intensity about the shock. I have to say I yelped like a girl! 'Yeeeaaaahhhh!' It was a firm old grip as well, I had to yank both my legs out of this grasp and shot out of the door. My security was standing outside.

'What is it, Matt?'

'There's someone under my bed, mate.'

I left him to sort it out and went next door to my PA's room.

I don't know how they'd got in there and I don't know how long they had been there. What I do know is that to this day I check under my bed before getting in – that sort of experience stays with you.

Equally as freaky is when you've got your dick in your hand and you are just about to have a pee when you hear the shower start. For me, that came to mean only one thing: there's a girl in it. After a few times, you just got used to it. Some of my mates have said, 'Hey, did you shag her?' but that is not exactly what you are thinking! Just consider what's happened for a moment. This girl has been standing, potentially stark naked, in your shower for three, four hours, maybe more, just waiting for that moment to come . . . and don't forget, hoping that she has chosen the right room. That's not something that sits well with me. You can't just jump in the shower and say, 'Oh, sod it, this isn't gonna come back to haunt me!' That is *so* coming back! That kind of mind is going to kill your dog and boil your rabbit. You just don't want to go there, you are not going to get away with just sending her a Christmas card.

Conversely, there have been a few occasions when I've just enjoyed the moment. When we were just becoming massive in Canada, there was a knock at my hotel door and a very attractive older woman was outside.

'I noticed you downstairs earlier, I know you are in a band, and I think you are lovely. I would love to give you a blowjob.'

I thought about it for a very brief moment and said, 'All right.'

I just thought, *Why not?* It felt incredibly decadent, she just came in and, even better, shortly afterwards, she left. I didn't

113

have to get to know this person so I'll be honest, it was fantastic.

As I've said, you might be surprised to learn that I wasn't actually over-active in that area, despite what you might think. I didn't have the time. I always thought it would have been nice to shag around but I've never been able to get down to it. For much of my adult life, I've also been in relationships, so there's always been people I had to chat to on the phone at 5.30 in the morning! Having said that, I snogged a lot of girls because I could and it was fun. I didn't sleep with hordes of women because it would have been all over the place – but there were definitely a few moments when you might be in a club and fancy a kiss. (I must say that compared to those Bros years, the fans now are definitely more direct. I get women in their late teens to late thirties and early forties being, how shall I say, more blatant. They don't just want hugs any more. Still, I appreciate the honesty.)

It's not always as simple as you might think. I was placed in an awkward situation when I went on a date with a girl in London. I'd known her for a couple of weeks when we went out together – after me she also dated Liam Gallagher. Her name was Cadamber and she had a very beautiful face, like that of an old-school actress. We had a lovely time on the date, but the very next morning the whole thing was published verbatim, literally word for word, in one of the tabloids. It was so violating, I can't tell you how disturbing that was. The whole date was detailed from start to finish, even with exact times. It was embarrassing and left such a lasting bad taste in my mouth. There are other similar situations called honey-traps, they are just newspapers trying to mess you up. Women are planted, and sometimes you fall into the snare.

Some time later, I was doing a casting for a girl to play a role in the video for my 1996 solo single, 'If You Were Here

114

Tonight'. We couldn't find anyone suitable but then my director said, 'I know this girl who is really cool, lovely and easy to be around.' We called her down and it turned out it was Cadamber.

One of the first things she said when she saw me was, 'I am so sorry, it's been with me so long, I was young,' and you could see it had been lying heavily on her. I just said, 'It's all right.' I think if somebody has the courage to apologize then you should have the courtesy to accept the apology. She must have apologized three or four times more during the trip. It actually turned out to be a lovely video, shot in Barbados. We worked the budget so that we got a holiday out of it as well and it was a great week (we stayed in the house of The Who's manager Bill Curbishley's wife).

The sad thing was that a few years later Cadamber was found murdered. That was very sad to hear. We didn't really stay in touch after the video so I found out like everyone else, from the press. It is strange when I watch that video we made with her, it almost gives me chills, but at the same time she is captured there on film, and that makes me glad that she did it.

On a lighter note, there was a time when I was actually having sex in a room at the Halcyon Hotel with a well-known celebrity. While I was with this girl, a journalist started to make her way up to my room for an interview. Let's just say my security man Johnny had to do a bit of 'creative shuffling' to extricate me from the predicament, bring the journalist in, sneak the girl out of a wardrobe and resolve my dilemma, otherwise it would have been a much more juicy interview than she thought she was going to get!

Another time I was getting into bed with a girl who had followed me around for some time. I thought she had a little something about her, because she had her own car, was definitely a bit more womanly and seemed to be an interesting person. We were just getting into bed and she said, 'It's really strange because I met "so-and-so" here,' so-and-so being another really famous singer.

I said, 'Excuse me?'

She explained, 'Oh, yeah I met so-and-so when he was playing here . . .'

. . . and I went 'Get the fuck out of my bed!'

I am big enough and ugly enough to work out who is around me for what reason. Of course I've had times when women have got off on the fact I am well-known, and even that other women dig me, but isn't that part of the fun? That makes you more of a desirable person to them, they get off on it, what's wrong with that? And besides, you get to know the women who are not going to hang in there through thick and thin, they are after money and gifts and they are more 'in love' with you if you are playing the bigger venues! But that's not the woman you are going to end up with.

My girlfriend Daisy Fuentes is a bona fide star in her own right. In recent years, I have found that there is an element of truth in the notion that being with another celebrity can make both your lives easier and more mutually supportive. It means there are some elements of bullshit in the business that you don't have to keep explaining away at the end of the day. When someone just knows that maybe you don't want to go somewhere too public, but maybe stay in and chill, then it is a lot easier.

The opposite of dating a celebrity is being with a fan. I never slept with Brosettes and this is why: it always amazed me how high they put me on a pedestal. As a young man there were a couple of fans you looked at and thought, *Oh my God, she's beautiful and this would be easy.* But the problem is these girls have an idealistic fantasy of what it will be like, they think there are going to be smoke machines, strobe lighting, music, thunder, sound effects. THX-quality sound, the earth rumbling and . . . the bottom line is I was only a young man and much of the time I was in bed with a girl I had to concentrate on Black and Decker power tools or my football team's line-up so I didn't come too quickly. I just feared it wouldn't have been as monumental for them as they would have hoped. They have this look in their eyes and it is a nice feeling to know that someone holds you in such high regard. I'm not being pious but I did feel a strange duty not to mess with that perception in any shape or form. So I just never went there with the fans. Ever.

Also, I didn't need to. There were enough surprises and little offerings around many corners, whether that was making a video, doing a TV show, in the studio, I have definitely had my fair share of rock-and-roll moments. I didn't have as mad a time as I could have done, but I've never ever had a problem with women. It's been great.

THIRTEEN

When You're Not Here

I have always been a massive animal-lover, right from those teenage days of wanting to be a vet. One of the first loves in my life was a dog called Billy. I'd made the decision I was going to get a dog and drove to the Battersea Dogs' Home in south London. There was a well-established routine of having your every waking moment surveyed by hundreds of girls, so I was inevitably tailed by about ten cars, chock-full of fans. I parked up and wandered towards the Dogs' Home, and I could see all the fans were whispering excitedly between themselves, 'I wonder what dog Matt's going to get?' Remember, these girls kept scrapbooks of my favourite boxer shorts, so a new dog was big news.

I walked in and one of the first dogs I saw was a dishevelled mutt that they had kindly named Scrappy. He was just like Tramp from *Lady and the Tramp*. He had no hair at all from his waist backwards, and what fur he did have looked like it had been in a tumble dryer for five hours with a bag full of spanners. He just looked really rough.

I looked at him and said,

'Oh, you are lovely aren't ya? I'll be back for you!'

He just looked at me as if to say, 'Yeah, fuck off.'

He was gorgeous in his own way, so I said, 'I will come back to you.'

He didn't move an inch and looked at me, his face saying, 'Yeah, whatever. Talk to the paw because the muzzle ain't listening.'

I carried on around the Dogs' Home and saw some majestic, beautiful dogs, pedigrees, dogs in peak condition, dogs with magnificent coats, some real stunning animals. But I couldn't stop thinking about Scrappy. When I eventually walked back to his pen, he jumped up as if in surprise, with an expression that quite clearly said to me, 'Fuck! You weren't kidding, you're back!'

I had him identity-chipped and strutted out of Battersea Dogs' Home as proud as could be. When the gaggle of fans saw me heading around the corner, I could hear them saying, 'What's he got? What's he got?' Then they saw me with this absolutely ragged, alopecia-riddled, scrawny little dog under my arm, and there was a tangible sense of 'Er . . . Oh.'

I put him in the back of my prized silver 7 Series BMW, ready to drive off to introduce him to Mel. I was merrily chatting away to him, really pleased with my new friend when I heard Ffrrrttt! I sat there in that pristine piece of German engineering, thinking to myself, *Wouldn't it be lovely if that was just a fart, I would love it in my heart if that was just a release of ecstasy, of relief, Scrappy saying in his own doggy way, 'Ah, I now have a new owner.'* Unfortunately, the next thing I thought was, *Wouldn't it be nice if that smell was just the remnants of the fart.*

You know you are in a situation when you see brown foot-prints on the back seats of your 7 Series. Scrappy just looked up at me as if to say, 'What? I'm a dog, this is what I do. I shit.' I opened all the windows and stopped off at the first car wash I encountered, bunged a load of money at these guys and said, 'Please can you clean this up and sort this out for me?'

They set to work busily returning my car to mint condition while I sat with the dog – whom I had re-christened Billy – watching them. When they were done, I got back in the car and continued on the journey to see Mel. Just before I got there, I heard Ffrrrttt! *Wouldn't it be nice if that was just a fart?* However, the fragrance was familiar now. I didn't even bother looking, I just drove straight back to the car wash. On the way, I said, 'Come on, Billy, give me all you got mate.'

I loved Billy. He ended up being pictured on the inside of the third Bros album cover. I managed to rid him of the acute alopecia and eventually all his hair grew back. I bought him a little bandana for his collar. He meant the world to me, he would open doors in the house, he was so clever and lovely. Mel loved him and I adored him. Unfortunately, when I later went to live in America, he couldn't go with me so Mel's parents took him and looked after him very well. I missed him desperately. It was very satisfying later on when I did *Hell's Kitchen* to give all the money I raised to Battersea Dogs' Home.

Unfortunately, there would be a much more serious mess to clean up in the first half of 1989. Craig Logan left the band. The schoolmate whom we'd waited an entire year for played his last-ever gig with Bros in Berlin in the winter of 1988. The show was part of our world tour and we'd already been to Japan and Australia. The famous moment when Craig actually left the band is quite a strange story to recount. This is my opinion of how it went down.

Being the singer of the band, I know for a fact that my workload was heavier than Craig's, undoubtedly. When you do radio, TV or media interviews, if they only want one person in the studio or on tape, they want the singer. It's just the way it is. In our specific case, Luke also had an unusually strenuous workload because we were 'the twins' so he was involved in far, far more PR and work than many drummers ever are. We were both constantly working. The spotlight on Luke and me was such that some parts of the media christened Bros 'Matt, Luke and Ken' by way of being sarcastic about Craig's lower profile.

Add to that the demands of a live show on a singer, performing, holding a crowd, singing. Bear in mind, I didn't just come on stage and swan around or sit on a bar stool with a drink, it was a full-on physical frenzy. I've seen photos of me eight feet up in the air with a mike in my hand! When you are doing four or five shows in a row, the way your throat hurts sometimes is excruciating. You can almost feel the lacerations weeping in your throat and you think to yourself *There's no way I can sing a note tomorrow night,* but somehow the adrenaline gets you through it. Occasionally, you suffer actual physical damage. I remember the time when I had to be literally carried off the stage. An inch-long nail from the sole of my shoe had pierced through the inner and sunk into my heel. As usual, I was jumping around like a mad man and running up the ramps and so on, so by the time we'd finished, I was in agony. I managed to shuffle almost to the side of the stage where John Buckland was able to carry me off.

It wasn't just me. Luke was such a physical drummer. You only had to look at the size of his kit and the way he used every square inch of it for the whole performance to know that his job was no picnic. He would often be completely shattered and frequently had to tightly bind his fingers and palms with tape to provide some sort of barrier for the blisters and sores.

However, bass playing is not notoriously the most energetic part of a show. Nor indeed are most bass players renowned for being in high demand with the media. It is not unfair to say that Luke's workload and mine were much greater than Craig's, so when it transpired that Craig had myalgic encephalomyelitis, ME or 'yuppie flu' as some more cynical observers called it, events started to turn peculiar.

Any band that has been on the road will know that you are almost permanently knackered, that's just the climate of travelling around for work, the *modus operandi* so to speak. When our tour bus pulled up in Berlin, Craig had already been feeling unwell for some time and said he needed to rest, but obviously he still wanted to be able to get around for catering and so on. Most venues have wheelchairs available so we said, 'Let's get him one of those,' to be brutally honest almost for a bit of a laugh. He didn't need a wheelchair, he was just exhausted, which was fair enough.

We sorted out a wheelchair and said, 'Rest yourself until the gig.' Time went by and we were all ready, with 12,000-odd fans waiting in the venue in anticipation. Just ten minutes before we were due on stage, we still didn't know if Craig was going on. We had to say something.

'Craig, this is ridiculous man! Just tell us yes or no. We need to make an announcement of some kind.' I don't think that was unreasonable.

'We've gotta prepare ourselves, we've got a show in ten minutes, just tell us, are you going on stage or are you not going on stage?'

If he could just say no, then we'd know we would have to change the sequences he played to suit the new line-up.

Anyone who works in an environment where there are deadlines will appreciate the pressure we were feeling. Then add to that the fact that thousands of people were waiting on that deadline, you can perhaps understand why the atmosphere was getting a little tense.

He was saying, 'I don't know . . .'

Perhaps inevitably, tempers frayed and Luke and Craig started arguing. Words were exchanged. Craig was being pretty rude to Luke and Luke was reciprocating, but even then that's fairly typical in a band on the road. Trust me, it is definitely what happens on tour. Before long, they were shouting at each other.

Then Luke pushed Craig – and over went the wheelchair, with Craig sprawled on the floor.

If Craig had genuinely had no feeling from the neck down, then what Luke did would have been well out of order. But it was treated exactly like that. It was like, 'Oh my God! You pushed Craig out of a fucking wheelchair!' Yet to me it was all rather comical. I probably sound like a right sadistic bastard now, but I felt Craig could have easily just stood up. It was like watching a scene straight out of *Airplane*. If you'd seen Craig, the way he didn't move his legs or anything . . . I was just like, 'Mate, get up!'

Next thing I know, Luke's own bodyguard grabbed my brother and tried to put him in a headlock! I was outraged, how dare he even touch Lukie! So I dived in and actually put a headlock on the bodyguard. And I wasn't letting go. It was really heated. I was squeezing as tight as I could and the bodyguard was starting to wheeze. I actually wanted to squeeze the head off his interfering body.

For me, there are certain unspoken rules of the road. These rules are part of what can be a very fragile dynamic within a touring band and certain things should just not be done. One of those is that if a band wants to have a ruck, it is their right to have one. Seriously, many bands have had fights in dressing-rooms, you don't need bodyguards to intervene, your life is becoming surreal enough as it is. So when I saw this bodyguard jump on Luke, I was shouting, 'Fuck off, we don't need to have bodyguards within our own circle!' We don't need to be protected from each other, we're not going to harm each other, we probably just needed to let off some steam.

Eventually things calmed down with literally a few minutes to go before we were due to perform. Craig did make it on stage that night on a stool.

I am not denying that we were all exhausted. We had, after all, been on tour for seven solid months. But there are bands out there that tour for eighteen months, sometimes far more, without stopping. Some of the older rock-and-roll bands and the established stadium acts can do a seven-month tour in their sleep. It is extremely demanding, incredibly tiring and it really puts you through the grinder, but that is what we did, we toured, *we were a band*. In one three-month period we stayed in forty-two hotels.

The day after his fight with Luke, Craig flew back to the UK from Berlin and effectively left the band.

I honestly don't care what Craig says about it, touring is hard work, it is obviously going to be difficult, there are dynamics you need to be aware of. There were definitely things about us that drove him mad, there were certainly things about him that drove me mad. But that is the nature of being in a band. Look at Oasis, Liam and Noel. I am sure that at times they can't *stand* each other but they are brothers and I am sure they love each other to death. But that friction and intensity goes with being in a band. Bands are not perfect text-book line-ups, you can't have a seamless lifestyle if you are in a working group. And you know what? I don't want to be in that kind of band. I want to be in a band that's got a bit of rock-and-roll to it, a bit of an edge, a fire in its belly.

I also didn't want to start being an old man before I'd even finished my first tour. This sounds a horrible thing to say, but

I'd begun to feel that we needed to cut Craig away. With him, there wasn't the laugh factor and the 'fuck it' attitude of being a young musician on your first major world tour. Craig wasn't one of the boys, never was, never will be.

At first we didn't see Craig for several months after Berlin and much of what we found out was through the many reports in the newspapers about his sickness. Initially, it seemed there might even be a possibility of him returning to the fold. We were due to collect a Brit Award for 'Best Newcomer' at the February 1989 ceremony (made infamous by Sam Fox's and Mick Fleetwood's compèring). Just prior to that, Tom organized a meeting for all of us to talk. Credit to Tom and everyone at the management, they genuinely wanted us to get back together. For my own part, when the dust had settled after Berlin, the crazy thing is I'd have taken Craig back in the band there and then. I just wanted to prove that we could be a unit; but it wasn't to be.

This meeting was all very cloak-and-dagger, we had to rendezvous at a secret location, like something you'd do in the FBI, at this hotel with security everywhere. It was the first time we'd seen Craig face-to-face since he'd left in Berlin. What people don't realize is that Craig agreed to come back to the band at that secret meeting. Sure enough, Craig turned up at the Brit Award ceremony – he went on the stage that night, collected his award with us and that was the last time we ever stood on a stage with him. Bollocks, isn't it?

Inevitably, with the great success and the revenues that were being created by Bros, lawyers became involved in the aftermath of Craig's illness. The press tried to portray us as the hard-nosed former band pals and Craig as the injured party, which was obviously not how we saw things. Strangely, Craig turned up at one of these legal meetings where the money and

125

various rights were being discussed, and announced that he wanted to take part of the name Bros.

I wanted to resolve all the issues amicably and come to some sense of mutually agreed closure. So I said to Craig, 'Look, what is it you feel is fair? What do you need to get from this?'

Craig barely flickered in acknowledgement and leaned over to whisper in his lawyer's ear.

The lawyer said, 'If you wish to propose something to my client, then you must do so by speaking to me.'

I was incensed and yet distraught at the same time. This was our old school-friend, we had been through so much together. Luke and I had waited *a whole year* for Craig to finish his schooling, because his parents wanted him to join a bank and insisted he finish his exams. We rehearsed on our own for that year, waiting for him before we took Bros to the public. When Mum and Tony moved to Commercial Way in Peckham, Craig lived with us and Mum treated him as one of her own. And yet, here he was, sitting with a besuited lawyer treating us in this manner.

Then his lawyer said his 'client' wanted 'one-third of the use of the name Bros'.

I said, 'What does "Bros" mean?'

'It means brothers,' said Craig, without a hint of irony.

'Yes, it does, and you are no fucking brother of ours.'

I had to leave the room.

I gave Craig plenty of opportunities to deal with the situation by ourselves and the disagreement never made it to court, we settled with him before that. We had to have several of these tense meetings with lawyers. The biggest royalty cheque I ever received, I signed and gave straight to Craig. He did very, very well out of Bros, he got a beautiful settlement, and in hard cash. Knowing what was about to unfold, if I could have left Bros with a cheque for the amount he did, without having the overheads, liabilities and all that was to come, I would have been very happy indeed.

I certainly don't want to fall out with Craig. If he ever wants to get on stage with Luke and me, then he is welcome. But I do want him to know how I feel; when you complete an album, you have a section in the liner notes called 'special thanks' . . . Craig could definitely be in the 'thanks for nothing'. I am not just saying that to be argumentative. I feel I can say that to him because I do have warm feelings for Craig (and his brother Grant), but at the same time I have my reasons for feeling as I do.

One future development that was really disappointing for me was when Craig came to LA and had a beer at my house, back in 2002. I am a very private person and I rarely ask anyone for anything, that is well-known. However, I was just about to come back to the UK with my new record and the prospect was very daunting to me (you will see why later). Craig had left Bros and gone into artist management – at the time of writing he manages Pink – so he was consequently right in the thick of the music industry again. Craig Logan might be Pink's manager to thousands of industry people, but you have to understand that to me and Luke, he was this kid that we went to school with, he was our best mate. Even if he became Prime Minister, to me he will always be Craig whom I went to school with. So I thought I was in the right company – in my house sharing a beer with an old school-friend – to say what I said.

'Craig, I know you've got Pink, I don't want you to manage me but it would be nice if there's anything you can do to make England a little bit less daunting to me, you know, that would be much appreciated.'

'Yeah, man,' replied Craig, 'no problem, I'll definitely give it some thought and get back to you.'

127

I never heard back from him. Not a word. I don't know why.

In my opinion, I have definitely given Craig a lot in his life; many good things have happened to him because of being in that band. I believe in repaying debts, with regards to friendship, I am not talking about money – if I give somebody a chunk of money, they don't have to pay me back, I don't need it. If you give and expect something back, then you are merely exchanging, not giving. If that person chooses to return the favour, then so be it. For me, if I was in Craig's position, it would have been a privilege and an honour to help out my mate in return. If you can help one of your friends and do so effortlessly, I think that is an absolute blessing. That's just how I view it.

I never had a history of being nasty or showing bitterness towards Craig publicly and privately. That couldn't have been further from the case. I think Craig will be the first to say that I've always been a gentleman to him. For example, Luke and I were invited to an industry party one time and when we got there, Craig had also been invited. You could see a few people were a little wary, thinking, *Matt's gonna knock Craig out, what's going to happen here?*

I went up to Craig and I will never forget his face, his expression really hurt me because he did look almost afraid of me, that genuinely upset me. I was wearing a pair of silver cufflinks in the shape of a dove, so I gently took one off and gave it to Craig as a gesture of reconciliation. As I handed it to him, I said, 'No matter what the media says to you and me, about you and me, or any of us, this is how I feel.' I don't even know if he remembers that, but I have always tried to be a gentleman towards Craig.

When he came to my house in LA all those years later, I thought there was an understanding between us. Maybe it's that working-class London mentality where you help your boys out. For me, I was simply asking a mate for a bit of a leg-up but it just didn't come. In my mind, I would be saying, 'You know what? I will always be grateful to these guys for this.'

It's hard to argue against the fact that Craig gained financially from Bros with the pay-off that we gave him. I gave him a break, that is undeniable. Furthermore, it was well into the new millennium before the final vestiges of the Bros split were cleared up and laid to rest for Luke and me, whereas Craig cashed a nice big cheque and a firm line was drawn under his responsibilities thereafter. There was a not inconsiderable amount of baggage and repercussions that he did not have to deal with at all.

But I heard nothing back – silence. That was difficult to understand. Perhaps worse still, when I bumped into Craig about a year later, he never mentioned our previous conversation in LA. I also saw Craig at a party for Pink in 2003 and the paps wanted a picture of him and me but he was very uncomfortable with it, which I found extremely odd.

I also think that Craig will be one of the first to say he didn't really do a lot in Bros. He played on stage live, of course, but he didn't have much to do with making *Push*, the one album that he was around for. There was a lot of programming on there and that was Nicky Graham. I cannot recall having a creative conversation with Craig in the studio. To my knowledge, Craig hardly played a note on that Bros record. That might be a bit of a revelation, but I think it's an important point to make. Nicky took charge of that side, really. Craig, in my opinion, was just an okay bass player. That's why his acting as if he was an equal third of Bros was frustrating to us.

When you think of my efforts in the vocal booth and Luke

slogging his arse off drumming and programming, it does seem incongruous, yes. I have always made a conscious effort not to be the bitter arsehole who says 'you got a load of money out of Bros and you didn't even do that much in the band', but those are the facts. There's very few things that I feel an inner need to say, but this is one of them.

So to be blanked in such a way by Craig was jolting. To me it's bollocks, there's no other word for it. If you want to leave a band then that is always your prerogative, totally and utterly. That stands for Craig too. But the way in which he did it? Not cool at all.

FOURTEEN

When I Wake I Must Do More Than Exist

So Bros was now down to just Dukus and me. I have to be honest, when I think of being on stage in Bros, that's how I think of it anyway. In the immediate aftermath of Craig's leaving, we completed a twenty-five-date British tour, threw a lavish party for family and friends on our way through before barely pausing for breath and heading out on an extensive European tour. The British trip included a series of dates that I still regard as one of the pinnacles of our career – multiple nights at Wembley Arena. Once Craig was out of the band, the momentum accelerated – we made two more albums, all those nights at Wembley Arena, Wembley Stadium, the big tours, with just Luke and me.

We recorded most of our second album, to be called *The Time*, at Miraval in the south of France, in a château studio called LaVal, which is about forty minutes' drive from Provence. It was a beautiful, isolated studio in the middle of 100,000 acres of vineyard, a serene place to make a record, and to this day those weeks in the spring of 1989 remain the best experience of recording I've ever had (on its October 1989 release, *The Time* would reach Number 4 in the UK charts).

At that stage, Bros's profile was such that we couldn't have made the record in London because there'd be a tendency to finish a song and then somehow, usually within hours or a few days, it would find its way out of the studio and get reviewed.

The fact the château was so quiet meant we weren't bothered at all, but it also meant the sizeable parcel of French countryside it occupied was our playground for a few weeks. We had so much fun. We all had motorbikes and would go scrambling up the hills, racing each other and generally having a great time. We also bought some quad bikes, which on one occasion very nearly lost Bros another member. I was hammering a quad up a very steep hill but as I neared the top, it started to lose momentum, then, almost in slow motion, it tipped over. I was thrown out of this machine and tumbled down the hill, closely followed by a quarter of a tonne of quad bike. I was very lucky that it never actually touched me, otherwise it could have been very serious. As long as they were driven well, those quads were fantastic fun – when we'd finished the record and left, we gave them to the kids who lived at the studio complex.

Strangely enough, that wasn't the only accident I had during our stay in Miraval, although the second incident wasn't my fault. While we were there I had a new Mercedes SL delivered. It was an awesome car and my guitarist at the time, Paul Gendler, asked if he could have a drive. I said 'no problem' but warned him to be careful as the five-litre engine was a real beast. Luke jumped in his car and followed us out on to the French country roads.

Next thing I know, Paul is doing 120 mph. I said, 'Hey, slow down a bit, mate, take it easy.' It was too late. We were screeching up to a contra-flow system which was effectively pointing this speeding bullet of a Mercedes into the path of oncoming traffic. We were still doing 120 mph when we reached the first traffic cone. A crash was unavoidable. We clipped the central reservation, went up on two wheels and spun around about five times. As we were spinning and spinning, I saw a juggernaut coming straight towards us. I looked across at Paul and he was frozen, so I grabbed the wheel and deliberately steered into the central reservation, away from the lorry, and ground us to a halt.

We got out and Luke was rushing up to the car to see if we were okay. It must have been a very scary thing for him to see from directly behind. He was livid with Paul, he went mad. He said the car resembled a dust ball violently spinning around, bless him he was so frightened. I managed to calm him down and we made our way back to the studio in his car. Shortly afterwards the garage phoned to say my brand-new Merc was a total write-off. I was disappointed but not too upset. It is, after all, just a piece of metal and we are all here to talk about it, so I thank God for that.

Back at the studio we continued with our antics. Our A&R man at the time was Gordon Charlton and he came out to see how the record was coming along. One night we all went out with Gordon, as well as my mum who was over visiting. A few drinks were imbibed, shall we say, and on the way back Gordon puked up in the back of our limousine all over my jacket. We took him back and waited for him to fall asleep, then everyone in the band and involved in the recording kicked open his door and pelted him with dozens of raw eggs. It was straight out of *Bugsy Malone* and just great fun. The entire recording sessions were extremely enjoyable. To be honest, the fact that Craig was no longer in the band didn't really change the process at all.

I've already mentioned that any young band should really revel in their privileged position and make the most of touring, being famous, enjoying their job. One aspect I have always truly found fortunate is the opportunity Bros and my own profile has given me to meet people I have admired. Many bizarre moments have come my way and I've enjoyed all of them.

One of the more surreal times when I met someone I had known about all my life was the night I went out with Liza Minnelli. Neil Tennant from the Pet Shop Boys – who we used to bump into a lot on tour and shared management with – just said to me, 'I am going out with Liza, do you want to come?' He didn't need to wait long for an answer!

We went to Liza's suite at The Savoy, where I was introduced and she was just lovely from the first moment. She said she needed to get ready for the evening, so she went into her dressing area and shortly after returned in a fabulous outfit, stood in front of me and said, 'How does this look?'

'Fantastic.'

It did, believe me.

Then she went away and tried on more dresses, each time asking my opinion. I felt like I was in an old black-and-white movie with her. It was very charming, because she was so humble and even a little under-confident which, considering her legendary status, is remarkable.

We went to Ronnie Scott's for some drinks and after a while she got up and sang to us. It was such an incredible moment. She didn't sit there and talk about herself all night either, she was stylishly gracious, but at the same time she had so much history and so many stories that I wanted to hear. Neil, as usual, was such a gentleman, and we just sat and told random stories all night, it was a lovely evening.

Not long after that night, she very kindly invited me to be her guest at a show she was doing with Sammy Davis Jr and Frank Sinatra. We were given front-row seats and, although we were very well-known at the time, when I walked along the aisle, past Sean Connery and a veritable *Who's Who* of celebrities of the time, it felt amazing.

I found my way backstage before the actual performance and headed for what I thought was Liza's dressing-room. I pushed the door open and walked in to see . . . Frank Sinatra standing there with some of his boys. He was exquisitely suited and booted, as were all his boys. He looked up, tilted a glass of whisky and his head at me, as cool as you like. Exactly as you would want Frank Sinatra to be. I am not afraid to admit I was totally intimidated, so I just nodded my head and walked out.

I went and found the correct dressing-room for Liza and she was in there preparing for the show when Sammy Davis Jr walked in, as casual as that. We sat down and chatted and then he asked if he could wear my jacket! He joked that he didn't think he would actually be able to lift it up as there was so much decoration on it! What a night that was.

We continued to bump into Liza across Europe when we were promoting and appearing on certain TV shows, as she was doing a record at that time. It was nice to know somebody like her.

Another time I felt I was in the middle of some surreal dream sequence was when I went to Ireland and a friend introduced me to The Edge. U2 were massive at the time and I've always been a huge fan. I believe they are a defining moment in music and always seem to be able to stay ahead of the game. And they have masterful management – I dream of having a manager like Paul McGuiness. We shared a few drinks when we met and after a while The Edge said, 'Why don't you come and stay with me in my house?'

I accepted his kind invitation to stay at his home even though I felt not quite worthy. He'd just put us at Number 4 of his

'Best Ten Pop Albums Ever' in *Rolling Stone* which to me was bewildering. His humility was so amazing to witness because he is The Edge! I was in Ireland, his home patch, yet he was very protective of me, waving people gently away and intoning in that soft Irish accent, 'Leave him alone, go on with you, leave him alone.' I felt like I was out for a beer with Ireland's father.

We went waterskiing on his new speedboat and later took a drink in this little pub by the Irish Sea. With my short, spiky hair and jacket, I looked rather like Larry Mullen Jr at that time and some people seemed to think I actually was him. To be fair, it must have made a sight for sore eyes – he'd gone out dressed as The Edge from U2 and I was dressed in my famous red jacket as Matt Goss from Bros, the most unlikely double act you could imagine. That night we really brought Ireland to a standstill.

I love Barbados and it seems to be a place I often bump into celebrities. I was sitting in first class, chilling out one time on the way there when I noticed that behind me was Russ Abbott. At the time he was massive, with his own TV show and a huge profile. We got chatting and both Russ and his wife were lovely, really friendly. I told them where we were staying but Russ wasn't sure where he was heading, so I said, 'If you don't like it when you get there, you are welcome to come over and stay with us at our villa.' The plane landed and we exchanged numbers, said it was nice to meet etc. and let's share a drink if we meet again in England. What a lovely chap, I thought.

Two days later, I was sunning myself by the pool when the phone rang and it was Russ.

'Hi Matt, I just wondered if you meant what you said about coming over to your villa?'

'Of course I did, Russ!'

Russ and his lovely wife came and stayed with us and they

were both an absolute pleasure to be around. It was a nice feeling for me, because I was so much younger and here I was mixing with this much more established star. He was such a funny man. One morning I came down to the pool and there was Russ sitting in the sun, with his white socks and sandals on and a white hanky on his head, all for my benefit of course. It was everything you would want Russ Abbott to look like, with that hanky tied into a little square on his head. I pissed myself laughing.

Michael Barrymore was at the hotel down the road and I don't think he could quite understand why the guy from Bros was hanging out with Russ Abbott. We were two very different generations and from two very different genres but we got on so easily. Towards the end of the holiday, we went to a café by the beach and Russ told me that to say thanks for the hospitality, he wanted to show me a trick from the Magic Circle. He showed me the trick and, of course, I have never told anyone the secret but to this day it is one of my best party-pieces, I took that bit of magic all around the world with me. I love magic and since then I have become quite good at it.

Several years later, I spent some time in Monte Carlo and while I was there I hung out quite a bit with Mickey Rourke and Mike Tyson. The most striking thing I noticed about Tyson was that in Monte Carlo he was being treated like a gentleman, and therefore he was acting like a gentleman. And I mean an absolute gentleman. So many people came up and asked for his autograph and every time, without complaint, he stood up, gave them the pictures and had a quick chat, always very softly spoken and very cool. He was a gentleman, no question.

Having spent so much time in America, I know that they talk of him over there as if he is an absolute animal and I think that sometimes if that is all you hear about yourself, there is a danger that that is what you become. I recognize that he has been convicted of a very serious crime, but I am speaking only about my own personal experience of him. I genuinely felt for him in a way, he was a real gent and he couldn't have been nicer to me. Every time I saw him, he would say, 'Whath's up Matt?' with that distinctive soft voice and lisp. I always feel weird when people go on about Mike Tyson, because the only experience I have of him is that he was absolutely cool. Mickey Rourke was cool too, I still bump into him in LA; he loves his dogs, like me!

Meeting Princess Diana was incredible too. Luke and I had lunch with her and the Bee Gees. She said she loved Bros and our music and talked about us in a way that showed she really knew what was going on. It was only a small dinner, but I can still picture her eyes, the most beautiful you've ever seen. The second you met her, you would start to fall completely in love just by looking at them. She was so very engaging and gracious, I feel privileged to have met her.

It is very important that, no matter how famous or successful you are, you can still enjoy experiences like that. Just because you are doing arenas and stadiums yourself and are known all over the world, you've got to allow yourself to be a kid, enjoy meeting your idols and the people that matter greatly to you. If you don't, then your life will be incredibly dull. Mine was never dull, not for one second.

FIFTEEN

The Best Part Of Me

We knew we were selling tickets, we were charting with our singles and anticipation for our forthcoming second album was growing apace. We knew we'd played one of the longest stretches ever at Wembley Arena. Even so, it was still a shock when we took the call saying, 'You're going to play Wembley Stadium.'

The date was set for 19 August 1989, heralded as 'The Bros in 2 Summer'. Sky Television was screening it as one of their earliest live gigs. We had weeks and weeks of rehearsals ahead of us but wild horses wouldn't have pulled us away from preparing for that show. The day before the Wembley date, we did a secret gig at the Marquee under the name of The Terror Twins. It was an incredible night, talk about an eclectic audience! We had punks with full Mohicans, Brosettes, record-company presidents, Marquee veterans, skinheads, all sorts. It must have been one of the year's hottest tickets. The queue for the show, which was only announced an hour before the gig, snaked all the way up Charing Cross Road and west round the corner into Oxford Street.

At the Marquee we used the full band that was playing

Wembley the very next day. It was a superb gig. I remember putting my legs over the side of the stage and people in the front row leaned on my legs, there was a real vibrancy in there. What made it even more amazing was knowing that tomorrow we would be playing Wembley Stadium. It was the most rock-and-roll feeling.

The day of that ultimate stadium gig is still one of the most extreme experiences of my life, always will be. Unbeknown to us at the time, it was also the last big British gig we ever played, so in a way that was how we went out: a 70,000 sell-out. It was mad to pull up to Wembley – whenever we'd played the Arena, we would drive past and look up at the two towers with awe. So to actually drive into the stadium complex when it was empty was a thrill in itself. At the same time, it was one hell of a reality check – you just think to yourself, *There's not a chance in hell we're ever gonna fill this place.* No way, it was too vast, 70,000 people, that's a lot of bums on seats. I shouldn't have been so worried.

It has to count for something, having a band that gets to the point where it can play that venue. It's different even to filling out fifteen Wembley Arenas, because with multiples you very often get repeat entries, people going three or four times. This was a one-off; that's a very difficult thing to pull off but we did it. Harvey Goldsmith promoted it and he did a very good job, so thank you Harvey!

We had about ten security men each wherever we went, because it was so manic and there were thousands of fans there from very early in the morning. Once we'd driven into the complex, we got out of our limos and walked out into the venue itself. I was speechless.

I was told that we used even more speakers than Michael Jackson had when he'd recently played there. I stood by these speaker cabinets, they looked about ten storeys high, and was just amazed at what we had to use to cope with the gigantic venue. These things were like skyscrapers nestled on the stage. Then I walked . . . and walked to the far end of the venue to soak it all in and survey the stage. When I turned around to face those same gigantic speakers, they looked like a small pile of black matchboxes.

They might have looked tiny from the last row but those enormous speakers certainly packed a punch. Obviously with a venue and production as massive as that, there were a myriad technical difficulties to iron out to ensure the show went smoothly. It wasn't just a case of plugging your mike in and saying '1–2, 1–2'! Mid-afternoon the sound technicians did a special type of soundcheck where white noise was pushed through a spectrum analyser to test the sub-bass in these towering speakers, essentially a very low bass tone. As they did so, this almost unearthly, primitive rumble started to ooze out of the bank of speakers which themselves seemed to be coming alive, like a giant awakening from a deep slumber. It was quite an incredible thing to see and hear.

I can still taste the sense of anticipation that built throughout the day. Backstage the VIP area was rammed with celebrities and the goodwill shown towards us by our music-business peers was very heart-warming, people were genuinely wishing us well for the show. Kylie was even sitting with my mum in the Royal Box! There was obviously a host of media there, and talking to them, other stars, family, friends and management contributed to the build-up of excitement. However, one of my most vivid memories from that day was the low throbbing that grew out from the pitch itself. At first it was almost imperceptible, but then you started to notice this warm, voluminous hum, then you realized it was the thousands of fans slowly pouring themselves into the venue. Remember, these weren't football fans just sitting around the edge of the pitch;

70,000 excitable people chatting and singing and shouting makes one hell of a noise. Every square inch of Wembley Stadium was filling up – the countdown was on.

The moment finally arrived when we were ushered down below the stage to prepare for our entrance. The reason we were in the bowels of that famous venue was that Luke and I were to be catapulted up through a trapdoor on to the stage in a big explosion of sound, light, pyrotechnics and smoke. This is Bros remember, you didn't expect us to just walk on stage?!

The catapult system we were each strapped into was a complicated set-up that was essentially powered by weights and gravity. It was almost like a reverse bungee jump, so once we were strapped in, we had to have five stage hands each holding us down until the moment of truth. Luke and I were on opposite sides of the stage, I was coming up on stage right and he was coming up through stage left. I desperately wanted to catch his eye before we launched, literally, into the biggest show of our lives. But I couldn't see him, I was straining to look but I never got to see him.

I was also keen to catch a peep at the audience, just to somehow prepare myself for what was about to come, but once I was strapped in I couldn't. The noise around me was a cacophony of activity: ten security guys talking to each other, walkie-talkies going off all over the place, the roar of the crowd as our entrance was introduced, then audio from the section that starts the show, it was sheer bedlam. To this day, I swear you could actually see my heart beating through my chest. I had to pull back for a moment, so I said, 'Wait, wait, wait . . .' I tried to breathe in and dissipate some of the nerves. As I did, I heard, 'Clear for pyros! clear for pyros!'

This was it.

The stage hands holding down our catapults nodded to each other then . . . let go . . .

I've been hit with some roars in my life when I've gone on stage, but this was other-worldly. I didn't know that so much noise could physically be generated in one place at one time. We both shot up about ten feet in the air, the trapdoors closed behind us, we came back down and when we landed . . . just imagine 70,000 people shouting at the top of their lungs at precisely the same instant . . . at *you*. It's a tidal wave of noise, an insane amount of energy being directed your way. Even today I cannot get rid of that moment, it is in my blood, indelibly inked into my psyche. I can't ever imagine feeling particularly normal and one of the reasons is that bloody show.

It's not that I hadn't performed in front of big crowds before. We'd done all those shows at Wembley Arena. We'd travelled to the Eastern Bloc and played the biggest production ever to be set up in Russia. That event was so massive that we even had the Russian Minister of Culture there to see it. In Budapest we had 33,000 people crammed into a record-breaking capacity for an indoor venue. We'd played at an Asian Award show – the equivalent of the Grammys – to a TV audience of one billion people. Big crowds were not new to Bros. Yet none of it prepared one single ounce of my body and mind for that second when I was propelled through the trapdoor and into that atomic reaction.

I have to tell you the noise level did not die down. As we played our set, starting with 'I Owe You Nothing', the fans chanted, sang, shouted, cheered, cried and screamed for the entire show (St John Ambulance crews dealt with 1000 'fainters' that day). It was just amazing. I later found out that the decibel levels registered at the show were some of the highest ever recorded at Wembley. Picture yourself standing on a runway directly behind a 747's engine as the pilot opens the thrust . . . that was Wembley.

I have never done drugs, but I do know that at Wembley I

experienced a natural and very intense high. We all did. There's a shot of my sax player Jim Turner (who'd introduced me to Mel) with his mouth wide open. He also doubled-up as a backing vocalist but in this TV shot he is not singing his lines, because he was just in awe of what was happening.

My brother had a Tama drum kit, a caged kit with shells strapped to every inch of the frame, a drummer's wet dream. Luke's a phenomenal drummer and he showed it on that day. He was on a riser that rose up thirty feet in the air before spinning round with strobe lights wired all over it, while he was doing his drum solo. His drum riser alone cost fifty grand. I was watching all this happen and I was so proud of him that I actually said out loud, 'Fucking hell! That's my brother!' I think in Luke's eyes that show will also make it hard for him to ever feel normal again.

We played several encores and then we were gone.

We'd played Wembley Stadium.

We'd done it.

And yes, I did say, 'Hello Wembley'.

Now that Wembley Stadium has been demolished, there's something final about our having played there; no band in the future can do so and that only adds to the pride I feel. There are certain things that Luke and I did in Bros that no one can take away from us, no matter what people say, and playing Wembley is one of them.

As with so much of my life, there was contrast, extreme contrast. Elements of that day were some of the most lonely I've ever felt in my life. Why? Within a couple of hours of leaving that huge stage in front of 70,000 people, I was sitting in my hotel suite at The Mayfair, alone.

There was an after-show party, of course, but that was at Wembley and was essentially more business than pleasure;

there wasn't anywhere for Luke and I to switch off and just digest the gig. There must have been 1000 people there, so it was hardly a private family moment. Management had taken care of that party, but for us there was nothing. It definitely felt like nobody really cared about us – I don't mean pampering our egos with an 'exclusive' party, just somewhere quiet and peaceful where we could rest and let the events of the day sink in, privately.

It wasn't forthcoming.

When it became apparent that the after-show was all that we were being offered, we decided to head off. You can imagine how much attention and focus there was on us at that after-show, everyone wanting to meet us and talk to us and be around us, which is understandable after such a big event, of course. But we needed some headroom.

I was staying at The Mayfair so I headed back there. I had been living there for a while and the staff were always very courteous and friendly, they were great to us. We'd often have to leave by the back door to avoid the waiting fans but the staff never grumbled.

I went to my room and lay on my bed thinking to myself, *How can I have just played one of the biggest venues on earth, and probably the most prestigious, and there is no one in the bar or at the hotel to share it with me?* I have already said that I am a big lover of comparisons – but this was just a bit too extreme. It was just too silent. It was a psychological bout of the bends.

Any musician will tell you that after a big gig your head is exploding with excitement, adrenaline, thoughts and energy. You can be buzzing for hours, sometimes days afterwards. This wasn't just a big gig, it was Wembley Stadium. Ideally, you want to talk to a few select people about the show, digest it, discuss it, but in a controlled environment and that is the consideration of your management, your professional parents, to organize. You've got to understand I was a young musician and within five years or so, I was playing Wembley Stadium. I wanted to talk about it, to be with our immediate circle and management after a gig like that. But here I was, holed up in a hotel room on my own, my head thumping with the night's experience yet, unless I'd started talking to myself, there was total, numbing, deafening silence.

Personally, Luke and I ended up heavily in the red on that day. Why? Because our management commissioned us on the gross. That is what their contract said, commission on gross. However, we didn't think it would happen on this show.

Why did it cost so much to put the show on? Easy. What people might not realize is that to play Wembley Stadium you had to rent it. You don't just wake up one day and say, 'Oh, yeah, we're gonna play Wembley because we are a big band.' It costs a quarter of a million just to rent the venue, which is fair enough because it's Wembley Stadium. We had to rehearse for weeks and weeks and weeks – which included testing all our production, dress rehearsals and so on – for just those two hours. Then add to that the cost of the lighting rig, the stage, the security, the promotion of the gig, an endless list of vast expenses. It costs an absolute fortune to play that one show.

So we roughly broke even, which is an achievement in itself. However, the defining moment of that show, and in many ways one of the key conversations of our entire career with Bros, came when we spoke to our management about the commission. The way I looked at the management then was that we were all in it together. Playing a show like that is usually an enormous loss-leader, yet somehow we had grossed enough to break even. As a management team, you can build on that incredible achievement. It could be seen as a mutual investment.

I looked at them and said, 'Come on, we're family. We've not made any money out of this but you've got a band under contract that has just headlined Wembley Stadium. Are you going to commission this? Are you sure? You are going to put us massively in the red on this show because of management commission?'

The management simply said, 'Yes.'

SIXTEEN

Chasing Demons

Two days after I played at Wembley Stadium to 70,000 people with Bros, I was a supporting act at a San Francisco venue to a crowd of indifferent Americans. I do like my comparisons!

We were supporting Debbie Gibson who, at the time, was big news over there. She is a good friend of mine, and a very talented woman who means the world to me. Unfortunately, through absolutely no fault of hers, when we toured the US with her in the autumn of 1989, it proved to be a very ill-advised combination. Despite having just played the stadium gig back home – which was lauded by almost all the press, even our most entrenched critics – we were packed off to grind around America in anticipation of the release of our album Stateside. Accordingly, we were given this slot supporting Debbie by our US record company. She had enjoyed two hit albums and was a bona fide teen star in her own right.

In retrospect, it was probably not a good idea to get a massive band opening as a support act, even though we had a relatively low profile in America. I think it was also a misjudgement on the part of the record company in terms of the type of people going to see Bros shows as against Debbie Gibson shows. Her core audience were younger than ours, *much* younger. And our show was *extremely* loud – after Wembley, there were laughable articles in the more middle-aged sections of the press about the dangers of loud concerts for 'the youth of today'. Bear in mind, we'd gone from Wembley Stadium to playing to crowds of maybe a tenth of that, seven or eight thousand, in America.

When we rolled into San Francisco for the first show of the tour, 'Hello Wembley!' was still spinning in my head. We were sent on stage in the middle of the day when the crowd seemed more interested in buying hot dogs than listening to our set. The whole atmosphere was utterly demoralizing. Worse still, the very young audience couldn't bear the volume. But anyone who knew our live show was aware that it was actually very loud and pretty hard – Debbie had supported us at Wembley so her management team knew what to expect. The whole set-up of supporting Debbie was, in hindsight, wrong.

Then I noticed a kid in the very front row, who was no more than maybe seven years old, sitting there with a grimace on his face and his fingers in his ears. Despite what preconceptions people might have had about our fan base, most Bros fans were aged from about thirteen to eighteen. We certainly did not get many seven-year-olds in our crowd. Paul Gendler, our brilliant guitarist who went on to play with The Spice Girls all over the world, was in the middle of a breath-taking solo and here was this little brat with his junk-food-stained, greasy fingers stuck in his ears.

I was singing and thinking to myself, 'What?! We've got twelve weeks of this ahead of us . . .' So when the first song had finished, I said, 'Thank you very much, good night,' and walked off the stage.

Almost telepathically, the rest of the band dropped their instruments and followed me without so much as a word between us. We all knew instinctively that we should walk off. The American management were yelling at us to get back on the stage and we were saying, 'Throw us off the tour! Go on!' It was farcical really, but completely disheartening at the time.

Things went from bad to worse. At each side of the stage were what are known in the trade as 'ego ramps'. These are ramps which extend out from the main body of the stage in front of the speakers and into the crowd, so that the frontman can go out to the crowd and really stir things up. Anyway, at the next show, I found that my path to the ego ramps was completely blocked by piles of flight cases. Clearly certain people behind the scenes didn't want the support act to be sufficiently energized or confident – or indeed popular – to make use of these ramps. So they were blocked. Naturally, I pushed all the flight cases out of the way and said, 'I am using these ego ramps, this is what I am used to, I need the full stage to do what I do.' Cue another argument.

We argued about it every day, it was so draining. Every afternoon I would find flight cases in the way, an argument would follow and eventually they would back down and remove them. Then, the very next day, the same cases would return to block my path once again – stalemate. I never understood that mentality. I felt that if a support act was warming up the crowd that much, then the headline act would surely benefit from a more vibrant and excited andience. My argument fell on deaf ears.

Our stage manager on that tour was a guy called Steve Martin. Those US dates were very trying for all of us and Steve was confronted on a daily basis with a lot of issues. Luke and I would later buy Steve a Rolex and it was lovely to see many years later when I bumped into him, that he was still wearing the watch we gave him.

The fractured atmosphere persisted for three long months.

In Canada, our following was getting really big and as Debbie was singing her first song, the crowd were still chanting 'We want Bros! We want Bros!', which of course just added to the tension. When combined with the well-documented physical and mental demands of touring America, it was so exhausting. I must make it clear that these events were no reflection on Debbie whatsoever; it was just the workings of touring and life on the road. It can become very, very stressful.

The contrast between playing Wembley Stadium and finding yourself as wallpaper music for overweight and apathetic American pre-teens was just too stark, it was too great a culture shock. Debbie's management kept ranting on about how 'Hendrix supported The Monkees, man, Hendrix supported The Monkees'. That line haunted us.

Worse still, our American record company seemed incapable of getting our promised new single out on time . . . or even at all. Every night of that dreadful tour I would introduce 'Too Much' by saying, 'This is our new single, you can buy it on Monday,' and week after week went by with only excuses from the record company when it failed to appear yet again. They were making me look like a fool and I wasn't pleased. They'd told us that playing this support tour was crucial and they would make sure the record would come out. You know what? It did, but weeks later.

Luke and I were at each other's throats as well, it was a horrible tour. While on the road out there our costs ran to about £500,000. Most of that money came out of our own pockets. That's a hard lesson to learn, because it boils down to the fact that if the corporation you are involved with believes your face doesn't fit, you lose your record – it has nothing to do with the music you are making. That's very frustrating but a fact of the business unfortunately. In many ways, that US tour was the straw that broke the camel's back, it was too hard, too problematic and too exhausting.

Fortunately, despite the difficulties behind the scenes, Debbie and I have always managed to put that into the background and remain firm friends. I went to see her when she was in *Beauty and the Beast* in New York and I stayed at her apartment for a few nights.

It never ceases to amaze me how dedicated some of my fans can be. When I played to a 3000 crowd in the West Country in the summer of 2004, a girl came up to me who I recognized had been at that hot-dog-plagued gig in San Francisco fifteen years earlier. I am a very lucky man.

Fortunately, there was a very positive comparison waiting for me when I arrived home from the US. We'd swept the board at the very influential *Smash Hits* Awards, winning pretty much every gong we could, and as that magazine's biggest draw, we had been invited to play at the ceremony. Coming off the back of those twelve weeks of touring at least meant that we were super-slick as a cohesive unit; and you could physically see how relieved we all were to be back on home soil and playing to a crowd who understood what we were trying to do. We played our nuts off! Watching the video, there is a point when I must have done about five spins in a row, I was so excited!

For Bros, America was never a very good experience. Of course, the first time we went there with the band was fantastic, looking at all the sights in New York, the Empire State Building, the Twin Towers, the yellow cabs, all that tourist stuff. We were only kids, barely out of our teens, so yes that was great fun. But once we got down to the harsh reality of selling a record out there, it was not one of my favourite Bros experiences.

There were some highlights for us during our various stays in the US however. For one gig in America, our entourage stopped off at a plush hotel that belonged to one of the biggest leisure chains in the world. All fifty or so of us checked in and went to our rooms to unpack.

During the course of our stay, a hotel security guy called one of our PAs a 'nigger'. We were disgusted and couldn't believe what had been said, so immediately we called the hotel's manager. The whole entourage was absolutely livid. The manager came down to speak to us and we told him how shocked we were about what had been said, how deeply offensive it was and asked him what he was going to do to rectify the insult. 'Your security has just called him a nigger!'

'Well . . . he is, isn't he?' came the reply.

To say our blood was boiling is something of an understatement but faced with such bigotry and ignorance I am very proud to say we chose to make a strategic retreat. As we walked away, you could almost hear our tour manager whispering, 'We are so going to fuck you lot right up . . .'

Rather than checking out in disgust, we stayed at the hotel for three days and nights. Bros would very often take entire floors of hotels. Fifty people, fifty bar bills, fifty servings of three meals a day, fifty calls on room service at least, we are talking about a great deal of money. On the final night we ran up a colossal bar bill just to finish with a whirl.

The next morning came and we were due to check out. Our tour manager was in charge of such matters so we went to the front desk with him, supposedly to settle our bill – he was just like a sergeant-major and so perfect for the job. We asked to speak to the manager who had behaved so appallingly earlier in the week.

As cool as you like, our tour manager had this to say:

'We are disgusted by you. We are absolutely appalled by the behaviour of your staff and yourself. What has gone on in your hotel is a disgrace. Now, see this bill? We are not going to be paying one cent of it. Not one penny. What is more, if we receive so much as one fax, one letter, one phonecall, even the slightest hint of communication from you or anybody to do with this hotel over this bill, then within a few hours every single news channel in the United States will know that this hotel chain thinks black people are called niggers.'

And with that, we all moved out *en masse*. Suffice to say, we never did receive a red reminder.

A very privileged moment in America for me was when we met the Rolling Stones. When the Debbie Gibson tour rolled into Kansas City, we were invited to a Stones concert that was also in town. It was welcome relief because by then I really wasn't enjoying myself at all, so to get the Rolling Stones invite in the midst of all the record company politics and on-tour tension was a great lift. We were invited backstage and as we wandered into the network of corridors behind the scenes, Keith Richards came round a corner walking towards us, looking exactly how I wanted him to look, dragging on a cigarette. He clocked us and with a little grin on his rock-and-roll-weathered face, he said, 'What the fuck are you lot doing here?' I just laughed because it was exactly what I would have wanted Keith Richards to say to me.

The Stones were really nice to us, very relaxed and friendly. It might seem like an odd combination, but the fact was that many of their daughters and family members were massive Bros fans. So many kids they knew coming to see us meant that the two bands shared a strange affinity with each other. We talked about the tour and some of the problems we were having and it felt good to hear advice and opinions from a band that has been touring for ever. They listened considerately to us and you could see, without saying a word, that they were thinking, *Yeah, we know that's true, we've been there,*

154

got the T-shirt and the lunchbox, mate. To meet them as part of my own band that was also selling out stadiums and arenas made it feel much more comfortable than if we'd just turned up as fans. Considering they are all founding-fathers of rock and roll, I was surprised at how humble and friendly they were, there was no side to them at all.

We all hung out playing table tennis and chatting. Then Ronnie Wood said to me, 'Can I wear your jacket on stage?' I was dumbfounded and said, 'Can you? Will you?!' This jacket was an incredible piece of workmanship, it was covered in jewellery, crystals, studs, a Bentley sign and was impeccably tailored, worth about four grand (it was the same one that Sammy Davis Jr took a fancy to). To go into the auditorium and see Ronnie Wood on stage wearing my jacket was just something else. What's more, he rocked way better than I did and looked much cooler in it than me! Bill Wyman wore one of Luke's jackets too. We went backstage afterwards and found that all of the Stones had signed the jacket for me (if the Hard Rock Café want that jacket, they can have it with my compliments!).

I've stayed in touch with Bill Wyman all these years – in 2004 he appeared in the video for a remixed release of my 1995 solo single 'The Key'. I've eaten many times at his Sticky Fingers restaurant and done a few events there for him too. I love talking to Bill. You will find yourself listening to some tale about life on the road or 'when I was in the band . . .' but then you catch yourself and remember that the band he happens to be talking about is the bloody Rolling Stones. Sometimes I feel like saying, 'All right Bill, just say "the Stones" one time, if nothing else it will make me feel good!' He's a great guy and still cracking on with his music after all those years.

The photograph I had taken that night with the Rolling

155

Stones is one of the favourite pictures that I own. I've been fortunate to have photos taken with so many famous people over the years, but that one still holds pride of place in my house.

SEVENTEEN

All Those Who Don't Believe

On 29 September 1989, we turned twenty-one. We were on the road in the US at the time, in Dallas. Shortly after, the tour bus rolled into New York and Dukus and I went into Cartier to buy each other a gift. We were just a couple of young guys in ripped jeans and T-shirts so the security guards latched on to us like limpets, they were convinced we were about to nick something. The assistants were also a little guarded but when I pointed to a gold chain with a panther holding an emerald and said, 'Can I have a look at that please?', the atmosphere changed very quickly. Luke bought me a magnificent Pasha watch which was just beautiful.

Unfortunately this very special watch vanished when we were completing the second album. I put this watch on a piano and next thing I know it's gone. Strangely enough, in my heart I think the guy I believe stole the watch wasn't a bad person but he was just totally the wrong man for the job. He made some bad judgements during that time.

There was a bodyguard I worked with who sold a picture of me in the bath. We had just done a twenty-four-hour-long video shoot for 'Cat Amongst The Pigeons/Silent Night' and I was exhausted and fell asleep in the bath. Imagine how you would feel when the picture turns up in the tabloids within a day or so and you know that there is only one person who could have taken it, and that that person was in your inner circle.

When you are at the head of what is effectively a very big business, you have to trust people; your career is often, to a certain extent, in the hands of others. The Bros empire was such a well-oiled machine that every minute of every day was allocated for something. You'd wake up in a hotel and there would be a sheet of paper pushed under the door detailing the entire day down to fifteen-minute segments, and always for sixteen, seventeen, eighteen hours a day, often more, so the people who were behind this sort of precision scheduling were vital cogs in the machine.

There was another person who worked for us who was a particularly trusted colleague. This guy would sometimes stay at my house. What I didn't know was that he would then smuggle a Bros fan into one of *my* bedrooms. It later transpired he was doing this all the time. When I found out, I went ballistic, I went for him and had to be restrained. It's an incredibly invasive moment the first time a fan tells you what the inside of your house looks like. The betrayal was so cutting, so disappointing, I can't tell you.

When you turn twenty-one, you are often given a silver key, to represent the opening of adult life and a whole new future ahead of you. Unfortunately for us, the year after that important birthday – through most of 1990 – was an absolute, unmitigated nightmare.

We felt very proud that after Craig had split we had gone on to play our biggest concerts, our biggest tours and increased our profile. That involved some very hard work but we had done it. However, it was becoming apparent that all was not well behind the scenes. Looking back, the pivotal moment that effectively catalysed our collapse – financially, commercially and as a working band – was when the management stood opposite me and said 'Yes' to commissioning the Wembley gig. It wasn't that their decision specifically caused all the problems, it didn't, but it certainly helped put us in a very big hole from which Bros never clawed its way back. We were backed into a corner. If someone says they are going to commission you, that's that; if the contract says they can, they can. At that point, we thought they had feelings for us. They obviously can't have done.

When we came back from America, the problems within Bros began to unravel. We wanted to renegotiate our contract with the management – as many successful artists do – but in the process, it started to become apparent that there were big difficulties financially. The exact details have been pored over by the press a thousand times, not least during court cases when exact amounts of money were detailed as having been spent by us. The press made out we were arrogant money-wasters, which upset me deeply, but the sums they quoted were predominantly the costs of running a big band.

Suffice to say, we were earning a huge amount less than we expected. The management contract allowed them to take commission on the gross of earnings, not the usual net figure. That meant we could play a show like Wembley, which costs vast amounts to put on, and lose a fortune.

I remember when the Pet Shop Boys left the Massive Management company. Tom travelled out to America when we were doing that Debbie Gibson tour and he was devastated by that band's departure from his roster (to his credit, despite his upset, he gave us both an inflatable jukebox and said, 'The real full-size ones are waiting for you at home'). He was gutted, though, about Neil and Chris. One of the things that had been said was that the Pet Shop Boys 'didn't want to be involved in his circus any more'. It's always stuck with me, that phrase, I've never mentioned it before but I think it is entirely relevant. I'd always viewed the Pet Shop Boys as so *together*, so wise and calm and that sentence really made me think about our own position.

In February 1990, we also left Massive Management. That month was the Brit Awards ceremony and I distinctly remember an advert in the programme for Massive Management. It was beautifully designed by Mark Farrow and mentioned all the acts on their roster. But both we and the Pet Shop Boys had gone, their two flagship acts. I recall Steve Wright on the radio saying, 'It's not quite so massive management now, is it?'

Tom issued a writ for breach of contract and we countersued. There was a complicated legal argument for two months which reached a resolution with an out-of-court settlement in June 1990. Our time with Tom was over, but in a sense, our problems were only just beginning.

I am sure that many people will expect me to bitterly criticize Tom Watkins. I can honestly say I don't harbour any animosity towards Tom or Mick at all, mainly because I don't have the energy but secondly, I have too many fond memories of Bros. What use have I for bitterness? It doesn't serve any purpose. I have a philosophy that says, 'Fear is never the creator of dreams, it only destroys them.' I think the same can be said for harbouring bitterness and malice. That path will only destroy one person, *you*. In the aftermath of splitting up from Tom and realizing our financial predicament, I had a very important choice: whether to be consumed with anger and bitterness or to follow a different journey. I chose the latter. I have faith in my life and that has been proved well-founded.

I do believe in forgiveness. Don't get me wrong, I don't think you should be an idiot or a sucker – if someone screws with you once, then give them a chance, but if they do it twice then it's probably best to part – preferably amicably – and say that's not an energy I need in my life.

What I will say about Tom is that he was a great manager but he became bored too quickly. Sometimes in long-term management you and your act will go through lulls, periods when you have depressing or difficult times. The sign of a really good manager is one who hangs in there and says, 'Let's ride this storm out.'

Obviously, there are certain practicalities to being in a huge band that I know how to handle now but didn't back then. You shouldn't really have the same accountant as your manager, that's a basic conflict of interest, I know that now. You shouldn't have a limousine on hire all the time – buy two cars and employ a driver, you will save a fortune. It makes good business sense. Even the small stuff can save you a fortune. *Never* feel bad about asking to see contracts; question specific clauses, individual words. For example, 'recoupable' is a very, very important word to understand. Don't feel afraid asking to see proof of payment, where the money's gone, where it's going, transport costs, who's billing what on your time. You are running a business and you need to know what is happening within that business. I was part of a band that did multiple nights at Wembley Arena – that's a very complex and costly operation. When you are playing Wembley Stadium you don't think you will have any financial problems. It can happen, believe me.

I would have liked the management to have been more personable, to have taken a little more care of us. It goes back to being a professional parent again. I think people like Mick probably knew exactly what was going on but to me, he could have said, 'Yo! Guys, think about the future.'

There are things that Tom did that I disagreed with, of course. I don't think that he was very supportive of Luke's relationship with Shirley, in fact he was blatantly rude sometimes. But Tom's always been like a caricature to me. He had an amazing presence and energy, there was no messing with him, but I think he became aware of that.

Bros was not the first band to work hard and come out at the other end with much less money than was expected. It is nothing new in rock and roll. One thing I always say when people ask me how I make decisions about trust nowadays is that you have to accept that *at some point you must trust somebody* and that could be the somebody who is going to rip you off. There is no other way around it, you don't have a choice. At some point in your life and career, you have to trust somebody otherwise you are going to end up burnt out. If I was to never trust anyone again because I might have felt wronged in the past, all I am doing is empowering that negativity, consuming myself with the bad side of my past. I constantly remind myself of that. Of course, be careful, but at some point you have to hope that the person you trusted is worthy of your trust and is not going to take the easy buck behind your back.

Tom's contract allowed him to commission us on gross: fact. Towards Tom and his team, I do not hold any bitterness. I can't invent anger. I don't hate Tom, I don't hate Mick. I just feel absolute sadness, complete disappointment. That whole circle of people and those events feel in many ways like a lifetime away, yet it's still a huge part of my heart. I've just found it easier to fall in love with those times.

Bitterness? No, none.

* * *

I woke up one morning in March 1990 to find one of the major tabloids running the front-page headline 'Amex Sues Bros for £58,000'. I was sickened. The most disgusting thing about this for me was that we'd spent hundreds of thousands of pounds on Amex, hundreds upon hundreds of thousands, all our tour managers used them and stacks of our personnel. God knows how much money went through Amex and then they sued us for that late payment. Worse still, someone at Amex must have leaked it to the press which was appallingly unethical. At that point, we could have easily paid that credit-card bill off by playing one or two gigs. Looking back, this was the first real taste of the *glee* that people seemed to revel in when berating us in the papers. In some ways, that betrayal by Amex was the start of the torrent of venom that was shortly to come pouring our way.

The battering that Bros took from the press around late 1989 and through all of 1990 and after was absolutely horrifying. It felt like emotional torture, our hearts and minds were pillaged. There was nowhere to hide and nothing was sacred, nothing. We'd had all our financial problems made public through the courts, and the press couldn't believe their luck, they saw it as such a fall from grace, these guys who were so rich, loaded, famous . . . they loved it.

It's hard to explain how painful and damaging it was to be on the receiving end of so much bile. Having said that, I really do want to preface this by saying that I understand why they were so barbarous with their stories about us. It is a long-established process in the UK to build someone up, then knock them down: pop stars, sporting celebrities, politicians, all manner of people. That is especially the case in the entertainment industry. So having my manager's or PR person's head on, I understand why it happens, I really do.

What I don't understand and will never understand is why

there was such vindictive glee. The 'pretty boys who've lost millions' vein seemed to be heaven-sent to them, they mined it thoroughly and with such disturbing vigour.

We didn't spend nearly as much as was alleged, and I will never feel bad about having fun. What was never reported was the fact that my brother and I were working 24/7, we didn't stop, our schedules were so insanely hectic. I often hear people say things like, 'Ooh, look at Britney! She hasn't got her make-up on quite right, she looks knackered, oh dear . . .' The chances are – and I speak from vast personal experience – she probably is totally knackered. She will have been working her arse off and won't have had a break for months. But that doesn't make headlines: 'Pop Star Works Really Hard and Spends Sensible Amount of Earnings.'

Yes, we were very decadent. Yes, we bought the flash cars, we wore beautiful clothes, we stayed at fabulous hotels. My God, we lived the pop star life, but I have never denied that or been ashamed of it. Despite the battering we took because of the money situation, my advice to anyone who is thinking of spending a bit of money or having a nice time but isn't sure if they should . . . *do it*. If you can afford it, have what you want. You don't know how long you are going to be here. Also, what are you supposed to do when you are barely out of your teens, touring the world, topping the charts and regularly seeing sacks of cash emptied out in your dressing-room? If they were totally honest about it, most people would do exactly the same.

There was also much selective reporting. They'd say things like we'd blown hundreds of thousands of pounds on a tour 'entourage', as if we were paying for hangers-on. But for example, when we went to Australia we had to take nearly sixty people. If you look at the price of *one* flight to Sydney, you might balk – well, we had to pay for *sixty*. Then there are hotels, food, transport, insurance, wages – I was told we were paying £70,000 *a week* in wages at one point. Why the big entourage? Not for fun I can tell you, it was because Bros was a mini-corporation, a massive touring machine on very expensive wheels and it had to be kept running. You take that machine out for seven months on the road, you have to know that it is going to cost serious money.

A lot of our stage gear was very expensive and that was something which certain people in the media held up as an example of our extravagance. But we were musicians, performers, the clothes you wear are part of the tools of your trade; and we had to buy clothes for the entire band, it wasn't just for ourselves.

You also need to remember that we were standing in front of thousands of paying fans, seeing truckloads of merchandise shifting every night, being told about tour deals, radio play, record sales; there was every reason to believe that our income would far outstrip our outgoings, however extravagant we were being. But it didn't and the press had a field day. It was an open wound and they went at it with a rusty axe, laughing as they did, as brutally and as coldly as that. It reached a point where I didn't even recognize the people they were describing. The early Nineties was a horrible time for many people and we seemed to have our recession a year before everyone else. The only difference was that ours was played out on the front pages of the tabloids. At one point, our financial woes made headlines in the tabloids daily.

To the credit of a few, I have had about ten journalists come up to me over the years and apologize, saying things like, 'I was really gleeful when you were having problems with the band. Sorry.' That takes courage and I respect them for that. It helps a little, but in terms of the pain they caused as a whole, it is like trying to fix a mortar wound with sticky-tape.

The repercussions of all this very often manifested them-selves on the street. People spat at us a few times and the more cruel members of the public would make loud jibes about money. It's amazing the depths that some people will plumb to have a go at you if your face is known. One night when we were getting a lot of shit from the press, I decided to wander down to my local petrol station, just to get a can of Coke and a little quiet time. It was pretty late so I thought I'd be all right. As I was waiting at the till to get my change, I saw in the window the reflection of five guys who'd just walked into the shop and were approaching me from behind. I just thought, 'Oh, God, here we go . . .' One of them started taking the piss out of me but then he said something about Carolyn and I just went for him. I smashed the Coke can into his face almost instinctively – you've never seen a nose so broken, completely wrecked, blood all down his shirt.

He got up and was shouting the odds, saying he was going to sue me and phone the tabloids – cheap threats. I said, 'Do me a favour, tell 'em that Matt Goss broke your fucking nose and tell 'em why. You mock my dead sister, you can come to me any time and I will break your nose again.'

Even the guys he was with saw in my eyes that I had passed the point of no return for all of them. The next day I had five policemen knocking at my door; they took statements and that was that. I don't understand why some people behave like that, what do they get out of it? Towards the end of Bros, I was frequently getting in fights and I didn't particularly like the person I was becoming.

Living in America, one thing that you quickly learn is that success is a bloody good word. As long as money is not the centre of your universe, you will be okay. I am not moti-vated by money, I am motivated by my family's happiness. Money provides freedom for the people you love so that's why

I like money, but it doesn't motivate me to do what I do. I don't think you should ever feel ashamed of enjoying a new car. I think if you see your mate buying a new car, then sure enough, think *I wish I had that*, but be pleased for him, *enthuse*. When I am driving around LA in my Aston Martin, people, more often than not guys, stop by the window and say, 'Hey, cool car man.' You won't get that in the UK and we certainly never saw that in Bros. I don't want to sound like an idealistic hippy because I am a realist, but I don't understand or like that 'Let's put a key down the side of his car' mentality.

You could almost taste the enthusiasm with which some of the papers berated, ridiculed and scoffed at us. It was so painful, I don't think I have the words to ever adequately describe the distress those media attacks caused us. I wouldn't wish it on my own worst enemy. It scarred me for years, perhaps for ever.

Ironically, particularly in light of the controversy over Princess Diana's death, the paparazzi nearly always come in for criticism whenever privacy issues and press freedom are discussed. I have to say now that the paps have *always* been really good to me. Always. Don't misunderstand – I am a shy person; my friends say I am annoyingly shy at times, so walking into certain situations, a film première for example, is pretty intimidating and uncomfortable for me. A part of me would just like to hide, come in to the studio or go on stage (where by contrast I *never* feel uncomfortable) and do my work. Literally, I'm not talking about an obscure address, I am talking about *no* address. Part of me craves that.

Unlike many celebrities, I have always had a good relationship with the paps. I have never felt like screaming, 'Get out of my face!', all that nonsense. You have to be realistic if you are in the public eye. You chose to do this job, it is a life that comes with a public profile. The paps' assignment is to get pictures of you. There's an on-line aerial picture of my house in LA. You just have to live with things like that, they are unavoidable parts of what you do, so just go along with it. The bottom line is, don't complain about being a public figure and wonder why people are snapping your picture.

Of course, I was often very shocked by certain pictures they'd take. For instance, I'm chilling out by a pool and there's nothing for miles except wilderness. The next day there's a tabloid running a picture of me up real close. Then you know there was someone out there in a tree with a huge lens pointed your way. Yes, that's disconcerting, naturally, but it is part of the job, that's all it is – you have to accept it.

I've known the paps for years and many of them have become notable photographers in their own right. I think there is a certain way of being a successful pap and that is to be polite. There are rude fuckers doing that job, as in every profession, but the good ones know how to be considerate. Many years ago, I was out with quite a famous woman, leaving a restaurant in my car and out of nowhere a camera appeared. Had that picture been printed, it could have caused plenty of trouble, because she was quite well-known. I just didn't want the publicity. I said, 'Mate, not this one, please,' and he said, 'Okay, you owe me one.' I said, 'Fair enough.' In early 2004, I saw this same man and I said, 'Remember that night? I haven't forgotten that, so if there is anything you want . . .'

But it wasn't the paparazzi that were so unbearably cruel to us, it was the press. Some of the press wanted to kill us . . . and I don't mean metaphorically. Literally, people wanted to see us turn to addiction and so on. We had money and we'd lost it and they were thinking, 'Oh yeah, good, build 'em up to watch them fall and we've done it.' I felt that if we hadn't eventually got out it would have killed us. There isn't a word to describe how violent it felt.

The tide had turned quite some time before we split up. It's a time in my life that I can't be philosophical about. There's no room for philosophy there, I can't use it to learn, I can't see an ideology in there, I still don't approve or use that for anything positive in my life. It was wrong.

I understand they want to cover you because you are in a public job, but I don't think it is acceptable to constantly try to screw with someone's private life. That need to interfere with your life is so distasteful, I don't get that, despite everything I have just said about being a public figure. Everyone in life deserves a little privacy.

EIGHTEEN

I Can't Hold My Breath That Long

There were other shocking revelations that unfolded at this time, alongside the financial issues. When the press started to turn against us, it was very hard for all of us, most directly Luke and me, but also for everyone on our team. For example, my PA Shaun would always get very frustrated. Around this time, he lost his mum and I was with him when he found out that she'd died. That particular bereavement is one of my biggest fears, so I knew I had to be there for him, he was someone really close to me, there was a real bond. It is not an easy job and with a schedule like ours, he had to be on call twenty-four hours a day, effectively.

There was a member of our management team who was teetotal, very strait-laced and always very cautious and careful about his behaviour. During that time, I was told this previously quite conservative person fell asleep on a radiator for hours under the influence of drugs and subsequently woke up with half of his ear burnt off. It was so shocking (for the record, I would like to state categorically that it was not Tom or Mick, absolutely not). I mention this not as some gory rock-and-roll incident, but because it shocked me to the core

170

to see the one element of our career that was supposed to be in control, stable and capable of steering us through all the madness, had a person within the ranks who was so out of control in such an extreme fashion.

You have to be strong to keep moving forward as an artist; it's easy for people to say, 'I can't handle all this, I'm not going to be an artist any more and I'm going to disappear into obscurity.' Part of the process that helps you steel yourself for that is your management.

What made the whole incident more disturbing was that I had introduced this man to his future partner, a dear friend of mine. So for us both to be visiting him in a drug rehab clinic was almost too much to comprehend. The actual day of the first visit to the ward is etched in my memory. We were sitting by people who were dying with anorexia. I kept noticing a woman who was so gaunt that her glasses kept falling off her nose, she couldn't keep them on. Yet here's someone from my former management team, among all these people who were truly desperate, because he'd taken drugs and lost half his ear through lying on a radiator for hours upon hours slowly having it burnt away.

I think the world of this guy and it was a really hard phase of his life for him to go through. The strain was so much, the press onslaught became so intense that even this person who wasn't directly in the line of fire suffered so badly. At the time I couldn't help thinking, *Where the hell do we stand? What else can happen?* By now, as each kick in the teeth homed in, I constantly thought, *Is this going to be the thing that finally breaks my back?*

People would sometimes say to me, 'Why are you and Luke looking so serious?' It was because we had a lot of shit to deal with, there was so much going on.

*   *   *

171

After we'd left Tom, for a while we were managed by John Reid who most famously looked after Elton John for many years. We completed production of our third album, *Changing Faces*, while with John and to this day I think that is the best Bros record we ever made; that dreaded third album, notorious in the music industry. We made it with Gary Stephenson, who also worked with Go West. I loved the way *Changing Faces* sounded, and I am still very proud of it. Unfortunately, by then so much mud had been flung our way that it was difficult to resurface. Our previous two albums had reached Number 2 and 4 respectively, whereas *Changing Faces* only managed Number 18. That was directly out of proportion to how good that album was, believe me.

There was also an undercurrent at the time implying I should go solo. The problem was that I wasn't ready to become a solo artist, I was unprepared to be without Lukie. Thinking of working without Luke was incomprehensible to me; I always feel at a loss when I am not around him. To this day he is the only human being who remotely understands what I have been through. The best way of putting it is that we are from the same seed, what more can I say? My beautiful brother and I went through a lot, a hell of a lot together, and I wasn't about to jump ship and head off on my own. It was never an option. By now, however, the writing was on the wall for that third album and there was just too much baggage and too many preconceptions to battle against. So, after only a short time, John Reid and ourselves parted company.

However, although our professional relationship did not work out, John was only ever an absolute gentleman to me. I was fortunate enough to have some great times with him, including being invited to Elizabeth Taylor's sixtieth birthday party which, in typically Hollywood style, was held at Disney-

land in America. In fact, Liz actually had the whole of Disney-
land closed down just for her party, which was held in the
main castle itself. I went in a limo together with John and one
of my favourite photographers of all time, Herb Ritts. When
we arrived at the park, all the guests were driven to the castle
in old *Chitty Chitty Bang Bang*-style cars. The castle had been
dressed for the occasion and looked spectacular.

I walked in and within minutes I could see David Bowie,
Michael Jackson and Cindy Crawford. There didn't seem to
be a face I didn't recognize, so many faces, everyone who was
anyone in those circles was there. I've always liked John Reid,
he's always been very straightforward with me and I enjoy his
company; Herb was a good friend of John's, so it was an
interesting group to arrive in.

John had bought Liz a $50,000 necklace as a birthday gift,
and when we walked into the castle's main hall, I was aston-
ished to see him place this amazingly generous gesture on a
table on the left-hand side of the hall that was allocated for
presents.

'John! What are you doing?' I said.

'What do you mean?' he replied, seemingly oblivious to
what I was about to say.

'You should give her the present in person, John! That's a
fifty-thousand-dollar necklace!'

'Do you know what?' he said, a smile stretching across his
face. 'You're bloody right!' He went back and collected his
gift and shortly afterwards presented it to Liz in person. I
was delighted to meet her and not surprised to find that she
was incredibly beautiful.

Later on in the night, there was a big group picture – one
thousand stars and friends had been invited so it was some
photograph! I couldn't help taking a small souvenir of the
party back home with me, a lilac napkin with 'Elizabeth

Taylor's Sixtieth' scrolled across it (there were plenty of other things I could have nicked). You might be surprised to hear that far from being a huge room full of proportionately big egos and attitudes, everyone was very gracious. I felt very privileged to be a part of the whole night.

It is a popular misconception about Bros that we declared ourselves bankrupt, but it is simply not true. People think they know all about what happened with Bros, how much money we spent and all that tabloid nonsense they read. But *we never declared ourselves bankrupt*. This was an absolutely massive choice we made which, in one respect, I am very proud of. Why? We were young men from a working-class family and the word 'bankrupt' held such a powerful stigma, it was like a cloak of fear coming into the room whenever it was mentioned. We just would not do it. On top of everything else we had had to deal with, the prospect of being bankrupt was just horrendous.

Instead, we entered into what is called a 'VA', a 'voluntary arrangement' where you work out a payment scheme with creditors to make sure your life gets put back in order. This was very strenuous on Luke and me but we knuckled down and worked our way through it all. It was a long road ahead – it was as recently as 2003 that the last financial overhang from Bros was resolved. It took that long for the last issue to stop rearing its head; these particular people were relentless, on a mission. I just felt like saying, 'Leave me alone, fucking vultures.' But what people have to know is that Luke and I *never* whinged about what happened with the money. We've just cracked on trying to remedy our situation. Hopefully we've been quite dignified about it and taken care of a lot of stuff.

In hindsight, we probably should have gone bankrupt. Being

older and wiser in these matters, which are very complicated and intimidating when you are much younger, I realize bankruptcy is just what it is and we should have done it. We should have simply said, 'Yes, we are bankrupt,' served our time and moved on. It was far, far harder on us not making that decision, but our self-respect would just not allow us to. You live and learn.

One day during the *Changing Faces* project, the phone rang.

It was Luke.

He said, 'I've had enough.'

Luke wasn't content, he genuinely didn't seem satisfied. I was very unhappy. We both felt the tide was changing – I will always remember not long after Wembley Stadium, our single 'Chocolate Box' charted at Number 9 and, as it wasn't Top Five, the press were all asking, 'Is this the end for Bros?' Things never really improved after that, but it was still a massive phonecall to take. When I was speaking with Luke, at that precise moment there were two hundred people outside on my lawn. He was adamant – he wanted out. The band – the love of my life – had finished with a single phonecall. I put the phone back on the base and sat there, taking it all in. I felt shattered. I was by myself again.

To be honest, I felt very frustrated with the band during those closing months too. If we dared to object to stories in the press or proffer an opinion, they said we were arrogant or obnoxious; it was so frustrating. They'd retaliate with *who do they think they are?* Yet we were musicians who'd been around the world several times and played music since we could remember. I felt very stifled by certain things in Bros and, as the singer, I had to front a lot of that. Luke probably doesn't realize that his frustrations were very similar to mine.

When he said he wanted to end the band, it was the statement of a realist. I didn't say 'No!' I just said, 'Okay.' It just wasn't worth it any more. I was with him – 'Enough already'. Every morning you would wait to find out what attack was next. He was the one who called up and said it and I am glad he did.

Having said all of that, I was completely devastated.

I'd lost my day job, my passion, everything I knew about, and it seemed that I wasn't going to see my brother onstage with me, ever again. The loss extended beyond Luke too. When you are in a big band like that, you have little families of people you get to know all over the world. Record company people, PR staff, TV and radio people, all sorts of acquaintances are involved in a band and many of those you become close to, you have dinner, chat, learn about their lives. There is a whole massive network. Then suddenly, that was finished too. I wouldn't be seeing them again either. In the aftermath of that phonecall from Luke, we both underwent a huge change of life, of emotion, of pace. It all came juddering to a halt.

I can honestly say with my hand on my heart that we could have learned about the business and become more savvy and taken Bros on to greater levels, we genuinely could have gone on and on. Luke and I had so much in us that we wanted to do. The sky could have been the limit, I truly believe that. We were just getting into our stride.

It made the *Nine O'Clock News* that we'd split. Each night for weeks I would go to my house to find people crying, hundreds of people mourning out there. Newspapers talked of how to counsel your child through the loss, radio shows did phone-ins for people who were upset. A whole episode of their lives had ended, suddenly.

It was the same for Luke and me. Everything we had known

for five years wasn't going to happen again. It was a very sad day for me and I just wanted to be with Luke.

The massive machine had stopped.

NINETEEN

So Many Miles From Here

Although many observers might think that the day after Bros split, I was free to go and start a new career and life, it was, in fact, at least five years before it all started to die down. The question was often asked, 'So, Matt, what did you do straight after Bros split?', but that was a query so far removed from actual reality that it was hard to answer. For starters, we had commitments all over the world spanning months ahead of us – remember, we were in the middle of promoting our third album. In Spain, for example, that record was our biggest. The single 'Are You Mine?' was so popular that they ran a competition to write the Spanish translation of the lyrics. It was backed by a huge radio campaign with national coverage and a massive promotional push behind it. But we couldn't go to Spain to finish the project, which was awful.

It wasn't just Spain, we had scheduled releases all over the world. Just because a band splits up, it doesn't mean they lock the doors and sweep the floor that very night. It's a beast that takes a long, long time to go to sleep.

What I did do was decide to move to America. Within thirty days of Bros splitting, I was in America plunging back into music. With Bros's profile and my role as lead singer, it was perhaps inevitable that the industry buzz was about whether I could be 'the next George Michael'. That was flattering, but I have to be honest; at the precise moment I decided to fly out to the USA, my mind was not thinking like that. The events of the past few years were not something that you could just neatly package up and say, 'That can go over there, I'm off to start afresh.' If only it had been that simple.

Once I'd finally made up my mind to head to the States, a very traumatic period in my life began. When I woke up on the morning of the flight, just after Christmas 1991, I was petrified. I drove to the airport almost in a daze, contemplating what had been and what might be in the future. The hardest thing for me was the absolute deafening silence. I was in the Virgin Atlantic lounge, sitting with my sunglasses on and my baseball cap pulled down over my eyes and I am not ashamed to admit it, I cried. I sat there motionless like a stone and tears racked my body. I was careful to hide my emotion but the Virgin staff, who have always been amazing to me, sensed I needed some space and left me alone. I have to give them credit, their warmth and concern for me was the reason that I could muster the strength to get on the plane (to this day I always fly Virgin, and because I am lucky enough to virtually commute at times between LA and London – two of the most wonderful cities in the world – I know the staff on both sides of the Atlantic very well!).

I am a dreamer, I can sit and dream for days, I admit that. But I also have a fierce streak of realism coursing through me and at that moment it was the realist in me that was most acutely aware of what was happening. I knew I was going to LA. I knew in my heart of hearts that I would not be coming back for two, maybe three years. I just knew and that was devastating for me.

There were a few hundred fans there to see me off and they were all crying. They knew it too, I wasn't coming back.

It was a crushingly sad day for me. As it transpired, I wouldn't return to British soil for five years.

I touched down in LA in an alien land far away from Bros, Lukie, Mum, Tony, Adam, the tabloids, everyone and everything. When Bros came to an end, I was still with Melanie Sykes – we'd been together for five years. We had an amazing relationship, we were the best of friends but when I moved out to LA, Mel did not come with me. She found a little place of her own and, looking back, I can see that she wanted to spread her wings, gain some freedom and experience more of the world. That decision not to fly out with me was probably the beginning of the end for us.

She did come out to LA a few times but the lasting memory of Mel in that city was her final visit. When it was time for her to go to the airport, she got in the car and I knew that this would be the last time we were together. I knew in my heart and I was proved right. Shortly after she landed back in the UK, she phoned and we split up.

I took it very, very badly. That was probably the first time that I had my heart broken. I genuinely thought she was the one, and I think she felt the same too, so when it all came crashing down and I was on the other side of the Atlantic from my family, it knocked me for six, it really did. Now she is happily married and I wish her all the best, she is a lovely person and I will never speak ill of her. I'd already lost Bros and my working relationship with my brother, as well as all those people I've mentioned that I was used to working with. When Mel and I split up, another foundation block in my life was pulled from under me. I was beginning to teeter.

I may have moved country but I thought at least I can get

my own personal belongings out quickly and that will help to settle me in. So my dad and Luke very kindly arranged to have my furniture and all my worldly goods shipped out in a crate to LA. They were given a price and the shipping was booked. The day came and the crate with my life in it set sail for LA, but when it arrived at port, the company demanded a price that was three times what they had quoted, and I couldn't afford to pay. It was an insane amount of money to get stuff back that already belonged to me. I was being asked to pay again for what I had already paid for.

On two levels, that was devastating. First, there were many very expensive items in there: beautiful crystal vases with copper inlay, handmade furniture, exquisite sofas, elegant and stunning furnishings that had taken much time and money to acquire. However, because of the financial repercussions of Bros, I was no longer in a position to simply replace like for like, it was just too expensive. But second, and worst of all, there was indefinable sentimental value to those items. There were personal things that could never be replaced that hadn't cost much, as well as more precious items that I adored. The composite of these things was my life, these were the practical wrapping around my soul, they were part of me and now, along with so much else, they had been taken away.

I set about replacing what I could but I knew that I had to be careful with money because of what was happening with Bros. Most galling perhaps was that no one really went mad about it at the freight company, my life was in a crate and it was just left there to rot. It was also a great shame for Dad and Luke because they had gone to a lot of trouble to organize this all for me, they'd made a genuine effort.

Losing all my belongings was a very brutal metaphor for what had happened to me so recently, severing ties with so many cornerstones of my life. I was so disappointed and genuinely depressed. I was sitting on my own, in a strange city, in an unfamiliar apartment, surrounded by impersonal furnishings. I was alone even in my own home. It just felt endless, bloody endless.

I've never had a guitar or piano lesson in my life. I didn't pick up a guitar until after Bros had finished. For a long time, not knowing music theory was something that made me feel that I wasn't a proper musician, but now I am older and wiser I'm really glad that I don't. What I do know is when it is wrong. I don't think any musician in history knows when it is perfect – and as they say, once you've written the perfect song, where do you go from there?

I've been blessed with really good pitch and I play everything by ear. As far back as the infamous Pulse 2 ('No, we're Ice!'), I wanted to write songs. I was only in my early teens but I had ideas in my head and the only way to get them down was to find a keyboard and start programming.

But over the years you learn, you adapt, you pick up tips on the road and gradually you shape your own way of writing songs. By the time I left Bros, I was writing all the time. The nature of modern music technology is such that the writing process can be very fragmented – you programme stuff, you play in the guitars, keyboards, vocals and backing singers and so on, but the very first time you play that same song back to yourself, that's when it really feels like it's yours. For me, being able to write songs is a blessing. When I moved to America, I knew I could write great songs. What I didn't know was how hard it would prove to get those songs heard.

You'd think that a young, single man in his early twenties, living in LA would have been in seventh heaven, but after the split with Mel happened, I felt terribly alone; I really did not want to be single, as mad as that may sound.

I was insanely determined to have a life without all the Bros/ pop star element. Yet I became convinced that I couldn't get a woman in my world without Bros. In hindsight I can see that I've always had very beautiful women with me both here and in America. But you might find it surprising to hear that I wasn't that confident with women when I was in Bros. Now I was in the USA, my confidence was being eroded on a daily basis and then my girlfriend of five years split up with me. I thought there was no chance of finding someone else.

These insecurities were exacerbated by the feeling of being 'just a number' in the US, which was a severe culture shock. America can be a strange place sometimes. There is often an assumption that unless they know you, you must do nothing. You couldn't help but notice it, coming from Brosmania to being unknown in the space of a twelve-hour flight. It's not like I had to work on being humble, humility is a really nice quality and because of my mum, my family have always been very grounded. But I think you'd have to be Superman to walk in somewhere, after five or six years of Bros madness all around the world, and be treated like a number, without it feeling odd. I'm just being honest.

I'll give you a specific example. I was at a dinner with quite a few people in LA and I was sitting next to a very well-known music manager. I spoke briefly about being from England and playing music but I really didn't go into very much detail.

'Ah!' interrupts this manager, before setting off on a wave of advice I hadn't asked for. 'There is a moment when you'll know you've really become an artist and do you know when that is? When you truly know why you do what you do?'

'No, when's that?' I said. Remember, I had just played Wembley Stadium and toured the world three times.

'When you do some live gigs, man.'

'Oh, really?'

'Yeah, man, that's what it is all about.'

At this point, I could see a few of the people around the table who knew me starting to wince, before burying their heads in their own conversation out of embarrassment.

But this guy was only just starting.

'Yeah, you are really gonna find your feet and realize the reason why you are actually doing what you are doing when you get some live concerts booked. When you go on that stage and feel the crowd. Of course, you won't get a full production at first, that will come, don't worry, but first and foremost just get out there and play some gigs . . .'

And he just went on and on and on for over half an hour.

At first it was a little amusing, but as it became apparent he wasn't stopping, I had to say to myself, 'All right, take a deep breath, he doesn't know what you've done.' Finally, I couldn't listen to any more. The table was almost hushed by now and tangibly uncomfortable, so I excused myself from my seat and went to the bathroom.

When I came back, a few words of wisdom had obviously been passed on to this manager in my temporary absence. You have never seen someone so red. The blushing looked terminal!

He said, 'Oh my God, man, you just played fucking Wembley?! Why didn't you tell me?'

Softly, I just said, 'You didn't ask me.'

This guy said barely another word for an hour and a half of the dinner. You could see him mulling over those four words. It was one of those comments that you knew would stay with someone for a long time, probably for ever. And I have to admit, it was a very nice feeling to have sufficient poise and self-awareness to say it with such calmness. I didn't go to America to shout out I'd done this and that, toured here and there and sold this many records. So it was warming for my soul to relish that moment of humility.

Apart from perfectly highlighting the anonymity you can experience in the USA, another reason I tell the story is because whatever you do in your life, whatever your career, if you've done well and you've seen a lot, then I think you deserve respect. No matter if what a person does is your thing or not, whether you like it or don't like it, respect them for it. Experience is becoming a scarce commodity in certain circles, people are very transient in their careers, especially in the entertainment business. 'Oh, I can sing, or I could dance, I do a bit of acting as well.' I have been offered TV jobs and West End roles but I want to be a master of one trade, not a jack of all.

That dinner has stayed with me to this day. On one level, it says a great deal about LA in particular. There are plenty of know-alls. They don't ask, they just talk, opinionate, ramble. I learned very quickly that if you try to talk back, they will talk over you, through you; it's pointless. They might even know you were in a band, but to many of these people, Europe is just a quaint little place with lots of fog and people with bad teeth. Even if you have been successful there, it's not considered very valid. Not valid? We sold sixteen million records.

But it is more than just an Americanism or a parochial quirk. It highlights something that is very important to me personally. You have to have faith in who you are as a person, knowing who you are in your life. I am fortunate enough to have a wealth of experiences in my life, both good and bad, and that's what keeps me calm sometimes when faced with such myopia.

At least I had Shaun, my PA, with me. But even that was about to change. Shaun thought the world of me, respected what I had achieved and knew what I had been through. So from that point of view, it was very reassuring that he was there in America with me. Unfortunately, Shaun found it increasingly difficult to tolerate the American way.

It was during this time that I became involved with a producer in LA who was to have a very negative and undermining influence on me. I'm not going to mention his name, because, quite frankly, I don't think he deserves it. I was in a somewhat fragile state of mind at the time and, of course, was looking to make a record. This guy had a studio of his own, so we agreed he was going to write half the record and we were going to work together. Sounds simple enough. Far from it. It might well have been the single worst environment I could have immersed myself in after Bros.

He was a strange character and I don't mean that in an eccentric or endearing way. He was not a good person. He was very poisonous towards me at times too, making me paranoid, saying I was fat, making me self-conscious about my weight and my hair. Remember, I didn't think I could get a girlfriend without Bros and within a few months of splitting up the band, this relative stranger was chipping away at what few small strands of self-esteem I still had left. It was all incredibly destructive, this drip-feed of malice. Looking back it is not surprising that my confidence and self-worth were not just eroded but completely dismantled.

I became a hermit.

I became agoraphobic.

I was spiralling downwards and fast while one of the few people who could have steered me clear of danger was actually accelerating me into the abyss. The severity of my situation became abundantly clear one day when I plucked up the courage to go to a shopping mall. That might not seem like a big deal, but it took a whole mountain of courage to walk out of the door, never mind mix with so many people. I remember finally getting into the mall then next thing I know, I am coming to, outside the shopping centre.

I had blacked out.

I was distraught. I pride myself on being someone who is in control, and always have done. I had never relied on anything to get me through difficult times except my heart, faith and mind. Blacking out was an eye-opener. Matters had deteriorated to the degree where I couldn't even go to a shopping mall. Only a matter of months previously, I had been standing on stage at Wembley Stadium with not a care in the world. I was so relaxed and excited that day at Wembley, I could have been down the pub. Now I couldn't even walk into a bar.

I just kept saying to myself, *This cannot be me. I will not be beaten by this.* I was determined not to let this consume me. Unfortunately, it was around this time that I had to fire Shaun. As I've said, he cared for me and we had seen a lot of the world in a very decadent, extreme, superstar way. The problem was, he could not get used to people who knew nothing of Bros saying to me, 'Hey man, good luck with the music thing,' as if I was just starting out. That whole environment got his back up. He was beginning to be short and rude to people, I must say only because he felt defensive of me, but nevertheless I knew it was going to be a really big problem if it was allowed to continue. I gave him a month's money and a plane ticket home and that was that.

There was no animosity whatsoever between Shaun and myself, I was genuinely sad to see him go. He was a tough black guy whose mum had died while he was working with me, so we'd been through a lot together. He was a close friend as well as a PA and I loved him. But I knew that if I was to progress in America I couldn't take the safe option and that was to keep Shaun. So I let him go.

It says much about my frame of mind that the second that Shaun actually left, I was so afraid. Now I was drifting without an anchor. Part of the reason that certain people make you feel safe is that they know what you have been through, what you are about and there is so much unspoken understanding. I was lost in LA without an angel for six thousand miles.

TWENTY

Freefall

The LA producer continued with his sniping, his unnecessary Chinese whispers boring into my head and allowing my confidence to drip out. I thought this person with whom I was staying cared for me, but he categorically didn't. I should have probably gone on holiday for a couple of months rather than try to get back into recording. But, as they say, hindsight is a very powerful thing.

Then one of his closest friends – whom he was actually dating – took me to one side and said, 'You're a really nice guy, he's behaving awfully, he's very jealous of you, and you should just leave.' Without him even knowing, his friends were telling me that. If ever there was a damning verdict . . .

At this point, my money situation was pretty dire. Straight after Bros I had no cash at all. We had our assets frozen and weren't allowed to touch anything until the various disputes were resolved. Living in LA can be quite a money-pit at the best of times, so my limited resources quickly started to evaporate. Fortunately, I had acquired quite a collection of watches but it had come to the point where I had to sell one every month just to get by.

At least I had those watches to sell, but it was so demoralizing. Watches along with cars and tailoring had been my passion when I was in Bros. I can't remember not loving watches. I think there's something incredible about an automatic watch that you never have to wind up. It's the most secure thing that you don't have to buy a battery, it's self-contained, it will do what it does for ever, the ultimate in reliability. There's something so eloquently tranquil about such a watch on the surface, but there's the purest form of perfect mayhem underneath. I adore that.

Pick a number when buying watches – you can spend a million dollars on one if you so wish. One of my very first was given to me by Tom Watkins. When 'I Owe You Nothing' went to Number 1, Tom gave us each a Rolex. Mine had the inscription, 'Matt, Bros, Number 1' and the date of that achievement. It was irreplaceable. Unfortunately, Mel later lost it in a theatre when it fell off her wrist. It would mean the world to me to find that watch, so if anyone knows where it is, please let me know.

Pretty quickly after I first started buying them in Bros, my watch collection was vast. I had everything, all designers, manufacturers, an accumulation that I was very proud of. Now it had been reduced to something that I had to sell off to keep me afloat. One watch would get me through a month or so. That was not a nice feeling.

There was one in particular that I was deeply troubled at having to sell. To this day, it upsets me greatly that I had to dispose of it. I have to be honest, I don't really feel comfortable admitting this. It wasn't so much the watch itself – an elegant, solid gold Cartier Panther – it was what that timepiece represented. Elton John's manager, John Reid, had given that watch to me as a gift. We were about to do *Wogan* and John gave us each these beautiful watches. For a brief moment there,

I thought it was all going to be all right. The giving of that watch was the first time in a long while that someone had shown faith in me. John simply walked up to us and said, 'I want you to wear these.' They were a very generous, sweet gesture, not to mention a very expensive gift; there was absolutely no need for him to be that generous.

That was the last watch to go. I was mortified. When I recall the things I did to eke out a living, to just get by so that, more than anything else, I wouldn't have to sell this one watch, it tears my heart out. Not for anything would I ever want to be in that position again. So alone, so skint, it burns just to write it down.

My guilt at selling that watch was exacerbated tenfold by the fact that John Reid – and indeed Elton John – have only ever been true gentlemen to me. When they parted company I was really sad for them both. If I can say this here and now, forgive me John. I think the world of both of you.

My neighbour Joe bought that watch from me for $5000.

I was damaged. I was emotionally and financially spent, but I had hung in there. I knew that I had to change my circumstances if things were to improve. Somehow I gathered the courage together to strike out on my own again. I left the valley and all the negativity that had been infecting me. Remarkably, within a month, I had a lucrative record deal with Polydor in America, a great new management team including Michael Lipman, who'd managed George Michael, along with Rob Cohain, through the *Faith* period. The record deal brought with it a very sizeable advance, enough to keep me writing and working for some time and even some extra cash to buy a spanking new Lexus.

Somehow, I was still in the game.

*   *   *

I have two tattoos on the front of my shoulders. The one on my left side, near to my heart, is for Carolyn and the one on my right is for a man called Johnny Ashie. I had them done when I came back to England in 2003 because they are two people that I really wish were still with me.

Johnny was somebody who made me feel safe. He was my bodyguard and he went everywhere with me, a big brother. He knew that Luke and me were tough little fuckers, that we've got that element to us – I'm going to go out swinging. Johnny always encouraged that in us, he loved that in me, he's seen me have many rucks.

Luke had Kelly to look after him, who was massive, like a Mr T in real life. I had Johnny, who was the opposite. He was a black guy, slim, wiry and very strong. He was a phenomenal kick-boxer – he used to roll broomsticks up and down the front of his legs for hours to deaden the nerves in his shins.

He was priceless to have around. Inevitably, if you are in a huge band, there are certain situations when you need people like Johnny and Kelly. For example, one time we were staying at the London Hilton and I was excitedly waiting for a new Lotus to be delivered. There were a lot of fans at the hotel, predominantly teenage girls and young women. Someone spotted this old guy hanging around, but it soon became apparent that he wasn't just there to see what all the fuss was about. He was trying to touch up some of the fans. When Johnny found out what this weirdo was up to, he started to run down the escalator to eject him from the hotel. But as he got less than halfway down the moving stairs, he decided that wasn't quick enough and so he jumped . . . clearing the rest of the escalator and landing right on this sleazy guy, who was thrown out of the hotel before he'd even had the chance to realize what was happening. When Johnny said, 'If I ever see you again . . .' you didn't take the risk. I once said to Luke's bodyguard, Kelly, 'Who is the one guy that you wouldn't fuck with?' He said, 'Honestly? Johnny.'

Another time I was having considerable bother with a couple of really obsessive people, stalkers for want of a better word. I heard a commotion outside and when I looked these people were walking all over my car – or should I say stamping – on the boot, the roof, the bonnet, all over it. These weird situations have to be handled very carefully and professionally, so I phoned Johnny and said, 'Sorry man, this is freaking me out.' He lived on the other side of London . . . and yet he was at my home with three of his guys in twenty minutes to sort it out. Unfortunately, the car was already a write-off but Johnny resolved the situation superbly.

You might think that someone so in control and so strong – emotionally and physically – would be something of a rough diamond. Not so Johnny. He was so eloquent, so well-spoken, a Londoner who at times could almost be mistaken for somebody from Eton. He was so charming.

We used to take the piss out of him because he had a gap in the front of his teeth. I used to say he could suck a Big Mac straight through, and teased him to order a Happy Meal and suck it up in one go. We always had such a laugh. I genuinely loved Johnny with all my heart. He would say the same back to me and tell me that I was part of his family. He looked after me, he was one of my bodyguards but he was so much more than that. He was just my best mate.

Then I got an unexpected phonecall in LA. It was from Johnny's cousin, Sam. He said Johnny was dying.

Another sickening thunderbolt. A terrible sense of foreboding.

'What do you mean, he's dying? Is he definitely going to die? What . . . how . . . ? Tell me what's the matter.'

'He's got a brain tumour, Matt,' explained Sam.

'How long has he had a brain tumour, Sam?'

'Quite some time, Matt. He's really not well.'

'Why didn't anyone fucking tell me?'

'We didn't know how to get hold of you, sorry, Matt.'

My heart was just instantly in my throat. This was someone I had planned on knowing for the rest of my life. He was so strong to me, he was invincible, surely.

'Listen, Matt, Johnny is really, really insistent that out of everybody he wants to talk to you.'

'Of course, of course. Where is he?'

'He's here beside me, Matt. I'll put him on the phone but you need to know that Johnny hasn't really got any motor skills any more and vocally . . . he can't really talk.'

Tears just started dropping out of my eyes. I couldn't take in what I was hearing. 'Let me talk to him,' I managed to say.

The phone line went quiet briefly then I could tell that Johnny was there on the other end of the line.

'Johnny, can you hear me? Johnny?'

A faint, strained murmur was all I could make out. He didn't say yes or no, he just mumbled, 'Uuurrr.'

'Johnny, come on man, you can get through this. Johnny, I love you mate, I love you so much. Can you hear me? Johnny, I love you, you know that I love you.'

There was another brief pause then . . . somehow Johnny managed to say the words, 'I love you too,' into the phone for me. At that precise instant, if you could have cut me open and frozen time, you would have seen my heart breaking.

He could barely get sounds out of his mouth yet somehow he managed, 'I love you.'

Johnny died a few days after that. I did not go to his funeral. I need to say that the reason I didn't go was that I wasn't strong enough, I genuinely wasn't strong enough. I couldn't see Johnny put in the ground, it would have probably put me in the ground. I have an image of Johnny in my mind. I didn't want to see him with a swollen head and so ill. I love him desperately. He meant so much to me, more than people know. He said so much to me and did so many things for me that were genuine. *Johnny came through for me*, he didn't just make hollow offers. When he said 'I love you too' on the phone that day, I knew how much effort that took. He knew I needed to hear that. I needed to hear him say he loved me. It was a huge loss to me, Johnny dying. He was a superhero to me; he still is.

By now, I was on my knees emotionally.

I just thought, *Please, how many more losses can I take? How many more things have I got to face? For fuck's sake, I need a break here . . .*

TWENTY-ONE

My Heart Has Had Enough

I know every artist and songwriter is different, but I absolutely adhere to the school of thought that writing – whether it is songs, poems, novels, letters, whatever – is a cathartic process, a means of purging or dealing with things that have happened to you and your loved ones in your life. That is my artistic *raison d'être* for making music. I don't see how it can be any other way.

When Bros had disintegrated and I'd headed for America, my mind was naturally exploding with thoughts, ideas, stories, opinions, anguish, frustration, experiences . . . every emotion possible. I knew that I had to get all this down. At times it felt as if I needed a pen and paper more than I needed food. I started to write and it was like a torrent. I can still sense how purifying it was to put all my thoughts into song.

The vehicle through which I happen to express these ideas is music, so for me, having an album of material released is the ultimate way to communicate. But, catastrophically, the record I wrote in the immediate post-Bros era never came out; it was never fully released. In music-business terms, I lost the record.

196

My Heart Has Had Enough

Why?

Politics.

Business.

One man changed his job.

There was much excitement surrounding what was intended to be my first solo album. As I have mentioned, there was considerable attention focused on my next move, not least from many industry people and media observers. I certainly had enough material. I had all these words, lyrics and songs that I wanted to get across, numbers such as 'House Of The Accused', which was about my managers and what happened to us when we were in Bros. In that lyric, I likened this character to a general in battle, standing elegant and proud behind the trenches, but all the time with 'blood on his cuffs'.

That was just one small example of hundreds of ideas and songs and lyrics I worked on. It took me the best part of three years to complete the project, a mammoth task to try to capture what I was feeling and thinking and a vital piece in the jigsaw of putting my life back together. I was recording at all sorts of studios, alongside people like Nine Inch Nails, Prince and REM. One night, I remember, the owner of the record plant I was using came up to me and said he loved what he was hearing coming out of my studio. That was fantastic to hear.

Then I heard whispers that the record company would be having some personnel changes. The man who had been overseeing my album was mentioned as one of those who might be moving. I had been signed to Polydor by an English A&R man, something of a celebrity talent scout in those circles. He had effectively been headhunted by the president of the record company and came to the States with a big fanfare.

People outside the industry don't necessarily realize that an

A&R person can have an indelible impact on an artist's record. They can be intimately involved in the actual sound on an album. I would say that in the case of my first solo album, this guy A&R'ed my record to death. I remember on one occasion he walked into the studio and said, 'Have you added an open hi-hat?' This was the detail that he was involving himself in. To an artist that can obviously feel intrusive. It wasn't a question of deliberate malice, he just wanted it to be so right, in his opinion. I must say in the first instance he wanted it to be right for him . . . then me. I had been one of his big signings, many people in the industry knew or had heard about that record and the stakes were high for everyone.

People might look into that studio on the day when he queried the use of a hi-hat and ask, 'Why didn't you say, "Yes, we have added a hi-hat because it needs one," or "That's how *I* want my record to sound."?' Unfortunately, it's not as simple as that. Creatively, A&R personnel might not have the authority to tell you what your record should sound like, but in practice they can and they do. For the artist, it is a Catch-22. You have a vision and a concept for your record and its sound. You want your label to love the record – after all, they are the ones who will release it. If you are too difficult in situations like that, it can come back to haunt you. If the record doesn't sell as well as people had hoped, those sorts of battles, which might seem small at the time, are presented as reasons for the failure. You are stuck between a rock and a hard place.

So that was where I found myself. It was exhausting, the most debilitating process I have ever been through in my life. There were times when it didn't even feel like music, it became his record, not mine. Then, after all that, he was moved.

What did that mean for me? I lost my record. It never received a full release. What happened was that although I had gone to LA to break America, they then turned around

Above Classic Bros

Right The safest place in the world

Above A schedule so crazy I fell asleep in mid-autograph

Luke and me with the greatest rock band in the world . . . The Rolling Stones

Bros winning the Brit Award for 'Best Newcomers' in 1989

Left Me and Mel . . . dinner with the family

Below Bros just about to meet Princess Diana

Above A multi-platinum disc party

Right 11,000 fans waited for a signed album at HMV in Oxford Street

Below The infamous Brosettes

The power of performance ... unforgettable

A memory I will never forget ... my view from the stage of the legendary
Wembley Stadium

Right Me and
my dad in the
studio

Left My dear
brother Adam in
a Scottish studio,
while I was
recording a song
for my sister
Carolyn

Right One of the
places I feel the
most happy

Above Me and Prince Charles last year for Capital Radio's 'Party in the Park'

Right A great moment: making it to the final day of *Hell's Kitchen* with James Dreyfus

Right We did have a few laughs in Bros too!

Above My Kids

Below Me and Daisy by the River Thames, the night before my Shepherd's Bush gig in 2003

and said, 'Let's release it first in the UK.' I was flabbergasted. That went against everything that I went to the US for. So in June 1995 they put out the single, 'The Key', that was supposed to come from the album of the same name, which would follow shortly after. It reached Number 40 in the UK, which was another chart hit for me, but this was still totally against my original plan of action. Next thing I know, they announce they haven't even got enough budget for a full UK release of the album! Three years of work evaporated in front of me. It was as frivolous as someone opening a window and watching smoke blow out into the ether.

Sometimes, people say, 'Oh, you lost the record, why don't you re-record those songs and put them out now?' If only it were that simple. There was a part of me that really wanted to say those things *at that time* but they just don't feel relevant to me any more.

The album was never widely available to buy or listen to. Those songs, which had meant so much to me in their writing and recording, were never fully heard and I was never allowed to express my swirling emotions. It was terribly hard for me because there was such excitement in my heart for that record, I knew it would have been genuinely full of things to talk about, to discuss, empathize with, reveal, opine and so on.

But it was destined not to happen. That, for me, was a devastating record to lose, absolutely devastating. Part of making a record is at least thinking that it is going to be heard. That was the first time where I had, with every inch of my soul, every piece of me, to remind myself how to continue. I was just screaming inside, thinking, *How do I fucking keep going?* I genuinely didn't know how to keep moving forward. It took me what seemed an age to motivate myself. I didn't think I would ever make another record again.

I kept thinking of the Duran Duran song, 'Ordinary World',

which was brilliant. It seemed to me that Simon Le Bon was contemplating going back to an ordinary world, that's how I read it. That song really struck a chord with me because I would pray with all my heart that I wouldn't have to go back to the 'ordinary world' he talked of. I didn't want to and I feel no shame in saying that. Nothing to do with ego, it's just how I felt. That's one of the reasons why people have fun at my gigs, as I have already said; I don't feel normal, I don't want to be normal, there is nothing about my life that is normal, nothing, and it hasn't been for fifteen years.

Sometimes when I listened to that Duran Duran song on the radio it frightened me. I used to wonder if he was going through the same as me – after all, Duran Duran did have a period where there was something of a career void. Maybe that wasn't what he was thinking when he wrote that song, maybe I'm wrong. That was certainly the soundtrack to my frame of mind at the time.

A huge chunk of my life that I had put on record was lost. It was so insidious as well; six months had turned into a year, a year into two, two to three, then . . . nothing. That took so much momentum out of my career. It probably took me two years to get straight – the period after that, it was frightening how low it was for me, just trying to find love again for this industry, for life.

When the finality of my record being lost caught up with me one day, I was at my lowest ebb. I curled up on the floor under a blanket and just lay there – for hours. It gave me that sense of feeling safe, strangely secure on the floor. Many years ago, it was my little table, now it was the floor under this blanket. I remember thinking, *At this precise moment, I am one of the most famous people in the world, how come I feel so acutely lonely?* When I say 'famous', I don't mean that to sound vain or egotistical, it was just that Bros was so fresh in people's minds, there were many countries across the globe where I would not be able to walk down a street safely. Yet I was utterly isolated, physically and emotionally exiled.

I've had a couple of moments when I've thought, *Does anybody give a fuck anyway?* If things aren't how I want them to be, I just disappear. You won't see me trying to pursue alternative careers. If I don't feel I can do something valid, then I will disappear. Luke is the same. We have never milked our fame for fame's sake. At that point, I could have gone out there and used my fame to wrap people around me, make me feel wanted and important. But I would rather be a number in America and have some privacy than look desperate.

It's an old platitude, but one with a core truth in it: there's a big difference between being alone and lonely. Being alone is often self-inflicted, you might choose to be alone, you might be on your own and not feel sad at all. Loneliness is usually thrust upon you and it can be devastating. I've been down there, deeper than I ever imagined in my worst nightmares and I never want to go there again.

So I sat there for hours. I had a blanket on my living-room floor. A grey and sombre stillness filled the room. Hours blended into a haze until I lost track of time. Still I did not get up. It was absolute shut-down. My friend Trevor couldn't get hold of me for an entire week. No response. Out of genuine worry and concern for my well-being, Trevor came looking for me at the house. Fortunately, there was a window on the top floor I'd left open and he clambered through that and found me still lying there, starving hungry.

'Come on, Matt,' he said gently. 'Get up, mate. I know you've been through so much and maybe people will never know that, but I know it.' I was both embarrassed and yet relieved because looking back I guess I was testing to see if anyone did give a shit enough to notice that I wasn't around.

I dragged myself off the floor – it was like lifting lead weights – and went to the kitchen. I opened the fridge to get some food and pulled out a pack of bacon. It was covered in maggots. If I haven't said this to Trevor before, perhaps it's because there is that small amount of embarrassment. I haven't acknowledged how grateful I was – and am – so maybe this will let him know. Thank you, Trevor.

It was small wonder, in retrospect, that I ran out of steam. I'd lost my sister, my band, my job, my money, my possessions in storage, the items I'd had to sell, my girlfriend, my best friend, my record . . . I just caved in and said, 'Okay, I am not bullet-proof. I cannot go on.' I think unless I had literally stopped, I would have lost my mind.

Around this same time, I saw my brother Luke doing a lot of weed and that depressed me even more. He had his reasons to escape from his situation, I will say that. Luke wanted to have a crack at a solo career as well, understandably of course, but it was very difficult for him, he wasn't given a level playing field by the media or the industry. To see Luke at the front of the stage singing was quite strange – he was a drummer, I love watching Luke play drums, so yes, that was odd. But he had his plans for a solo career and they were essentially in a more rock-oriented vein than a lot of the material in Bros. Unfortunately, he wasn't even given a chance and was virtually hounded out of the record business. Luke was really into his new band but he was treated mercilessly again by the press and it never took off the way he wanted. It hit him hard. Having already been pilloried in Bros, to take it a second time must have been terrible. It was certainly hard for me to witness, so heaven knows what he was thinking himself.

After Bros split, we spoke constantly even though, quite quickly, we were both doing our own things. What really affected me was that when he was in LA during that time, I didn't really get to talk to him. Watching him suffer at the hands of the press again genuinely affected me, more than he knew, because we didn't *really* talk. I felt a little bit detached from him and sad. It was lovely having him near me but we didn't connect.

I know him and how in control he likes to be, but during that time he wasn't, to my mind. I knew he had much more to do (which he has obviously proved now he's a very successful actor). I don't care what theories there are out there, drugs are a crutch for most people. Some people escape by watching a movie, some take drugs. I know Luke was certainly only doing weed, but it still saddened me.

Part of me envied the fact that he had found something to help him through his own battles, to mask his pain, but mainly I just thought it made him boring and a little brain-dead. I felt anger towards his friend with whom he was doing so much pot and I was scared for Luke. Seeing him make a bong out of a Coke can, I thought, 'Luke doesn't need this.' I let him carry on, I didn't want to be uncool and say, 'You shouldn't do that,' but it broke my heart. That might sound stupid because it was only pot, but Luke was too precious to me, I didn't want anything to hurt my Lukie. My lovely brother, he'd hate me for saying this, but just purely based on the amount of love I have for him, I view him as my little brother; every bit of me knows that he thinks the same about me.

When I saw him in LA at this time, he was just someone I didn't recognize. Whenever we've met up or been about to go into a situation like a big gig, Luke and I would always look each other firmly in the eye, *firmly*, and share this handshake that was very powerful – it wasn't a funny handshake, just straight and normal, but we would hold each other's hand and exchange energy. There are times when Luke and I have had to be tough little fuckers and that look, that handshake had prepared us for hard times ahead on countless occasions. It was part of my lifeblood.

But we didn't have that moment in LA. It was like I didn't recognize him. Selfishly, if I am being brutally honest, I guess I needed that look and that handshake from him, that fierce look we used to give each other when we needed to get through anything monumental. But I could also spot the fact that Luke was escaping his own pain. Both Luke and Shirley have been through a lot. Shirley has always stood by him and I saw her living with it too. As any good wife would, she knew in her heart that it wasn't going to be anything permanent, it was just a moment in time that Luke needed.

Luke was based in the UK at that point and that was where most of his worst moments happened when he was trying to launch a solo career. Part of the problem for me was that I was making the record in the USA for Polydor and I wasn't around in the UK. I came back and tried to be there for Luke as much as I could be in my own way, but it was really hard to see Luke in pain.

To this day, I find it disturbingly distressful to talk about the events of this period. Aside from everything else that was going on in my head, I don't know how to accurately convey the pain I felt seeing my brother like that. Coming at a time when my own world had been turned upside-down and was spiralling out of control, it was deeply torturous. This is genuinely hard for me to write about.

Part of the reason for that is that, naturally, I never worry about opening up to Luke if I am upset or worried about something. Of course not, he is my brother. If you can't let your guard down with your own brother, then who can you do it with? However, that means that he tends to see that side of me, that softer side, quite often, but that isn't all I am about, that perception is not entirely representative of who I am. I have seen a lot of life and sometimes I don't know if Luke realizes that too. There's probably much in my life that Luke doesn't know about.

I haven't had a wife. Luke has a very strong wife in Shirley who has stuck by him through thick and thin and is his best friend. I know that means as his twin I have to let some of our former closeness go, I understand that, but I miss him, I miss having a beer.

Luke is an integral part of my soul. We have the same DNA, you can't get a closer blood-relation than my brother and I. But I have to be very conscious of not speaking for him because he means so much to me. He has his life and I am very respectful of that – there are many things that have happened in his life I'd like to talk about, because of how they have affected me, but if I discuss certain events it will encroach on his privacy. I can never do that.

For my own part, I never felt drawn to use drugs, or alcohol or women or whatever emotional crutch people may choose to lean on. Even when I had lost my record, I managed to steer clear. Each person makes their own choices and you cannot judge a man's decisions until you have walked a mile in his shoes, but I did not want to go down the path of drugs. Why? Because if I had, it would probably have been the end of me.

For one thing, I didn't feel I could mask what was going on, because I knew when I came out the other side, I would still have to face my demons. It was an incredibly raw, brutal and punishing way to deal with my problems: clean, alone and sober, but that was what I felt I had to do. Furthermore, the fact that I needed to escape so badly meant that anything that stopped me feeling the pain would become my life. I knew that. If I had started heroin at that point, it would have buried me, no question. I had to keep control and I knew if I slipped up at that moment, when there were times when all I wanted to do was escape, it would have been the end of me. That in itself was an extra burden. I admit I had a devil on my shoulder whispering. 'Go on, Matt, have something to take your mind off it.'

Somehow, at that time, I managed to push those demons away. But they would return and next time the battle would not be so easy.

With the benefit of hindsight, everything is for a reason. At the time of losing that album *The Key*, I had a Caesar haircut with a goatee, reminiscent of the look George Michael would later use on his *Older* project. However, I just wasn't comfortable with myself at all then. When you see photographs of me from that period, I have something of a thousand-yard stare. I wasn't happy with how I was coming across and I wasn't contented within myself, so maybe that record might have exacerbated that. Who knows?

Looking back, it's easy to say what I should and shouldn't have done. There were so many things to consider – I had been offered a solo deal to stay with Sony after Bros, but as I have said, I just felt it wasn't respectful to Luke to do that after everything we had been through. If I am being perfectly honest, there was a song called 'Never Love Again' on the last Bros record which I really wish with all my heart that Sony had released as my debut solo single. Rob Stringer, then marketing manager and later president of Sony, wanted that to be my first release. He was right, but it didn't happen, I went to America instead. I should have just gone with it, because it was one of those songs that just felt good, felt right.

But life post-Bros was so barmy, the fall-out was so intense, it wasn't easy to see through the barrage. There was plenty of pressure on me and in hindsight I should have perhaps signed with Sony and stuck it out in England. But I ran away to America and wanted to hide. I wanted to get out, so I did. Three years later, I'd lost my first solo record and my heart was on the floor.

TWENTY-TWO

Life Is A Slow Dance

The first album that totally rocked my world was Stevie Wonder's remarkable *Talking Book*. Just look at the track listing: 'Big Brother' is on there, 'Superstition', 'You Are The Sunshine Of My Life', it was amazing. He is astounding, my all-time biggest influence. To think that he was deprived of one of his senses in such a cruel way, being starved of oxygen at birth, then later lost his sense of smell in a car crash and yet is still such a creative, unique individual is remarkable to me.

As I've mentioned, my mum and Aunt Sally both had a very eclectic taste in music. It was good for me to be around such diversity. Like Mum, Aunt Sally was a bit of a rocker, she had Deep Purple albums, Thin Lizzy and so on, but most of all she was a Stevie fan. Sally was a really big influence in my discovery of music.

When Aunt Sally played me that *Talking Book* record, I was just blown away by Stevie's voice and words. I loved what I heard, and I fell in love with that album. To this day, I need a sense of love for the actual artist that I am listening to as well, not just the music – Stevie has always seemed like a really cool guy to me.

I often open my live set with a thumping version of 'Superstition', an immediate way of acknowledging the guy who is the reason why I do what I do. I truly think he is the reason I am singing. Stevie has endured. I don't think that clutch of albums he wrote in the Seventies will ever be out of date, and I'll tell you why. Because *he* played Rhodes keyboard, clavinova, Moog bass, harmonica and the drums – those were the key instruments in all the songs on those albums. Stevie has a certain way on harmonica, obviously, but also on all those other instruments. Then there's the lyrics, astounding – Stevie could write a song about a tree and make it interesting. His influence on my style and musical character is immeasurable.

So, when it was put to me in later years that I could meet Stevie himself, you can imagine my excitement. Fast forward to LA in 1994. I was with the president of a major record company and another record-business executive. I was asked if I wanted to sit with Stevie at a piano and play some songs to see what happened.

'Are you kidding me?' I said, in disbelief. 'That would mean more than the world to me.'

The exec said he loved what I was doing and that Stevie would love it too. So it was arranged for me to meet *the* biggest music idol in my life in two weeks' time. That was a long two weeks; I was so looking forward to it, I just couldn't believe that my path out of Grandad's flat in Crawford Road and out into the crazy world of music had brought me to a restaurant in Los Angeles where I could meet Stevie Wonder.

The day came and I was sitting like an excited schoolboy waiting for Stevie to arrive, with this major-label president and his wife. We sat down to dinner, waiting for the phonecall from the exec to say Stevie was on his way. Anyway, to cut a very long dinner short, we were there for about six hours. Eventually, the phone rang at around midnight.

'Okay, Matt,' said the exec. 'Stevie's around. You ready? You want to come down?'

'Are you kidding me?! Of course I do!'

I was so excited, I can't tell you.

'Okay. Listen, before you come down, I want five grand.'

The record exec I was with was ordinarily a quiet and mellow guy, but when he heard the words 'five grand', he went absolutely mental.

All credit to him, he said, 'Look, Matt, if you want to go and see him, I will pay for it.'

It was obvious that Stevie had absolutely no idea of what was going on, that much was clear. There was no way in a million years that Stevie knew about it. I had to reply to this demand for cash.

'You know what?' I said, as I went back on the phone. 'I will meet Stevie one day, but I will not pay to meet my heroes. It will be under my own terms. And let me tell you something, when I do finally meet him, I will tell him what you tried to do today . . .'

The exec butted in, flustered; 'Hold on, man, hold on, hey, look, it's a . . .'

I put the phone down on him.

I finally met Stevie Wonder in the late Nineties at Motown in New York. He was a complete gentleman.

Although my time in LA in the early Nineties saw me going through some of the hardest moments of my life, and losing my record was certainly devastating, there were also a few special days too. One of the nicest moments in my entire life was when my grandad came out to visit me on the West Coast. We have always got on brilliantly well and love nothing more than taking the mickey out of each other – I often rib him about hooking him up with a lady and he takes the joke, but he also always says he is married only to one woman and will see Win when he gets to heaven.

Anyway, Grandad flew out and I was so excited to see him, particularly as there were so many difficult things going on in my life. My neighbour Joe, the guy that bought the beautiful watch given to me by John Reid, had a so-called Ninja motor-bike, one of the world's fastest production superbikes. My grandad took one look at it and said, 'I want to have a go on that!' I love that about Grandad. I am always the one to buy him another packet of fags or another pint because, fuck it, what has he got to lose?

Joe agreed to take him out on this two-wheeled bullet. I was all for it. However, when Joe screeched off at about 80 mph with my grandad clinging on to his shoulders as pillion with no crash helmet, I must admit I was a little nervous! Within seconds the bike was a tiny blur in the distance, the engine revs soundtracking what looked like a real-life warp factor. By the time they arrived back about five minutes later, my heart was pounding away with apprehension. Grandad's full head of silver hair was standing on end and tears were streaking back past his ears. He was a sight to behold. He said he'd had the time of his life.

Our own means of driving around LA at that point was rather more sedate. We had a dodgy little Triumph Herald convertible, baby-blue with leopardskin seats and we would both go out cruising around checking out numerous places. We'd often go to a pub that I had discovered; it was the only place in LA that sold draught Bass ale. Grandad would go in every day and chat up the waitresses, saying things like, 'You know my boy? You don't know who he is do you?' He was so proud of me . . . and I of him. It was a wonderful time. Grandad was with me for about a week and we had a fantastic time, even though that was the week of the LA riots and then the flooding!

Grandad's visit was one of the few highlights of that draining period of my life. Although perhaps I should not have gone to America, the fact is I did. That led to certain events that have been very difficult for me to deal with and remain to this day very upsetting to talk about. However, and it is a big however, I think at the same time I was right to head out to the USA, it probably saved me in a way. I became more of a rounded person in America. I faced so many realities; it was almost the end of me, but I faced them and I would win. What fire does not destroy, it hardens.

In 1995, I came back to London briefly to regroup. I still wasn't feeling particularly comfortable in myself – sometimes I feel as if I have spent more years not feeling comfortable about myself than otherwise. Fortunately, there were plenty of good things happening around me. My single, 'If You Were Here Tonight', a cover of the Alexander O'Neal song, was a hit in the UK in February 1996, which was encouraging, and my previous single, 'The Key', had been remixed by a top Italian producer called Joe T. Vanelli and was at Number 1 in his native country. Joe is a genuinely wonderful guy who had his own label and production company in Milan, as well as being a very well-known DJ. He is something of a music mogul in that country.

With the success of the remixed 'The Key' in mind, Joe got in touch with me and said, 'Why don't you come over to Milan and we can make a hard-house album together?' I was flattered and intrigued – the prospect of living in Italy for a while pandered to my nomadic tendency, I was keen to see Joe's talent first-hand and the idea of working on a hard-house record, effectively a complete, underground departure for me, was very enticing. So I replied, 'Yes, why not?!'

Unfortunately, what had seemed like a colourful overseas

opportunity for me proved not to be a very good experience at all. From the day I landed in Italy to the day I left, I was plagued by loneliness. I didn't have a production team around me, like if I was making a movie, I didn't have a management team as I would have done in a band, it was just me, myself and I, again.

Joe and his staff were very caring towards me, but I felt as if I was in Italy making a record on my own. The language barrier proved to be more of an obstacle than you might think. At first, it was a bit of fun, I was very keen to learn Italian and asked questions about words at every opportunity. One night I was invited out to dinner by Joe and a group of his friends by way of welcoming me to Italy. Many of them knew who I was. Halfway through the meal, I leaned over to Joe and asked him, 'How do I say, "Can I have a glass of water please?"' Joe said, '*Scusi, mi piace la figa.*' So I raised my hand and said, '*Scusi, mi piace la figa.*' The whole place instantly cracked up, the waitress went bright red and I knew straight away that I had been stiffed. What I had actually said was, 'Excuse me, I love pussy.' Thanks very much. Can I have the check please?

However, after the initial honeymoon period, that inability to communicate with people started to wear me down. I love talking to people, about music, about family, work, life, anything. But I couldn't, or not as freely as I wanted. Don't get me wrong, I learned quite a lot and became reasonably fluent in my Italian but it was always a barrier. Learning the language was one of my top priorities but so was learning English for the people I was working with. Inevitably, because their English was better than my Italian, more often than not we ended up speaking in my native tongue.

At the time, I was initially in a relationship with an American girl. That was probably one of the most unsatisfying liaisons

I've ever been in. In short, it wasn't very loving. This girl had been through problems in her own private life but I didn't feel connected to her at all. That emotional estrangement was never very far from the surface. I didn't get the feeling that she was going to be a life-partner, she never really made me feel that way. Yet at the same time, I needed contact, I needed company.

I think she had flown over to Europe probably expecting the big, glamorous lifestyle, but I had to work and I constantly had the feeling that she was waiting to get back to LA, which was fair enough I guess, but it didn't make me feel very secure. She spent some time with my mum and came to Italy, but that relationship was always going to be temporary. I have always been the sort of person who, when I am with someone for a while, I like to think she could potentially be my life-partner. But being with this American girl just wasn't fulfilling at all.

When that started winding down, I began hanging out with Federica Moro. She was a famous actress and a former Miss Italy. Although the friendship was very sporadic and casual, we did have some pleasant times. However, again we were both working very hard and consequently I was on my own most of the time.

I'm not ashamed to say that I am a hopeless romantic. Milan is a very romantic city, Italy is an incredibly romantic country. Time and again, I would find myself walking around the beautiful city completely alone. I was learning the language and discovering the city by myself – what's more, the streets were always full of couples in love, having special times together as I walked past back to my empty apartment. I was sick and tired, absolutely sick to death of feeling lonely.

TWENTY-THREE

My Solitude Will Fade Away

My top-floor apartment in Milan had an amazing terrace with beautiful city views including the Piazza del Duomo. The Duomo is one of the most famous cathedrals in the world, and certainly one of the most exquisite things you've ever seen in your life. Right on the very top of the Duomo was a solid gold figure of Mary the Madonna and it was lit up every night. In a strange way I felt she was watching over me.

Being close to that special place was very uplifting for me; I used to go there every day, without fail. I lit so many candles, praying I would be okay, candles for my brother and my mum, especially for Luke and Shirley – I don't think they were particularly happy in their world at that time either. I also missed Shirley's daughter Carly, my niece. She was three years old when Luke first met Shirley. She is now a very beautiful young woman. It was quite strange because when she was about fifteen, people would say to me, 'Look at you, it's bloody awful, taking advantage of a girl of that age.' One time in Butler's Wharf wine bar on the South Bank this one guy became particularly heated and I just had to say, 'She's my fucking niece!' I always miss her a lot when

I am away and it would be great to spend more time with her.

Don't be mistaken, there were good times during those nine months in Italy. I flew Mark King, former bassist and frontman of Level 42, over for a short stay. Mark seemed to be very disillusioned with the music industry, rightfully so in some respects, but I would always say to him, 'You can't give up because you are too talented.' Level 42 was a great band in my opinion. Mark, as is universally acknowledged, is a phenomenally talented and influential bass player.

When he was over in Italy, we went out with a guy called Lorenzo Joe Minoti who is more widely known as Lorenzo. He is, I suppose, the Italian equivalent of Robbie, big news over there. Lorenzo's bass player was totally freaked out because Mark King was with us that night. It was nice to be the person that helped Mark meet musicians who were so unreservedly enamoured with him, I got a kick out of that. So Mark, if you are reading this book, tour with Level 42 again, mate!

Robbie himself was out there too, he came by the studio from a hotel round the corner and we hung out, I went back to his hotel and we had a little bit of a jam, which was nice. Robbie seems to be one of those people I bump into all the time, more often than not in LA, walking his dog. Debbie Gibson flew out to stay with me for a week too, which was lovely. The guys in the studio doted on her. One colleague in particular was making us laugh with his incredibly corny chat-up lines, which somehow he could get away with because he was Italian. My mum came over for a week to see me as well – we became stuck in a lift, which isn't the ideal situation for her, being claustrophobic – but then when she left I missed her even more, before she'd even stepped back on the plane. I missed Mum, Tony, Adam, Lukie, lots of people (when I eventually decided to leave Italy, I spent two days shopping for Shirley, buying clothes and nice things for her and Luke, I was so excited to be seeing them again). I had some great times with Joe and his band members too, but the overall tone of my time in Italy was not very positive.

I must say that was through no fault of Joe's whatsoever, absolutely not. Indeed, we would sometimes sit in his Mercedes and talk for hours about things that were going on in his life and mine – he had many issues to deal with himself. He is one of the music industry's true gentlemen and someone I feel very close too (although I can never forgive him for tucking his T-shirts into his jeans and he knows that). I would actually say that Joe was a Godsend in my life. It was other factors and my own personal circumstances that made my time in Italy a very taxing one.

Back in the studio, events had taken a twist that I wasn't entirely happy with. Perhaps understandably, Joe wanted to spread his wings and make a commercial record, whereas I was still looking forward to creating a whole album of hard-house music. The problem was, many of the musicians in his production team were far more talented than for just making house music, they wanted to make commercial music as well.

The dilution of the original concept for that record was just the first complication – unfortunately, after having already lost my first solo record in America and knowing what that did to me, I was gutted to find out that this Italian project would not be getting a widespread release either. It did get a soft release, but in mass-market terms that means it effectively didn't see the light of day. The irony is, the record is available in Italy and still sells to this day.

I remember on my birthday I was completely by myself. I'd got one card, from Mum. I'm not saying 'Oh, woe is me!', because it's just a birthday, but at the same time, a birthday can amplify your feelings, good or bad. I had that fantastic top-floor apartment which had gates to let you into my section. For whatever reason, these gates had been locked so I couldn't get out of my apartment – I was seven storeys up and stranded, on my birthday. I switched on the telly for a while but it was all Italian terrestrial TV, I was just channel-hopping out of boredom.

I began walking around my terrace trying to figure out what to do, pacing about aimlessly for two hours. Then I noticed the balcony of the apartment below. It was about two feet wide at the most but that was enough of an incentive for me at that point, I just wanted to get out. On this balcony was a metal office filing cabinet. So, still keen to get out, I climbed over the edge of my own terrace . . . and jumped.

It didn't go exactly to plan. I landed on top of the cabinet, which toppled under my weight, making me slip over the edge. As I fell, I somehow managed to grab the balustrade and stop myself falling seven flights to my death.

So, here I was, it was my birthday, I'd had one card, I wasn't feeling particularly happy about the change in direction of my record, I was lonely, tired . . . and hanging off a balcony seventy feet in the air by one hand. I felt like some oddball Woody Allen creation. I could just see the headlines, 'Rock Star in Bizarre Birthday Death Plunge'. The ranks of great entertainment conspiracy theories awaited me.

Not wishing to make light of it though, I was just suspended there, thinking, *This is fucking mad!* Just hanging there was difficult enough, so it took every bit of strength I had left in me to pull myself up. Somehow I managed to haul myself to safety, then I dusted myself down and opened the balcony door. It was a dentist's office, so I just said, 'Hello, sorry about that,' and walked out into the corridor.

That was not one of my best birthdays.

I think Italy was the most lonely I've ever been in my life.

The low point came one week when I was scheduled to do an MTV interview. I came round in my bed and to my horror realized it was the day *after* I'd been scheduled to go to MTV.
I rang Joe up and said, 'I've missed the interview!'
He said, 'No, you didn't. What do you mean? You did it.'
'You're kidding me.'
Shivers charged down my spine.

What transpired mortified me. Being an insomniac, interminable sleepless nights are a constant feature of my life. I was taking sleeping tablets, but somehow in my deep sleep, I had managed to lean over to the bedside table and take four rather than one. I don't even remember taking them, which is really worrying in itself. *I'd done the MTV interview* and even went into a shop and bought some sunglasses. I had no recollection of any of this.

I found the receipt for the glasses and went to the shop to ask them if I had seemed okay.

'Yeah, you were fine, really funny in fact.'

These were some of the most expensive glasses you could buy and they had given me a discount because they recognized me, which made it even more embarrassing. To these shop assistants, I looked as if I had it all, yet inside I was an empty shell. As I have already said, I pride myself on not searching for escapism or relying on drugs, so to sit there and realize I'd missed an entire day of my life was deeply embarrassing.

I have seen the MTV interview on video – I was dreading watching myself knowing what had gone on, but fortunately I was wearing the sunglasses to hide my eyes and I was generally reasonably coherent and mellow. Most of what I said was pretty valid. So I have that as a memory, but I don't remember getting there, doing the interview or going back home.

My body had been functioning but my brain was effectively asleep. Anything could have happened, I could have been killed. The walk from my apartment was about two miles, with busy roads and even a tramline along the way. I will never know how I got there and how I didn't get hurt. I'll be honest, I cried for two days.

I was terrified. There was no one there to help me or maybe take charge.

I became reliant on the tablets to sleep. I needed escapism, to switch off. I didn't want to feel anything. Those demons that had first whispered at me in LA had finally chiselled into my brain and got their way. I had found my Achilles heel. Later on, I would take tablets every day, just to relax and calm me down as much as to get me to sleep, not in Italy, but just before I came back to England in 2003. I became reliant on them. In hindsight, I don't think that compulsion was just about being depressed and lonely. With the loss of my records, I felt my creative purpose in life was being completely stifled and that was personally suffocating me. If I don't create, I get severely depressed, emotionally paralysed. I have to make something that wasn't there yesterday, whether that is a song or a painting or a storyline, otherwise I feel very odd.

Italy is one of the darkest periods in my life, no question. I needed some light in my life. Unknown to me at the time, my world was about to get a whole lot brighter.

I was eating sushi in a restaurant one day in 1998 when my mobile phone rang.

'Hello, is that Matt?' said a fairly soft, but gruff voice.

'Yes, it is.'

'Hello, Matt, this is Reggie Kray.'

This was definitely one of those moments. The environment I was in seemed so out of synch with the phonecall I was taking. I said 'Hello' back and we ended up chatting for about ten minutes, just about life. Reggie was telling me that he knew about me and felt a connection because we were both twins. We instantly started conversing as if we had known each other for ever.

That first call was soon followed by others, and before long I was having quite a number of conversations, every day at times. We would chat sporadically and talk about all manner of subjects. Reggie used to have this phrase that he would say to me, 'Hello, Matt, do you want to hear my words?' He would say that every day. And I would always say, 'Yeah, I would love to.' Of course I wanted to hear his words. He would read his poetry and his words, or just talk with me.

I actually feel very passionate about what happened to him. He was sentenced to thirty years and he actually served thirty-two years – the whole point was that he had done his time. I felt that in some ways he was a political prisoner. He wasn't a criminal who went out hurting the general public; to use his own words, it was 'within my own jungle'.

I made contact with his wife Roberta and eventually I went to see Reggie in prison. One of the first things I noticed was that he had a gold bracelet with 'Legend' on it, in sapphires. Reggie was so lovely and full of life, he had so many things he wanted to do. As well as poetry, he had designs he sent me for coats, jackets, he was constantly working on ideas. The hardest thing about visiting him in prison was that he wasn't able to walk out with you at the end. He and Roberta were just so in love. To see how much she loved him and he loved her was a wonderful thing. There was a picture in one of the tabloids of me walking out of prison with a book of poetry that Reg had given me. I just said to the photographers, 'He's done his time.'

Naturally, Reggie told me some great stories. I recall he said he didn't like the movie that was made of his and his twin's life, because his mum swore in the film and she didn't swear in real life. There was a strange affinity between me and him, obviously being twins but also our feelings and views on certain things. It was very strange, I felt relaxed with him straight away. Reggie later talked about a Hollywood version of the film of the twins' life and he asked me if I would play him. What a compliment.

I remember being in New York one time going over the Brooklyn Bridge with my dad in a yellow cab when the phone rang and it was Reg. I said, 'I am actually with my dad at the moment in New York, do you want to say hello?' Reg was always very gracious like that, you got the feeling he was always hungry for more experiences. So I am sitting there in a yellow cab on that famous bridge, next to my policeman father with Reggie Kray on the phone from prison. I handed the phone to Dad who said, 'Hello, Reg, it is a real honour.'

Roberta came to Luke's and my thirtieth birthday and Reg had very generously sent me a pair of solid gold cufflinks with the 'The Krays, London' and the handshake engraved on them, along with a matching solid gold bracelet. A very beautiful and generous gift. I learned later that there were only three of these made so I was incredibly honoured. I can't wear them very often because sentimentally they are priceless, it was just an amazing gift to be given.

I didn't want to bother Reg when he finally came out, I don't think anyone should have pestered him, to me it was just about him and Roberta. When he died it was very sad. He'd served one of the longest sentences in British penal history. It was very, very sad news.

TWENTY-FOUR

Waiting For The Light

The music industry can be a very unforgiving world to inhabit. After all my problems, I just had to put my left foot in front of my right. Success in the business has, sadly, become qualified by longevity. So you have a clear choice: you can either wallow and say to yourself, 'I can't get up today,' or you can roll with it, get up, dust yourself down and move on.

Around 1999, I received a phonecall from Universal Records in New York saying that they absolutely loved my voice and wanted to record with me. They openly courted me because of my voice. That was just what I needed; I said, 'Thank you God.' I knew this was my chance to regain some momentum. If you let the inertia take a grip in the music business, you will stagnate; stop for a minute, and you will stop for ever.

It was a big record deal instigated and signed out of Universal's New York office – which I was very proud of – and so I immediately moved to that city, where I would stay for three years. Life in the Big Apple for more than three years would prove to be one of the most crazy, fun times I've ever had, I had such brilliant experiences. I went there with no PA, no manager, nothing. Yet I was relatively buoyant, happily single

223

for the first time in years and in one of the most vibrant cities in the world.

I often went clubbing. One night I was hanging out in a cool club called Lot 61 when I started talking to an English guy called Carl Kennedy, who has since become one of my very best friends. He said, 'Hey, I know you from Bros!' and we just hit it off straight away. The next day we met again and pretty quickly became really close mates. He was a bit of a hooligan back then, a real football fan. He didn't seem to have much direction but he was aspiring to be a DJ. I helped him get some turntables and really encouraged him to go for it, so I'd like to think he would say that I supported him. Just a few years later he'd become a sought-after DJ with tracks being played on Radio 1 and all sorts of stuff going on. He's done brilliantly. I loved Carl, for the first time I felt that I had acquired a best mate again. He was just someone I connected with instantly, we were inseparable.

Back in those heady New York nights, Carl and I would be out clubbing virtually every evening. He'd come round to my apartment, which was a stunning place overlooking the Hudson River, by Tribeca, a gorgeous area of New York. I could see the Twin Towers from my window. The lady who ran the leasing programme which effectively vetted who could live in the apartment block (New York has some very strict traditions like that for homes) was called Evelie and she was just one of the sweetest, kindest people you could wish to meet. I really valued Evelie as someone that I could always rely on.

Within a few weeks there were many more in our crew besides Carl and me, eventually numbering more than a dozen. There was also Gavin, Simon, Steve, even a guy called Jesus, mostly English, this little Brit contingent roaming around New York having a great time. We would meet up and head straight for a place called The Mercer Kitchen at The Mercer Hotel, on

Prince Street just off Broadway. They always had very pretty waitresses which would help to get the evening off to a good start.

Luckily, most of us were okay-looking and a few, like Carl for example, were real ladies' men. Being good-looking, confident and mostly English was one hell of an asset in New York, so we were quite a deadly little force going out. We used to go clubbing in one place where Grandmaster Flash would DJ every Thursday night. We would be dancing – and I am talking proper *sweating* – with our little crew and the tables would be overflowing with drinks and conversation and good times. Then we'd go to eat somewhere and often see famous faces. Several times we ate at a place called Bubbie's which was JFK Junior's local (he lived virtually next door) and he would be in there too. We would always watch the England games at a place called the Tribeca Sports bar, we used to take over the place on match day!

It was a real lads' environment and great to be around. One time Steve accidentally shagged one of Gavin's girlfriends – he didn't know she was dating Gavin. We actually had a board meeting where it was discussed and everyone was cool with it, even Gavin! We were proper mates, just a genuine bunch of lads who felt invincible.

One of the best days out was when we got hold of Tommy Hilfiger's blimp and toured around the Manhattan skyline in this magnificent airship for hours, quaffing champagne and having a great laugh. There was something about seeing New York that way, the Statue of Liberty, the Twin Towers and all the sights, without the noise of a helicopter or airplane engine. There was this serenity about it, even though you knew that down on the street the city was as crazy as ever.

We ended up pretty much running New York in some ways, there wasn't a club or bar in town where we couldn't go and

225

be treated really well. I found out later many of the bouncers on the New York circuit were from Israel – Bros were massive in that country and most of these guys told me their sisters and girlfriends had posters of me on their walls. I seemed to get recognized continually in New York. I was still being stopped four or five times a day by tourists; Luke and I have just got one of those faces, people come up to you. After a while, we had our own nights in certain clubs, we would have tables full of vodka and cranberry mixers, dozens of pretty models with us, it was a really good phase of my life.

Our notoriety went before us. We actually started to get called 'The Hat Pack', because of our penchant for stylish headgear! We were even mentioned in a magazine called *The Hamptons*, a very trendy publication which featured all sorts of interesting and 'cool' people and places.

Carl and I would go roller-skating along Battery Park by the river, we were always out doing stuff, it was just fantastic. One of the few scarier moments was when a drunk pulled a gun on me in an attempted robbery. Fortunately I had the foresight to punch the gun out of his hand, which avoided a pretty sticky situation for me. It might all sound a little 'laddish' but to be perfectly honest, it was really nice not to be beholden to any one woman and so I have very fond memories of those single days.

I had my moments in New York when I craved being around my close family, despite this amazing bunch of lads of whom I was (sort of) gang leader. New York is a powerful animal and I think if you overstay your welcome, it can start to take away more than it gives. Having said that, it is an incredibly inspiring city and a great place to live for a few months each year. When so much is going on in your life, you want to share it with those closest to you, so on more than one occasion that did get me down. But Luke was going through his struggles, Mum and Tony were going through theirs. One time when I was particularly missing family and was upset, Carl was a rock for me. He was suffering turmoils of his own but he was selfless; he listened to me and said, 'I hate seeing you like this, Matt.' To feel comfortable enough to have a moment of weakness like that in front of Carl, when virtually everyone in New York saw me as this very confident, strong person, was very comforting.

As happens with friendships for many people, I don't see Carl very often now, which is a great shame, but when I do meet up with him it is always so good to see how focused he is on his life. He has a wife and a kid, and his DJ-ing just keeps progressing all the time. I'd trust him with my life. I entrusted Carl's dad to put the bracelet that Reggie Kray gave me in a safe in Birmingham for over a year. That's how much I trust Carl.

You'd think with all this partying I would have had no time for work. Far from it. I wrote *eighty* songs in one year during my time in New York. Most notably, the track 'Lucky Day' was included on the soundtrack for the Number 1 hit movie *Stuart Little* which was a welcome boost. I was delighted to see a review of the soundtrack in *Billboard* magazine which mentioned the other noted performers such as Bryan McKnight and the Brian Seltzer Orchestra but went on to say that 'the only hit is provided by Matt Goss'. I was getting a fairly good name for myself.

I was working with people like Denise Rich, who is a songwriter, one of Bill Clinton's best friends and a famous Manhattan socialite. She lives in one of the most desirable apartments in the whole of New York City. I went up there many times to work – the entire nineteenth floor of this ultra-prestigious, super-wealthy block was her first floor! Her second was all of the twentieth floor, and her roof terrace was the whole of the twenty-first floor. So that was amazing, to be able to write in her studio. Despite all her wealth and popularity she was always a very lovely person to be around.

I worked many times at Denise's recording studio in that apartment, so I was used to seeing pictures of Bill and Hillary Clinton on the walls. On one particular day, Denise said to me, 'Someone's popping round whom you might know . . .' I was recording in the vocal booth that day which had a glass door fronting on to the studio itself. As I was singing away, this lady walked in, smiled across at me and said, 'Hello.' It was Sarah Ferguson. I stopped the vocal, went and greeted her and we had a little chat. She was lovely. That was another one of those 'moments'!

It's an odd life, that of being a songwriter as against a performer. Some of the most successful and wealthy people in the music industry just write songs for other people. They have no inclination to perform and thus avoid all the pitfalls of fame and celebrity. In that way, it might just be a dream job.

But for me, it isn't. When you are writing a song for somebody else, there are plenty of aspects 'for' and 'against'. The good thing is you can invent any situation, go wild and be as extreme or as conventional as you want to. You don't need to worry about recording it, performing it, talking to the press about it, any of those complications. You just write the song, send it off, hopefully someone covers it and the cheques roll in. There's a lot to be said for that!

The trouble is, it can feel rather shallow. It can feel very unrewarding and, for me personally, doesn't feed any of my deep artistic impulses – after a while it becomes like a proper job which, for a lot of musicians and people involved in the arts, is a curse they have striven all their lives to avoid.

By contrast, writing a song for yourself, that is about your life and that you know you will be performing for people at some stage, is the complete opposite of that. It is very cathartic, particularly when you are dealing with certain subjects. It is immensely rewarding too – it gives you the opportunity to connect with people, those who have experienced the same feelings that you are singing about, or perhaps others who interpret your words in a totally different way which is equally valid for them. Those are the two worlds I sometimes straddle and there is no question which environment I am most happy in.

In New York it was crazy, I was writing constantly, it was a frenzy of lyrics, melodies, music and the muse. Writing and writing and writing. I wanted to build up a catalogue. I can write songs for any performer, so it was great to get all these ideas down. At first it was exciting because I love writing and it was incredible to see such a body of work being created. Eventually, however, it reached the point where I couldn't write any more songs, I was done. Eighty songs in one year, that's an average of one completed song every four and a half days . . . for twelve months. It was remarkable.

The problem is that when you keep writing songs, you feel like you are creating a bunch of orphans. Like little kids, every song belongs to you and they don't feel as if they have a home. It feels more than a song – if you put your heart and soul into something and it doesn't get heard, it hurts, it really does.

Fortunately, many of those songs were being heard. I was getting covers and doing really well. Unexpectedly, I heard one of my songs on American radio one day, which was nice. Another morning a CD from Japan arrived out of the blue with a very commercial song I had written included on it. It had become a hit in Japan without my even knowing. That made me feel two things: amused, because the translation sounded so funny; and dissatisfied because this simple piece of plastic in my hand was what that song had become. I didn't get to hear it on the radio in Japan, I didn't see it recorded or performed, then I received an envelope through the post with my name on it. I was the writer and I earned money from it, but creatively it didn't make me feel anything.

Eventually, I did get a manager in New York, in the late Nineties. One small incident sums him up for me. I was telling him about my dilemmas with writing and performing and how hard it was at times within the industry, just sounding off really to a professional associate who should be interested and have opinions on what I was doing – he was my manager after all. Do you know what he said? 'Why don't you get a job?'

Now I am not saying I'm above getting a job, but this is my job! I was writing over a song a week! In that one sentence, he showed an absolute lack of comprehension of my personality, what I do and my aspirations. I was so insulted. Once again, a professional parent failing in his duty, another skirmish in the minefield of artist management.

I also had a run-in with one of my management team, when I'd had one of my songs sent over to Tina Turner. I've had songs on hold with Diana Ross, loads of people, so this was nothing new. It was a fairly last-minute request, so to avoid delay, I spent two hours on the phone with one of the manager's assistants meticulously going through the lyrics. Unbeknown to me, the next day this assistant wasn't in work and hadn't left my lyric sheet where somebody could find it. Instead of just finding it, acknowledging their own mistake, they came on the phone to me and accused me of being 'unprofessional'. I was livid. Apart from the fact I had gone to such lengths to get this song to them on time, it seemed so inappropriate and I couldn't help thinking, *People write classic songs on a fucking beer mat!*

TWENTY-FIVE

Where You Are, Can You See The Moon?

I was back in LA recording parts of my new album for Universal at Conway Studios, a very striking city complex swamped in greenery and tropical plants. I was single, making music, feeling liberated and, if I am honest, attracted by the idea of sleeping around a little and having the life of a single man.

Then I met Daisy.

I was invited to the actress Tia Carrere's house for a divorce party which she had neatly combined with a house-warming – a uniquely LA experience. Luke was there, myself, Tamara Beckwith and lots of US celebrities. I saw Daisy and the first thing I did was just bury my nose in her hair, it was so beautiful. The people around her were laughing so she turned around and we began to talk. I thought she was a volleyball player, when in fact she is a former MTV presenter and TV star, who has also presented *Miss Universe* among many other shows. We had a lovely evening chatting and at the end I said, 'E-mail me when you get home.' I did wonder if she would play it cool and not get in touch, so I was delighted to get a very lovely little two-line e-mail from her the next day and since then we have been virtually inseparable.

Not long after, I started work on a track called 'Face The Wind' (which is based on my fear of losing somebody) and I invited Daisy down to the studio. For this particular song, I had hired the LA Philharmonic Orchestra for backing so I knew it would be a special occasion. In fact, it turned out to be probably *the* most beautiful moment I've ever had recording-wise. I had some friends, Julie and Michael, down as well as Daisy and the orchestra was just sublime. When we did the first run-through, they gave me an ovation, all tapping their instruments, it was fantastic. Some people in the control room were in tears – it was so moving to hear such a beautiful sound coming through the speakers, nothing was plugged in, it was all acoustic. An incredible experience.

We put on a massive barbecue spread for the Philharmonic after the recording and I chuckled when they told me, 'You are so much better than Barbra Streisand, all we got was pizza at midnight!'

I was at Conway making that record for a year and during that time, Daisy and I became very close. I was gradually staying at her house more and more, even though I still had my place in New York as well as a hotel room in LA. Eventually, we ended up getting a place together in the Hollywood Hills.

Daisy is half-Spanish and half-Cuban; she was born in Havana but brought up in New Jersey and that's how I see her – as a Jersey girl through and through, plenty of attitude, funny and very strong-willed. She is definitely a very fiery woman!

She had a place in Miami and invited me to stay there. I have to admit I was really quite nervous, it was the first time I had flown anywhere with the sole intent to meet a woman. Her apartment was right on the beach and shortly after I arrived, we both headed down to the sea. I found myself a little self-conscious getting into my shorts and going into the water, but after half an hour Daisy said, 'You're like a dolphin!' I loved it, we kissed and cuddled in the sea, I carried her for hours in the water and just chatted.

I was given a taste of how fiery she is very early on. I don't think that is a bad thing to say, though, because it is a facet that I sometimes love about her and at other times find difficult. Besides, I don't believe a relationship should have to be all hunky-dory and at the first sign of any problems you call it a day. You are either a quitter or you are not and neither one of us is. It takes a lot of effort to maintain a connection in a transatlantic relationship. This has definitely been one of the most turbulent relationships I've had, but it is also the most real one in my life. Daisy is the most real woman I have ever been with. Essentially she is the best mate I have ever had in a relationship. We've had some amazing times together. We once took my Aston Martin DB7 up to Big Sur with the roof down and it was just great. Daisy was one of the people who said to me, 'If you want the car, buy the car!' She has always encouraged me not to be afraid of having things and that is a great characteristic, she wants me to enjoy life.

She is also very thoughtful towards me. For example, when it was my birthday one year, she threw me a big party, something I was not really used to as an adult. It might sound banal and I certainly don't mean this to be taken the wrong way, but I love it that she often makes me dinner. Daisy is the first person to repudiate the view that 'a woman's place is in the kitchen' and I am with her on that, but sometimes I will come home and she will have cooked me a fantastic meal. One of the ways she first seduced me was with the most obscene sandwich you've ever seen in your life; I have an addiction to sandwiches, it had everything but the kitchen sink on it! I know it sounds silly but little things like that really warm my heart. In the relationship before Daisy, the only meal that my ex ever cooked me was chicken and four roast potatoes with mayonnaise!

We've had family holidays together, another thing I hadn't really done in my life. The time I went to Barbados with Mel Sykes, Luke, Shirley and my friend Rob Ferguson and his wife was, for years, the best holiday I had ever had. Untouchable. Naturally, Mel, Luke, Shirley and I all got on very well but Rob and his wife are very special to me as well. Rob has been one of the few people who has remained a rock for me, a true friend, just looking at him makes me laugh. It was an incredibly memorable break.

Then I went away with Daisy and it felt good to finally be on a holiday that topped everything before it. We went with Nicky and Steve, two English friends who run a pub in LA, and it was just an incredible time (those two will be my friends for life, no question).

A funny thing happened when we were checking in for the flight at LA airport. We bumped into Patti LaBelle and, as we both knew her, we asked where she was going. She said the same island in the Caribbean. We had such a great time, and I even ended up jamming with Patti one night in a beach-front bar where we wrote a song about the menopause called 'Internal Burn' with a bunch of women!

We have also stayed at the Sandy Lane Hotel in Barbados where we were lucky enough to share a dinner with Bob Monkhouse, a month or so before he died. I'd met him a few times in my life and he was always a gentleman. I explained later to Daisy that this guy was a British comic institution so that was a nice moment, but one tinged with great sadness too because he was so ill.

Another holiday we had that was special was when Daisy came to London and we stayed at the Lanesborough with my friends Michael and Julie Guzman. Mike came out with my mates down the pub and we all had a few too many. It was so lovely to have Daisy over here. It is hard for her to visit often because her work keeps her very busy. One of our plans is to set up a proper home in the UK which would be great.

Daisy's family live in Miami. Her lovely mother, like mine, is a cancer survivor. I remember sitting in their house for the first time for dinner and all seven people at the table were talking in Spanish at the same time – it was so animated and quite a culture shock. I am slowly learning Spanish but because they talk so fast I struggle to pick much up there, so I have taken to learning from CD packages.

Daisy's sister and brother-in-law, Roseanne and Bernie, are lovely, two people I found it very easy to connect with – at first I did feel quite daunted being introduced to a family with such different cultural ways, but they all made me feel so welcome. I make a pasta dish – which Gordon Ramsay would later award 'one out of ten for presentation, looks like something my missus would make' – which is actually delicious. In fact, Roseanne found it so delectable that she not only christened it 'crack pasta' as it was so addictive, but also asked me to make her up two jars of it for when she has guests round.

Both Daisy and I are homebodies and that suits me fine. Neither of us likes going out partying, we prefer to just chill. When the 2002 World Cup was on, all the matches were screened at 3–4 a.m. LA time. We would buy food in and wear England tops for all the games – I even bought two shirts for our dogs Alfie and Rita. When England had been knocked out but Spain was still playing, I wore a Spanish top as a mark of respect to Daisy's family. It was great, the two of us, staying in and having such an enjoyable time.

That said, on certain occasions we do like to make an effort. One year, on her birthday, I wanted to make a real effort for her big day. I woke her up with breakfast in bed and two or three little gifts. The previous evening I had waited until she'd gone to bed, then dipped a bowlful of strawberries in chocolate, so the next morning after breakfast I walked her down to the beach for strawberries and champagne – her favourite, Dom Pérignon Rosé. I'd secretly arranged for her dad to 'bump into' us on the beach, so to see her face when he came strolling along, as if by accident, was a picture. Then, after we'd shared a drink with him, Daisy noticed a plane flying towards the beach, and as it came fully into view, you could see the banner behind it saying, 'Happy Birthday, I love you!' which I had also arranged on the quiet.

We left the beach and went to a beautiful shopping mall called Belle Harbor for a spot of lunch and some more gifts. Then we went to a nearby hotel, a lovely low-key place called The Beachhouse and headed to the bar, where we found ourselves sitting with Michael Stipe of REM and Liv Tyler. It wasn't over yet!

Then we went to her mum's house in my car with the roof down, and unbeknown to Daisy, all her family and friends were waiting for a huge surprise birthday party. That was when I gave her my main gift, a five-carat diamond cluster ring. When we finally rolled into bed that night at home, Daisy was absolutely exhausted, she'd had such a big and exciting day. It was really nice for me to see because she fell asleep looking at her new ring.

She called that ring her 'disco ball' because it sparkled so much. Sadly, when she threw a birthday party for me the following year, it was stolen. However, that hasn't tainted the memory of that previous birthday, which to this day she calls her 'best ever'.

In some ways Daisy is very cynical and tough, which can be quite draining if that is not your natural inclination. Having said that, she has also helped me to be a little bit more resilient which can be a good thing. Fortunately she has not had to deal with any great loss and her career has been, compared to the rollercoaster I've been strapped into, a relatively smooth ride. So sometimes I don't see the reason for her cynicism, but everyone is different. The thin line I have to tread with care is that I can't allow cynicism to take over. I have been through so much in my life that it would be my downfall to allow negative events and energy to dominate me, because then I would become all the things that I don't like in my life. So I have to be careful. It is my own private rebellion, to say, 'No, I am going to stay positive and still believe in the human spirit.'

I'd like to think I have made Daisy a little bit softer too. When you get older, you date people who have a history – I have a past and Daisy has been married before – but I think I am probably better at dealing with that than she is. Daisy doesn't talk about that past, it seems all very black and white, but I think that she is slowly understanding that there has to be a mellow acknowledgement of those times.

Marriage as an institution is sacred to me, that's why I haven't yet married anyone. I need to know it is the right person. As Daisy has been married already, a little bit of the magic goes, in a way, but that can't be allowed to affect us. I guess because of Mum and Dad I want to be cautious, I do not want that life.

I have homes in LA and London and my work is predominantly in the UK so Daisy and I often spend time apart. I am not going to lie – the distance is excruciating at times, it lies very heavily on our relationship. The present and future are things that are dear to you and I hope people will understand why I have to hold that little bit back on this subject. I would love it if we could become a family and move to the next level.

Suffice to say, we have had our ups and downs but thankfully so far we have made it through.

One crucial part of my life with Daisy in LA is our two dogs. I used to go into a pet shop in the Beverly Center in LA quite frequently. I'd seen many bulldogs in there over the years, but on this particular day there was a beautiful dog that just had something about him that I connected with. As soon as I locked eyes with him, I knew there was no way I was leaving him there. So I made up my mind to go back later and get him.

Next thing I know, Daisy has been to the shop and bought him for me. It was just amazing. I called him Alfie after Michael Caine's character in the film. I was holding Alfie in my arms and I said, 'I give you my word that nothing will ever harm you.' When I am in LA, we are inseparable, he will not leave my side. Daisy says if Alfie could crawl up my arse and die he would!

Alfie is such a character. He weighs over sixty pounds but he seems to think he is a lap dog, which can be very painful if he decides to crawl all over you with one leg on the family jewels! When I fall asleep at night, for some reason he needs to feel me breathing, so I always wake up to his black nose and eyes looking at me, snoring. When I come away from him to London, it's the only time in my life I can honestly say I miss whiskers!

Around the same time, Daisy became obsessed with Wheaten Terriers. She'd also seen one of these dogs at a shop, so I reciprocated the gesture and went to get one for Daisy, as she'd done for me with Alfie. The terrier is called Rita, as in Rita Hayworth. Daisy is obsessed with Rita, and we love both dogs unconditionally, they are a very special part of our life. Funnily enough, when Rita arrived, Alfie was suffering with a

238

very bad leg and becoming quite immobile, but after just two weeks with Rita, his limp had gone altogether, she'd made him stronger and more agile within days.

During this time, I was contemplating coming back to the UK and that was a very important decision for me, a very big deal (more of which later). My LA home is in the Hollywood Hills and every day I would go hiking up there, it really was my saving grace. Alfie would come with me – it was a long six-mile hike – so I would have to be careful because bulldogs overheat very easily. As a puppy I kept him on a short lead so now he never strays more than a few feet from my side. We'd walk together up the hills and I would be chanting as I breathed, in, out, in, out, 'Every-thing-is-going-to-be-okay' and always Alfie would be there with me. I nicknamed him 'Ever Ready' because he just keeps plodding, left-right, left-right, relentless, he personifies what I want to do through my life in that way. There's a spot in the hike where you get a 360-degree view of the hills and I would stand atop there and, for want of a better phrase, put my energy out to the universe. It was so therapeutic out there on those hikes. I felt so at peace. Alfie was a big part of that, I love him totally.

I was with Daisy in LA on 9/11. Because I lived virtually next to the Twin Towers during my time in New York, that horrific event shattered me, as it did many New Yorkers, Americans and people around the world. It was the proximity of the towers to my apartment that made it seem so incomprehensible. They were so immense, so *permanent* – from my window you could only see a third of them, that is how tall they were.

I spent so much time in and around those towers. I often used to go to the 'Windows of the World' restaurant where one of my favourite meals was the short ribs. My mates and I would go to see the swing band play in the bar and I went on numerous dates there too. When you arrived in New York as a foreigner, the towers were your compass, you knew that wherever you were, especially if you were lost, you could realign yourself by these two mammoth structures anchoring the bottom of the island. Sometimes you'd get in a yellow cab and you wouldn't know where you'd want to go, you didn't know exactly how to get there either so you'd point at the towers and say, 'I want to go there!'

Every night I would see the lights go to dim as the workers headed home, these great chunks of floors all going to emergency lighting only, clunk, clunk, clunk. I came to know what time that happened. The towers were part of the air that I breathed when I lived in New York.

Oddly enough, I had been in LA when the earthquake hit in 1994. That was monumental for me, one of the most extreme things I've ever been through. At the time I was on the fifth floor of an apartment block and I was thrown out of bed, that's how I woke up. I was tipped out of bed on to the floor, my TV exploded, my windows were buckling and the walls were cracking. That apartment had a 180-degree view of LA, an endless expanse of glittering lights, but when I picked myself up off the floor, the whole of LA was in darkness. It looked as if the city had dropped off the face of the earth. Every car alarm in Los Angeles was going off, it was just this cacophony of terror. It was a horrible experience which took me a long time to get over. Some people never felt safe there again and left LA after that quake; a huge English contingent departed.

But, of course, as distressing as that was, that was Mother Nature – 9/11 wasn't. I was asleep with Daisy in LA when her dad phoned at 6 a.m. and said a plane had crashed into the first tower. We put the TV on and watched aghast as the second plane hit live on air. It was one of the saddest moments of my

240

life. I knew the geography of the news footage like the back of my hand. There is a very well-known shot when a vast cloud of dust is chasing people up a street and in the foreground of the camera's view is a mesh fence – that was right next to my apartment block. Then the phone rang and it was a former neighbour in New York who said all the windows had been blown out of my old building.

When the first tower started falling, I could not comprehend it. That awful day really affected me. When you walk down west Broadway now, they are not there and it is so weird. It has become a permanent scar. Daisy and I took a Polaroid of ourselves; we looked so distressed, but I wanted to capture what was one of the saddest moments in American history.

Carl Kennedy, my best friend in New York, was due at a meeting in one of the towers at 9.30 a.m. that very day to arrange, of all things, a party. He overslept.

TWENTY-SIX

Just Me And My Thoughts

I'd lost my first 'solo' record with Polydor in LA – bang, three years of my professional life extinguished; then I worked on that house record in Italy, which mutated into a commercial album, something I hadn't intended to be involved in, and then . . . another record was lost – another year snuffed out; at least I had my New York album with Universal Records to look forward to, because, after all, lightning shouldn't strike twice, so three times, never . . . or so I thought.

I'd had some problems with my record company in New York, even though I had been so prolific with my writing. The A&R woman assigned to me came into the studio one day and said the most ludicrous thing to me. She listened to one song and said, 'You've got to change the backing vocals, they sound too black.'

'Pardon me?'

'The BVs sound too black, we gotta change them.'

'Are you having a laugh with me?'

'Sorry, Matt, they will need to be changed.'

Remember, I grew up with Stevie Wonder, Michael Jackson, all sorts of black artists. I loved them as a kid because they were brilliant, not because they were black. I sang as I did on that record not because it sounded black, but because it sounded right. I am influenced by black music, so why wouldn't I want that to emerge in my work? All the harmony groups I am used to singing with and arranging are influenced by black music. I was stunned.

I shouldn't have been surprised, though. Unfortunately in America there is black radio and there is white radio, which is quite insane to me. This politicizes the making of a record even more than just the usual record company machinations, which is a great shame. When she said that, I felt like walking out of the studio there and then and saying, 'Fuck it, I will see you tomorrow and I'll put my "white head" on.'

It was really just insane, and I was incredulous. After a lengthy and heated discussion, it was decided that the backing vocals had to be changed.

Eventually, the record was finished and it was sounding fantastic. I was so excited. Then I spoke with a marketing executive at the record company and he said to me, 'We're gonna take this record, throw it at the wall and see if it sticks.' It was so insulting. No one is ever going to throw a record of mine at a wall. That is a good example of how incredibly rude this industry can be, reckless and offensive, very disrespectful.

The A&R lady who insisted I change the BVs departed from the record company at a later date and suddenly no act on the label felt secure. This particular set of circumstances I call 'step-children' syndrome. One person signs an act, they work on an album – and in my case the album was *finished* – then that person loses their job, a new face appears and wants only to bring in and work with their own choices. They feel no relationship to the acts already on the roster. Unfortunately for me, I was seen as a step-child, so I lost my third record in a row.

People outside the industry perhaps don't understand that

if you lose a record, the record company still owns the masters. There is such a thing as a 'technical release', which means that if a small amount of records – often no more than a few hundred – are put out into the marketplace somewhere, then that record is classed as released. I am telling you that my record was not released, whatever they say. It might have been a technical release, hence you can buy that record on the Internet where they are going for forty pounds, but it was not a release that I valued.

Fortunately, as the writer of those songs, I do at least have the option to re-record them – but to record costs a great deal of money. One song, 'Fever', took two weeks to complete. Multiply that by about sixteen songs that you record for consideration for an album and you are looking at about thirty to forty weeks in the studio alone. I might as well have taken that advance they gave me in the Big Apple and gone on holiday for three years.

Over six years of making records, working long hours in studios, writing passionately for month after month after month, spilling my heart out on paper and trying to capture those songs in the finest sonic detail. And what did I have to show for it? Nothing.

At this time, I would often bump into people from the UK, journalists, writers, people who knew of me. The one question they almost all invariably asked me was, 'So, what have you been doing for six years?'

The frustration of not seeing my records released was really grinding down my natural optimism for what I do. It reached a point where I started to have regular conversations with Daisy about possibly doing other things, like painting or just writing songs for covers. It seemed ludicrous to me that I was even thinking like that and in my heart of hearts I know now I could never have stopped being involved in performing my music. But we would have these chats and I would wonder where I was heading.

The weight of all these disappointments just became too much for me to carry any more. I was emotionally desolate. I went into the bathroom, quietly locked the door, ran myself a bath and stepped in. My head was aching with hurt as I lay there for a while, really not in a good place at all. I felt like the old pain hard drive was full and I couldn't store any more. I slid under the water, feeling the surface gradually cover the top of my mouth, nose and head until I was submerged, hidden. The pain and loneliness had become unbearable. I started crying under the water. I thought to myself, *All it takes is for me to breathe in under the water and that is that, I'm gone.* No more oxygen will come into my lungs, but I won't be able to feel any more hurt.

I heard my heart beating.

I contemplated breathing in again but my lungs wouldn't let me . . .

. . . then I thought of Carolyn and what an insult to my sister's death it would be.

I lay there for what seemed like an eternity . . .

. . . then, finally, I resurfaced and gulped in the air.

Do I lay convicted and will I drown alone,
my mind says 'please' but my lungs won't let go,
I am crying underwater, an invisible crime,
it's strange how my beating heart fills this silent time.

I wrote those lyrics about that moment in the bath for a song called 'Watch Me Fall' on my 2004 album *Early Side Of Later.* There's nothing wrong in having a couple of those moments when you feel like checking out. That is as literal as song-writing gets.

It took me some time to recover from losing yet another record. One particular night I was feeling really down and directionless, doubting if anyone out there actually gave a damn about whether I continued with my music. Daisy, bless her heart, said, 'Can I show you something?' and took me to look at her computer. She had logged on to a Yahoo chatroom and there were 1500 people talking about me, about where I might be and what I might be doing. Saying things about me, lovely things; 'I hope he is okay', and so on. It made me cry. Daisy doing that proved to be instrumental in my decision to return to the UK. These were simple words, from lovely people. I didn't know how to write a message back so I asked Daisy to do it for me and just said, 'You guys are so caring towards me.' They'd stayed loyal to me for fifteen years. That one little thing my girl showed me had such an impact.

For much of my life, I have felt as if I have been living on a major emotional fault line, just waiting for the ground to move and open up another devastating crack in my world. My childhood didn't feel safe, neither did Bros, and parts of my current life still don't.

Being on stage feels like the safest place in the world.

That might sound like a complete contradiction, coming from someone who is chronically shy, so let me explain myself a little more. On stage, I know the phones won't be ringing, my manager's not going to want a meeting, I don't have to do interviews, I don't have to be somewhere else . . . I know that for ninety minutes or so I won't be bothered in that way. Throughout rock-and-roll history, even if they are going to arrest you, they usually let you finish the show first!

Being on stage brings with it, for me anyway, an overwhelming wave of feeling safe – not just because there might be thousands of people screaming nice things at me, that's not the crux of it. It's just the performance. That brilliant holiday in Barbados that I mentioned with myself, Mel, Luke and Shirley had a great example of this feeling. We were in a local bar and the band was playing really hard reggae, some great music. We were all dancing, sweating and having a good old night. A couple of people teased me to get up and after a little bit of ushering – I didn't want to impose – I went up. I must admit that in secret I really fancied it.

The band leader said, 'Yeh mon, we gort someone here that wonts ta seng. Worts yur name, eh? Matyoo, yeh mon.'

I'm not kidding you, I bloody rocked the place! It was heaving. You could see the band were thinking, *Fucking hell, where's he come from?* I had a lovely moment with Lukie afterwards because he came over to shake my hand, looked me in the eye and said, 'Matt, tonight I realized you are a true performer.' That was one of the most touching things he's ever said to me.

I love music and performing with every inch of my soul, this isn't just something I do for the time being. I don't work on my abs in a morning, choreograph on an afternoon and then squeeze in two PAs on the night.

Unavoidably, something that feels so natural and so comfortable can become addictive. I understand that certain performers struggle to replace the buzz of live shows either after a gig or later in their careers when they retire. Some of the alternatives to that buzz can be poisonously destructive. I am fortunate enough to still be able to perform live. I cannot imagine being in a position where I couldn't, heaven forbid. I pine, I ache with every single fibre in my body when I don't play for a while.

Fittingly then, the other crucial catalyst during this period that encouraged me to return to the UK was a very special live show I took part in. I was delighted to be asked to perform in a charity gala at the legendary Carnegie Hall in New York. The head of the charity called me and said he'd been recommended to ask me to sing because of my voice. I didn't know it at the time, but it turned out to be the night that I realized I still had it on stage.

I was apprehensive, of course I was, but my inner self knows I can always deliver once I am standing behind a microphone. It helped on the day that I was treated with great respect. They gave me the so-called Maestro Suite, the most prestigious room in the venue which even had its own grand piano. Best of all, however, it has tiny square windows in the wall, peepholes effectively, through which you can spy on the audience and auditorium.

Also on the bill were Odetta, the jazz singer, the Harlem Voice Choir and the Tokyo String Quartet, the latter of whom I performed with. I sang two original pieces, one track I'd written with Denise Rich and another I'd penned with the man who was head of the charity. I absolutely *nailed* that performance. I could sense I was directly moving people in the audience and at the same time my mates were there having a laugh, it was incredible. The standing ovation I received started before the final note had rung out, it was overwhelming. I could feel my soul being nourished with every handclap.

There was a party afterwards and it was so full of women wanting to proposition me, older women, as well as younger! I'd flown Mum and Tony in to watch the gig and it was lovely to see them. The attention from women became so blatant that Mum was actually embarrassed by it. I don't mean to sound arrogant when I say that, I'm just telling the story and it did make us chuckle afterwards.

When I was about to leave, there were a few American fans from Bros's first time in the US, because Sony was close to Carnegie Hall. One lady came up to me and said, 'I've got your brother's autograph and I've waited all this time to get yours, do you mind?' Of course I signed it for her, I thought that was just amazing.

At the end of the night, I mulled over what had happened. Needless to say, I felt fantastic. I thought to myself, *You know what? I am not well-known here, I've just been given a standing ovation and stole the show at Carnegie Hall, what an amazing night ... what am I so afraid of?*

For the first time in a very long while, I dared to think what had, until very recently, been unthinkable.

Let's have a peek around the corner back in England ...

TWENTY-SEVEN

I Think I'm Gonna Fly

You may well ask why returning to England, my home country that I love, was unthinkable for me for many years. One word: *fear*. Quite honestly, I was consumed with fear. The battering we had taken in Bros had left such deep welts that I didn't recover for years. I can still feel the damage now, but the acute pain has subsided. Back then, with everything that was happening to me in America and Italy throughout the Nineties, the future loomed very bleak if I allowed myself to contemplate returning to the country of my birth.

The sudden sense of foreboding would strike me at the strangest times. In LA there are 'English' shops that sell baked beans, breakfast tea leaves, brown sauce, all those home comforts that expats miss. I would find myself buying something in one of these shops and if I caught sight of the red top of a British tabloid, I would get chills. My stomach would turn and I would have to leave the shop.

This absolute fear had kept me a prisoner in America for years. Over there, I wasn't so well-known, but in my memory I just kept going over and over events during and after the break-up of Bros. When everybody in the street seemed to know our problems, when people read such negativity about us and believed it, when we were hated by so many people.

I used to say to myself, 'Why?' We were a young, hard-working band, we didn't smoke, take drugs, sleep with under-age fans, we loved our mum, and all we really wanted to do was make music and communicate with people. For that we were mercilessly berated. How else could I feel except fearful?

The years in the US didn't help calm the fear but I knew at some point I would return and that scared the hell out of me. Certain situations – like asking Craig for a little help and his not even getting back to me – were also very quick and brutal reminders of what I would be coming back to. My whole body would tense and I would get extremely anxious just thinking about it. The fear would literally give me palpitations, flutters of distress, I would constantly break out in cold sweats.

But I still really missed England too. I had to go back.

A few incidents occurred which prepared me for the intimidating prospect of coming back to the UK. As I've said, Daisy showing me that chatroom and the Carnegie Hall performance helped me realize I could still deliver, and moreover that people wanted to see me deliver. However, there was still that grave fear of the press and that alone almost stopped me getting on a plane at all.

When I had finally decided to return to the UK, I booked a show in LA. The posters for the gig were printed on a background of Union Jacks and the venue was crammed with a host of expats, in fact it was quite a bit 'hooligan' in there. It was a raucous gig and I loved it. My friend Simon was there from New York and he started chatting to these black guys who were saying how much they loved my voice. They were comparing my vocals to all sorts of great performers, Marvin Gaye, Sam Cooke, all very flattering comparisons. Simon was intrigued by their knowledge of music and the way they talked about me so he asked who they were. 'Oh, we're the Gap Band, you might know of us.'

There were certain people who buoyed my spirits so much and helped me make the decision to face the UK. One of my closest friends who was always there for me when things were getting difficult with Bros is Jackie Brambles. I remember vividly how we first met. I was listening to Capital Radio in my suite at the Hilton Hotel as Bros prepared to fly out for a tour of Japan. Jackie Brambles played 'I Owe You Nothing' which was nice, but then she flipped the single over and played the *a capella* version of that song, after which she waxed lyrical about my voice. I was really taken aback. She didn't need to do that and no doubt it hadn't been on her playlist for that day's show, so I was really touched.

I called Capital but they didn't believe it was me on the phone. Eventually I managed to get through to Jackie and at first she didn't believe it either!

'I just heard you play our single and B-side on the radio and say all those lovely things about my voice. I just wanted to call to say thank you.' We got chatting so I said, 'What are you doing later? Let's go out.'

'Oh, I'm off out with some friends . . .'

'Bring them as well!'

So we sent two limos, one for Jackie and one for her mates! Remember, this was Bros!

That was the start of a fantastic friendship which survives to this day. We became really good friends and were even pictured in the press going out a few times. Although there was never any romance – we were just massive mates – a few of the more extreme fans were not always so understanding. In fact, it reached the point where Jackie had to have her own security to escort her out of Capital – some girls were saying they had Jif bottles full of acid and were going to spray it in her face. When we talk about those times now, Jackie just recalls how extreme it all was, having to have security for herself because she knew someone in Bros.

This was a classic example of how even people around us were very affected by the day-to-day mayhem surrounding Bros. Jackie would give me daily updates on how easy or hard it had been just to get through the door of Capital Radio. If we had three hundred girls outside our house, there'd be forty outside Capital Radio and another fifty or so outside the management. That was what it was like, they would be everywhere.

Over the years, Jackie and I have given each other much good advice. When I was debating whether to return to the UK from America, Jackie was instrumental in helping me make that decision. She kept telling me I had to come back and sing live again in the UK, she was so supportive. For my part, I tried to help her as much as I could when she broke up with her husband. I was on the phone from New York for hours and later when Jackie went for an audition at GMTV, I spoke with Michael who is the executive producer and said, 'Please look after her, she is a dear friend.' She got the job because she is a talent, but I hope I helped smooth the way a little. Jackie would always be on the phone while I was touring – by way of scant commiseration, my tour manager at the time said 'at least those phone bills are cheaper than cocaine!'

While I was still in America and going through managerial hell yet again, it was a delight to get a phonecall from an old friend of mine who was also one of the UK's top agents, Richard Smith. Richard is very direct, a real geezer, and he just came out and said the sentence that I had not dared to mouth for all those years, 'Listen, Matt, do you want to do some UK dates then?' I think he could sense the trepidation in my voice, it was hard to mask; I'd been trying to find love again for the industry for so long. But Richard is so full of positivity and energy, he was having none of it. He said, 'Matt, you are a fucking legend, get yourself over here and let's do some gigs!'

Richard, along with his colleague Steve Hume, were two great guys to come back into my life. They are both real fellas, British geezers, tough, loving and supportive. It was magic to have people like that back on the scene. Richard wasn't joking either – within a few weeks, he called back to confirm a sixteen-date UK tour.

Finally, it was time.

I boarded the plane with my hands up, fists clenched, ready for a scrap. What I didn't know then was that the only thing people back at home wanted to do was shake my hand . . .

I was expecting to be met back in the UK by a hostile barrage; instead there was a welcoming party. One of the first shows I was booked to play on my return was Birmingham Academy in July of 2003. I am not ashamed to admit that when I saw that gig on the schedule sheet, my instinctive reaction was, *Shit, I'm playing a gig as small as the Academy.* I was so convinced that I had to come back and play arenas, I'd think if I couldn't get into the arenas I was finished. That was a perspective solidified by Bros because my last big concert in Britain was Wembley Stadium. I really didn't fancy the Birmingham gig at all, but it turned out to be one of the best shows of my life and I loved every second of it.

I was just not thinking straight. When I arrived at the Academy and started singing, the audience went nuts and within a few songs I was crowd-surfing, the sweat was cascading off me and the whole venue was rocking, truly going berserk. I don't think people who haven't seen my live show really know what happens at a Matt Goss gig. It's so much harder and so much more full of energy and funkier than people could ever imagine – there are ten of us up there, a brass section, the whole deal! My live audience is changing, the 'lad factor' is increasing. There were lads there with their mates and their pints, singing away, which was a nice surprise. It's nice to have a lot of women at my gigs but it's also good to see lads enjoying the women! I want that energy in my gigs, I want blokes to think, *I'm gonna see Matt Goss live and there will be lots of totty there and I'm going to have a laugh*. Birmingham was such a buzz. That show proved to me that I could still rock it, and that it is an absolute thrill to play live *wherever*.

Barrie Marshall and Doris Dixon of Marshall Arts came to see one of my shows on that tour. You can't get bigger than them in this business. He said, 'You are amazing, Matt,' and we sat until five in the morning in a hotel in Manchester just chatting. They put so much optimism and belief back in my heart. I couldn't believe how good people were being to me.

That Birmingham show was a pivotal moment, a turning point if you like, but the highlight of that tour without a doubt was the gig at the Shepherd's Bush Empire. The week before the London show there was just one solitary preview in *Time Out* of a previous gig, saying the forthcoming date in the capital was one not to be missed. That was very nice to see but I had a fresh sense of context: 3000 fans is a lot of bums on seats. Bear in mind, at this point, I did not have a record deal. So my more cautious side was thinking, *That one little article is not going to fill the Empire*.

My manager at the time was Steve, brought up in Leeds but based in New York, and he came back to the UK with me. We both often used the phrase 'coming back guerrilla style' – it was nice to have somebody like Steve who really believed we didn't need a record deal to fill Shepherd's Bush. The funny thing is, doing that tour without a deal was liberating in a way; there was nobody behind the scenes telling me what I could and couldn't do and it made me feel very confident about going out there again.

So you can imagine how excited I was when I arrived at the Shepherd's Bush Empire and there was already a long snake of people curling around the building. The last time I'd been in that same dressing-room was on *Wogan* all those years ago in Bros and that night there had been a queue round the building too, so to see that again was a lovely feeling. I could literally feel the fear and anxiety in my body beginning to seep away.

When the gig was about to start, Neil Fox of Capital FM went on stage and gave the most generous little speech, ending with, 'The last time I introduced this man he was playing Wembley Stadium, so it gives me great pleasure to bring you ... Matt Goss!' The roar that went up when I walked out was amazing – that sweaty, raucous, heaving gig at Shepherd's Bush was one of the highlights of my entire career and, to my own surprise to be honest, it is up there even with Wembley Stadium.

I couldn't believe what was happening. I was back in the UK and loving every second of it.

Of course, I will always want to get back to the arenas. Once you've done a stint like Bros did at Wembley, that stays with you. I have always found arenas to be my favourite shows, that's where my gigs really come alive – you have to engage an arena as it's a vast audience and if you do, they will all reciprocate. An arena is intimate to me, believe me when I say that.

Fortunately, in September 2003, only a few short weeks after I had first returned to England, I was asked to support Mariah Carey at Wembley Arena and six other big venues. I *loved* all those dates but particularly the Wembley show. I had the place on its feet, people were singing their hearts out and I was lucky enough to earn some very favourable reviews when the critics were not always so charitable to Mariah. When I sang 'Famous', the whole arena was on its feet, it was fantastic! And it felt great to say, 'Hello Wembley!' again. For musicians, that is the phrase that they all want to say, and I have been fortunate enough to have said it twenty times or so. It never gets dull!

It was quite refreshing to find myself so quickly on the other side of the fence with the press. I was getting great reviews and Mariah was always being written about as a 'diva'. Because of all the intense fear I had suffered from the press treatment of Bros I cannot judge a person in the newspapers other than by how I have found them to be. Mariah is a case in point. First of all, she was never anything but very cool with me. I did those dates and she was always nice and later I went to her Halloween party and she was very sweet again. Second, there are always going to be divas in the music business. The beautiful thing about music is the characters it can boast. You need your divas, your punks, your rock dinosaurs. You need your fiery new bands, people who feel like your mate next door and you need showmen like Freddie Mercury or Elton John. That is what it is all about, variety, characters.

I judge things on what I know, I can't be guided by other people's opinions. People who let that happen are going to live very narrow-minded and shallow lives. It is absolutely vital that people form their own opinions on what they know to be true because, unfortunately for me, I have been judged so harshly in that indirect way. Millions of people made their minds up about what Luke and I were like over the years from stories in newspapers that were often either very misleading or completely fictitious.

*   *   *

And it just kept getting better. In November, 'I'm Coming With Ya', my first UK single for *seven and a half years* charted at Number 22, my highest slot for over twelve years. I was delighted. With that success came an invitation to appear on *Top of the Pops* again.

I've played that landmark show maybe fifteen times, but obviously when I went on there in 2003 it was my first appearance in quite a few years. I was so excited. When I arrived at the studio, it was great to see so many familiar faces: Andi Peters had just started out when Bros was breaking through, whereas now he was the producer of the most famous music show on TV (Phillip Schofield is another friend who was just beginning back then and whose career really took off – he and his wife would often come round to my house when I was living with Mel and just hang out). There were other people, too, backroom and technical staff who were still there. Those people working at the studio almost seemed to feel protective of me, they knew I was nervous and they did everything they could to make me feel welcome. It was nice to see them and several people said to me, 'It's good to have you back, Matt.' That was pleasing and my clenched fists relaxed a little bit more.

Also on the show with me were the Pet Shop Boys, Black Eyed Peas, and the video was Robbie and Kylie. In the previews in magazines it was nice to see my name flagged up for the show and I was later told that that episode had enjoyed two million more viewers than they'd had for several series. It was good to be back in the thick of it – appearing on that show is still a benchmark of your success and national profile – and there wasn't a shred of anxiety to be seen. Except of course, a few stage nerves! I don't think you can play an institution as huge as *Top of the Pops* and not get nervous, you have to want to do so well, it should make you a little edgy. Once I was on stage though the nerves vanished and I enjoyed every second.

It was good to go up to Chris and Neil from the Pet Shop Boys while they were rehearsing and catch up. They are, I will say, probably two of the nicest – if not *the* nicest – people in the music industry. They can play any venue they want, they have total control over their music, their image, their direction and yet I have never heard a bad word said about them. My experience of them is that they are two true gentlemen, they personify how you should behave as successful musicians and people and they make quality product.

That day at *Top of the Pops* made me feel so much better and, dare I say it, safer.

TWENTY-EIGHT

Gangster Or Spiritual Leader

By 2003, fifteen years since the days when Bros had ruled the charts, pop music had changed beyond recognition. I understand that more people voted for Will Young and Gareth Gates during *Pop Idol* than voted for the Conservatives at the General Election in 2000. Britain was celebrity-obsessed. It was apparent how much had changed by the tone of questions I was being asked in interviews on my return.

For a start, people would often say to me that I am the Godfather of boy bands, that Bros, Luke and myself are the godparents of the genre. That's a very flattering thing for someone to say, but I have to be honest, I never considered us to be a boy band. We never intended to be 'teen idols' or whatever you might wish to call us. We just went into a studio and started to make an album. Okay, we were cute and featured in all the pop magazines, but when you think about it, we were just a band like any other rock-and-roll band. Bass, drums and vocals. We played all our songs live, we wrote material, we toured frantically. That's what we did. Unfortunately, when you get screamed at it is assumed you have no talent (although they didn't say that about The Beatles!).

260

In my view, boy bands sing covers, dance to choreographed routines, do PAs. We didn't do one day of choreography. One morning in a central London studio, we were shown some dance moves, but I just remember thinking, 'Where the bloody hell can I use this?' You never saw Craig and me in a line working the stage, we did nothing like that. I always felt, what is more boy band, Bros or Wham!? What I do think is a fair comment is that the hysteria surrounding Bros set a lot of precedents for boy bands. That is unquestionable.

I am often asked by new artists for pearls of wisdom. I come across many very young, very inexperienced bands that know my history and are keen to bombard me with questions. I answer as far as I can but there is only a very limited amount of help I can offer. For example: you have four pretty girls dancing and singing onstage. With a very few and phenomenal exceptions such as The Spice Girls, it is either going to be massive for a very short time, or sink without trace. That is just a fact.

I am not overly comfortable giving advice and this is why: I feel that offering some snippets of guidance in a few minutes is like speaking to someone who's been thrown into a cage full of untamed lions and saying, 'Here's a Swiss Army knife.' The music industry is so vast and vicious and so insanely consuming, I don't think that five minutes, thirty minutes, an hour or whatever, of listening to advice is going to cut it. There is no magic pill, no quick-fix.

You have to get your hands dirty, dive into it and be realistic. It is a business fraught with dishonesty. Be prepared for it to come to an end but – and this is the sixty-four-million-dollar question for me – you have to ask yourself if it does come to an end in terms of public profile, will you still be playing music and finding a way of doing so on your own terms? Do you want to be a musician or do you just want to be famous?

You must be comfortable on stage; if an audience senses

that you are not, that will be magnified tenfold and ruin the gig. The audience is there to be comfortable and have a laugh. That's the one thing about performing that you don't ever have to worry about. There are audiences that you have to break but if you are willing to have a crack at it, then you will probably succeed.

That is one of the problems with TV talent shows. People often say Simon Cowell is too harsh – I don't believe so. I agree with ninety-nine per cent of what he says. He seems to want to find the cream: good songs, great performers and I think he is very good for the industry. But being auditioned – either through a talent show or by a manager looking to start a pop band – takes so much fun out of the equation. You lose all those years of having a band with your mates at school, doing some crap gigs, writing some terrible songs before starting to find your way, improving, getting signed, working early tours; there's so much to be said for starting from the bottom. You need someone like Simon Cowell to put a little bit of reality into these kids' heads and remind them how harsh the business can be because, God knows, the second they leave their cosy environment at home, things will become a lot tougher.

One piece of advice I can give is vital to the survival of any band: go into the music industry expecting to get injured, because somewhere along the way it will happen. The clever ones can work hard and find a way around those problems, and if they do – as I have seen – they can have the most astonishing life and times. The less clever ones or the ones with dubious motivation, or even the unlucky ones, will be cast aside like cheap shoes.

So all I can say to these hopefuls is, 'Here's your little pocket knife, go into the cage and be lucky . . .'

*   *   *

Events had definitely taken a turn for the better in my life. It felt like it was all falling into place once more – as the record-business executive Clive Davis once said, 'Once a star, always a threat.' If you've sold millions of records once, there will be a song out there that can do it again. I am always striving for that. I was hard at work, loving every minute of it and up and running again. With the very warm reaction I'd been getting from the press to add to my sell-out shows and chart placings, I really did think that everything was going brilliantly.

Then I got a phonecall from my agent. Another phonecall, but this time, it was not bad news. Far from it.

ITV were going to make a show with ten celebrities spending two weeks in a kitchen run by the infamously volatile Michelin chef Gordon Ramsay. It was going to be called *Hell's Kitchen*. In short, did I want to take part?

It was a no-brainer.

Thanks, but no thanks,

Not remotely interested.

No way.

In fact, I couldn't really think of anything else I would rather *not* do right at that moment. Apart from being concerned it might distract or complicate the delicate process of finishing off my new album that I had sweated over for the last four years, the prospect of being on a reality show had always appalled me – and I'd said so in the press. It always bewildered me why celebrities – or indeed anyone else – would want a camera in their face twenty-four hours a day. What on earth could possibly make that appealing? I wasn't confident enough physically to face that. I am a confident man but, as I have said, I am also painfully shy to the point where it hurts. That's why I like to wear a cap, because I can hide underneath it. I'm not a bad-looking fella without the hat, but with it I can sit and hide. I love people-watching, rather than people watching me. I am a big fan of corners in restaurants.

Then they phoned again.

I said no again, without hesitating.

It wasn't just my aversion to those types of shows; the dynamics of the programme weren't right, the money wasn't right, nothing was right. No, thanks.

Then they phoned a third time. They told me who else was going to be on the show but that had no real impact on my decision at all, if I'm honest. There wasn't really any one who I thought might rub me up the wrong way and I didn't know a couple of them, so it wasn't a major deciding factor. It was still a 'no'.

They came back with more offers – 'We'll do this and that.'

They seemed to really want me for the show.

So I asked my family, friends and manager what they thought. They all said the same thing: 'Do it!' I was vastly outnumbered and felt sure I was the only one who was right, but eventually I chose to listen to their reasoning. They all said essentially the same thing: 'We know you in a certain way, but you've been represented constantly by soundbites and headlines for many years. You've got the perfect medium here to make people realize that there is much more to you than they know.'

Eventually, my agent, my record company, my TV people and even members of my family were saying, 'You've got to do this!' I knew these people cared for me, they wanted me to do it and clearly thought it was in my best interests. I thought to myself, *At some point, Matt, you have to listen to the people around you.*

The phone rang again.

This time I said, 'Yes.'

They were all right and I was wrong.

The one practical thing that influenced my decision was that we would be working with Michelin chefs, not apprentices, but trained Michelin chefs, so I knew I could take something away from it. There aren't many practical applications in life once you've come out of the celebrity jungle and can say, 'I can do that for you, I can eat five bugs.' Funnily enough, I wasn't particularly into cooking *per se* before *Hell's Kitchen*. Having said that, I have always loved food and because of my job and success I have been fortunate enough to have the opportunity to eat in very fine restaurants for many years.

I didn't know that much about Gordon Ramsay apart from his reputation as a fiery man and a phenomenal chef. I had seen him on *Faking It* on BBC America, in the show when he and two other experts took a burger-flipper and turned him into a top chef in about four weeks. I didn't know if I liked him at first but then I saw how Gordon really cared about that guy doing well. Yet, against that, I had heard so many horror stories from other people that I had a mixed perception. As I have said, I was now being given the chance to make my own mind up from personal experience.

When you meet Gordon, you instantly realize he is very intense, very full-on, all the time. There is no question that he is an incredible motivator – he has his own individual style to say the least. There were things he said to Edwina Currie that in my opinion were without a doubt very close to the bone, but at the same time there have to be people like Gordon in the world, alongside more polite and subtle people, there is a place for all of them.

As I am a very private person, I found little ways of protecting some of that privacy. I would put my mike on last, I would only go to the loo at certain times. The noisy little motor in those bloody cameras as they followed us around was quite comical. I hated the cameras, couldn't bear it. Yet, my unease began to ebb away and by the time I came out, although I wouldn't say I was at ease, I was definitely much more comfortable with the cameras than before.

It was shocking how much hard work we had to do. I know in the jungle show *I'm A Celebrity, Get Me Out Of Here*, you have tasks and suchlike, but there is a lot of sitting around too. In *Hell's Kitchen* we would be up early getting the food ready for that night – the amount of prep we had to do was astonishing, it was so gruelling I can't tell you. We spent hour upon hour preparing all the fruit and vegetables, the meat, the dishes. And this wasn't prepping for any old cook, this was for Gordon Ramsay. That means, for example, when you are working on a rack of lamb, there can be absolutely no trace whatsoever of any meat on those bones. You have to strip them of every tiny shred and sinew. Remember, these bones were essentially aesthetic, but nonetheless the prep work on them was painstaking. You really learned what the term 'dead weight' meant from working with meat like that for hours. What most people don't realize is that restaurants usually have twice as many staff to do the work we did. I have since very kindly been given chef whites by the head chef at a Knightsbridge restaurant called Zuma and he chatted to me and said how hard we must have all worked.

After a few days of the show, I was chopping the food and saying to myself, 'Don't leave, don't leave,' putting a knife through a lobster's head, 'don't leave' and so on. At one point, James Dreyfus was in floods of tears, really feeling pain and it was an incredible, intense experience. You genuinely started to feel for these people. I made some good friends in there.

I saw Amanda Barrie's incident and felt really uncomfortable with that moment. My mum suffers from high blood pressure and I have seen her nearly faint because of it many times. Amanda had high blood pressure and when I saw her losing it, I knew it wasn't really her nature or for the cameras. I was genuinely worried for her. I could see her neck was flushed, and spotted the signs, so I put my arms around her and told everyone to leave her alone. She clung to me so tightly. I think Gordon regrets that moment, it might have made good TV but everyone in the kitchen was uncomfortable. This was a bit too invasive, Amanda is in her sixties and she was hanging in there. That experience was troubling and I didn't enjoy it.

There were plenty of laughs in there too. We all wore our hats in a certain way, like at school when you rebel by knotting your tie differently to the approved style. James had the big tall hat, I had what they called the sailor cap, Al Murray turned his into a flat cap, Jen had her Princess Leia from *Star Wars* look while Edwina's just looked like a plant pot on her head. Those little things were quite endearing to me, it was people expressing themselves in there, because at times it did feel like a prison.

What they didn't seem to show was James's 'pigeon' routine. James, Jen and myself were becoming very frustrated by Edwina at one point, because she wasn't really batting for the team. Furthermore, she would sometimes corner you at the end of a long day and talk about politics and we couldn't handle it! So, James started doing this pigeon impression every time she began talking, 'Bbbrrrr! Bbrrrr!' It was hysterical and Jen and I reached the stage where we couldn't even look at each other without bursting out laughing. I have to say also that Edwina was actually very caring, especially in the common living area, but I don't think people were shown that side of her.

I do miss some of the camaraderie, Jen and James and Al

especially. It was nice to be around people who were cool, and that applied to most who were in there. I felt closest to Jen and James because they were in my team the whole way, but generally it was a good bunch.

When I went in, I said to myself, 'It would be nice to walk out of there under my own steam' – and that's exactly what I did, job done. I was really happy with getting through to the final day.

I still haven't watched the show and I don't really intend to, although I do like the montages I see when I do talk shows. I have my own vivid memory of what happened and the actual televised version will just be what the editors saw. It seems from what I have been told that the programme-makers represented me well and I am grateful for that. I said to myself, 'If I don't try to be anything but myself I will be safe.' I had my few moments and one notable confrontation in particular – I am glad I had that, that's who I am. What people saw on the show was the real me.

It's strange how much I miss cooking food, and I am sure Gordon and Ange would chuckle at that. Gordon's colleague Sarge said to me, 'It must be like the adrenaline you get from a gig,' and it is exactly like that rush. Once service starts, you are on, you deliver and it is a performance. I would really love to be involved in a restaurant because I do miss the whole process. A few people have spoken to me about exactly that and I certainly do not wish to rule it out of my life – if the right situation comes along I will definitely consider it. As I've said, I am really proud to have been in a reality programme that wasn't about eating bugs. I don't think it was at all demeaning working very hard and being trained by Gordon Ramsay and Sarge and Angela, and I am quite proud that I can whip up an apple tatin among other things! I am not alone – people loved that show and as Gordon is implying he will not do another, I think he recognizes it was a unique TV moment and should not be messed with, and you have to admire him for that.

TWENTY-NINE

It's Good To See You Again

It makes me emotional, the way the public have been with me since *Hell's Kitchen*. That feeling of never being safe is finally starting to fade away, little by little. When I was in Bros, with the exception of the US, there wasn't a country on earth that didn't have that same manic reaction to us. Malaysia, Japan, Israel, South America, all over Europe, anywhere. But as I've said, it didn't make me feel safe.

The way the public are with me now makes me feel safe, or at least much *safer*. They seem to have taken me under their wing. People have been lovely to me, hugging me, shaking my hand and not letting go. A cab driver said to me, 'You're part of the furniture, Matt.' I could not wish for anything more, to me that is the ultimate compliment. (I love black cabs, to me they are one of the safest places in the world. No one looks inside a black cab.)

Shortly after I came out of *Hell's Kitchen*, I played a sell-out show in London as a warm-up to Party in the Park. The night before the gig, I had fifty people outside my house, including one girl from Sydney and one from Japan. They told me it felt like Christmas Eve because I was doing a show again. The

270

day afterwards, the press stunned me with their reviews. The tabloids were right behind me, but what amazed me perhaps even more was that the broadsheets lauded the show. The *Guardian*, for example, said I was 'an expressive pop-soul singer who demands to be judged on his own merits'. I was delighted reading reviews like that.

I thought that was special but Party in the Park was an amazing moment for me. I played as a Londoner at a London gig, in front of 100,000 people. I met Prince Charles and had a great day, even walking home at the end of the show. But without doubt, my favourite part was when I broke down 'I Owe You Nothing' to just the crowd singing vocals. I'd said to my band before we went on that I wanted to do it, and a few of them thought it was a little bit on the brave/foolhardy borderline. I knew it wasn't. 'Just watch what happens . . .' I reassured them. Sure enough, I broke the song down and 100,000 pairs of hands clapped and 100,000 voices sang the choruses for me. It was a magnificent moment.

Some friends have stayed the course for me. One of these is a man called Mark Hamilton. He owns a massive security company in Scotland called Rock Steady; I think it's the biggest operation of its kind in Europe. Mark looks after Paul McCartney and lots of stars, and he was in charge of Party in the Park. Mark gives me the same energy that I used to get from Johnny before he died. Mark is the person that Johnny wouldn't want to mess with. Yet, Mark is also one of the sweetest people and he is the one person that I would call if I ever needed anything. He feels like family to me, we don't speak often but he is someone for whom I have a lot of respect and a great deal of time.

There were daily signs that the fear which had gripped my body for years could genuinely start to dissipate. I came back to the UK absolutely ready for a scrap and slowly I have been humbled by the really warm and affectionate way that I have been treated by everybody: by the fans, the press, the public, the media, everyone, it's been a joy. I can now, finally, relax my hands a little more.

It's interesting coming back to England having lived in the US for years because you are able to have a much keener sense of perspective about your home country. I have a passionate love for England and, indeed, Britain. I do notice, however, that the Scottish and Welsh are fiercely proud of their flags and the English are not easily allowed to be the same. In the US they are too and I enjoy the freedom of being able to have the St George Cross on my Aston Martin dashboard without people casting aspersions on me. Luke's Shirley is black and Adam's Sam is Pakistani so don't dare tar me with that brush, I love them with every inch of my soul. We should be allowed to be proud of our heritage. We have to recognize that history is peaceful *and* violent, that's the very nature of it.

Unfortunately, the city that I love, London, suffers from a similar malaise. This is largely because of certain people in charge, who don't consider Londoners, they just think about tourists. People seem to want to turn London into some generic European city. Why do that? I don't want our capital or this country to be just generic, we are different. Take the Routemaster bus, for example. Why replace those with standardized vehicles? Why not commission a British company to design a new Routemaster and make a big event of the relaunch? People would love to see that.

Visitors come to Britain to meet a civilized people with a long history. I am an absolute Royalist, I really am. I feel so strongly about the immediate Royal Family, they do so much good for the image and welfare of the country. So many nations have chopped the heads off their royalty and still have ceremonies, but these are essentially pantomime. Our pageantry is based on a current monarchy and we should be very proud of that. Coming from the US, it is so striking to me what an incredible asset we have here. I am not saying we should cling on to the days of Empire, but there are elements of our past society that we should hold on to. Heritage is so vital for a healthy, cosmopolitan nation.

People might read this as controversial, but I look at this country as our home; if you come to my home, you have to treat it with respect. Maintain your traditions and your faith, of course, but if you are not proud of being in this country then you shouldn't be here. This is a wonderful country that is generous, readily opens its heart and lets people be what they want to be, so please respect that. Don't slag it off. I hate it when I hear waiters from overseas criticizing this country, I just think why are you still here then? Britain is an island and we can only accommodate so many, so we have to embrace people who will be proud of this country. Governments should lead the way. However, at the moment it is not politically correct to stand up for your country. That's not who we are, the Brits have always been proud of their home nation and long may that continue.

Britain has some wonderful ways that are often eroded or completely ignored. The lack of common courtesy you see, simple things missing like saying, 'Good morning', 'Good evening', holding doors for people, is a constant annoyance to me. That is not what Britain is famous for, quite the opposite. Basic civility towards people has to count for something and it takes no effort whatsoever. I am not being old-fashioned, I just feel very strongly about this. Forgive me for stepping up on my soapbox a moment, but I have opened up my heart and soul for you in this book and this is a very important part of my life. It embodies who I am as a man.

Another aspect I noticed on my return from America was how well-dressed people in the UK are! My love of fashion has always been *equal* to my love of music. Whether my styles in the past have been right or wrong – and often that is all a part of it – I have always loved fashion. I doubt I would win any awards for some of the looks we had in our early days, especially the soul-boy mutations and long haircuts of the band's infancy, but we were just kids.

I think you should experiment and have fun with clothes. I think this interest in fashion is something peculiar to the British man – even the toughest English bloke can love his clobber. I notice this particularly when I am spending so much time in America, where clothes are tediously generic. They just go into one shop and buy a whole wardrobe, they're done. There's so much more pleasure to be had from it than that. It is not all about function, there has to be some form too. And it isn't just for myself, I love to see other people beautifully dressed. To take one random example, I am a massive fan of David Bowie, the way he dresses, he's got it right. To me he is the best-dressed man in rock.

I love fine tailoring, style and trends. I always have done. I didn't have money when I was a kid but I still loved clothes – hence the Fred Perrys, DMs and Sta-Prest shirts when I was into Two Tone. I genuinely love fashion, now more than ever. I'm lucky enough to be starting a few partnerships in different ventures and one of these concerns getting involved in some high-end, beautiful tailoring (I already have my own Emgie clothing range). That is a dream for me to follow. In autumn 2004 I was invited to a gala dinner by the British Luxury Club and that was a very interesting night to me. I really think that the British male should be able to have high-quality luxury items around him, not necessarily expensive, but just high-quality, little accessories that make life more charming and more comfortable. That may be an old-school way of thinking, but I am really passionate about that, it's a big part of who I am right now.

Obviously, in my days in Bros and since, I have been fortunate enough to be around such things for many years, but I would very much like to explore that more, to involve myself in tailoring, lifestyle branding, those sorts of areas. I can't talk about it enough, I love it. Whenever I have a meeting about tailoring or fashion, I don't want the chat to end.

While all of this was happening, I was still working away at a new album. I'd agreed to do those UK shows, as I've said, without a record deal. After that tour I had a choice of three labels and I went with Concept Music, run by Max Bloom and Roseann McBride. They had been to see rehearsals and then one of my shows, which was absolutely manic. They were both so enthusiastic. Being an independent label, I knew that they couldn't afford *not* to work a record really hard, whereas some majors write money off without batting an eyelid. For someone in my position, that can't be an option, every penny needs to mean something. I was determined that this time it would be an incredible project and would *definitely* be released. I did a deal with Universal that allowed me to use some of the songs I had recorded for the New York album that was lost, numbers I just refused to lose. 'Face The Wind' and 'Fever' were vital, crucial songs to me and my life. When you've spent weeks on one song, it is frustrating – and expensive! – to re-record the track, but it was essential. I wrote 'Fever' sitting in Battery Park in New York by the Twin Towers. That song is about the worst kind of fever, the cold sweats, yet it was invigorating to me. I have had to learn to find the most daunting moments invigorating too. That song has one of my favourite lyrics. I wrote it with Hital Shaw who won a Grammy for the Santana song, 'Smooth', so there was no way I could let that song just sink without trace.

There were also some very simple moments making the new record, when a song just happened almost in an instant. Probably my favourite song on the record is called 'Just For A Change'. I did a guide vocal on that and it ended up being the one I used on the record (a guide vocal gives a track a road map of a song, but it isn't the final vocal – it is usually put down so that the instruments know where they are in a song and get the feeling of the track). I did one take and we used that because it was *right*. The drummer was from the local music shop down the road from the studio – he'd done some drumming for Simple Minds, so he came in and played brilliantly, I did pretty much one vocal take and it just worked.

When you are making a record, it becomes your baby, but it also becomes the child of people very close to it. Max Bloom felt this way about the album and he loved it when it was finished. We feel very strongly about it. That genuine partnership is a nice thing for me to be part of, especially after my experiences in New York and LA.

This time, I was not going to be beaten. I have my album *The Early Side Of Later* to show for all that hard work and perseverance and, to be perfectly honest, it was worth the wait. I have never been more proud of any record than I am of that album. I really don't think I have ever put more into a record in my life. I love Max and Roseann, they have been great, it's nice to be in a position to say that about a record company. I wanted to write a fairly mellow album and people seem to have hooked into that.

It was also written without any restrictive parameters of what suits radio formatting, a problem for many artists that I think is in danger of killing quality songwriting. Some pluggers tell you that your song should not be more than three minutes, twenty seconds long otherwise radio will not play it – but what sort of way is that to go about creating material? The Eagles' 'Hotel California' is widely acknowledged as one of the greatest songs of all time, but it is over seven minutes long. What's more, there is a guitar solo in there that is almost longer than three minutes itself! Imagine saying to Freddie Mercury, 'Listen, Freddie, this "Bohemian Rhapsody" sounds good but can you cut it down to three minutes please?' Artists need to be very careful about what constraints they allow to limit themselves and their work.

The lead single on my album, 'Fly', brought me another Top Forty hit and I found myself back on all the music television channels again. The album has garnered great reviews and the press seem genuinely into what I am doing. What's more, they appear to want to let me do my own thing, as an artist, singer and a performer. Having been on the wrong side of them so severely, you have no idea how liberating that feels. I don't think many of the public understand how hard it is to come out of a band that big, go away for so many years, then come back and have any kind of presence in the charts; it's nigh on impossible and I am very proud of myself and my team for doing that. If my career grows from here, then thank God, but if it doesn't, then thank God anyway.

Mind you, every time I walk into this bloody country it's called another comeback! That makes me laugh. The thing I know is that I make quality product, and since 2003 people have been giving me props for it. Given my past, that is very rewarding. However, I also get as much, if not more, satisfaction out of the opinions of people I simply come across in everyday life, rather than critics. The wife of someone I worked with during 2004 told me that she was playing my album constantly on her car's CD player. Then, one day, she thought to herself, 'Am I listening to this because my husband is working with Matt, or do I actually like it?' I was delighted to hear she concluded that she played it because she loved the record. Little vignettes like that mean the world to me.

One of the tracks on *Early Side Of Later* was called, simply, 'Carolyn'. Shortly after my sister's death, we'd recorded the song 'Sister' as Bros, and that brought both Luke and me to tears. All these years later, I felt it was time to rejoice over my sister – of course, I still think how amazing it would be to have her back for just one hour – but I wanted to celebrate her too. I wrote the track when I was feeling really alone, having travelled from New York to Nashville. I was in a splendid hotel room, a beautiful suite, a lovely place to be but I was alone again. I looked at the windows as I lay down on the bed and I saw a big white dot in the middle. I instantly felt Carolyn, she'd come to be with me again. The next day I went to a park with Tommy Simms, who'd co-written the Grammy-winning 'Change The World', performed by Eric Clapton and Babyface, one of my favourite songs ever. We took our guitars and it might sound far-fetched but as I started writing the chorus, the wind picked up, it was mad, this bright sunny day with all this wind. It was a lovely moment and we wrote the song that afternoon and everybody has loved it.

I wrote it in a way that it could be a love song from one perspective, but if you want to know more and are looking to delve deeper, then it is about the death of my sister. It was when we first lost Carolyn that Adam and myself started to get really close. I invited him up to Scotland to see me record the song I had written about our sister, so he was there in the studio when I recorded 'Carolyn'. He was absolutely in tears, something you very rarely see with Adam. He was crying his eyes out. If you listen to the track, when I am ad-libbing and just before the little jazz groove sets in, I say, 'Adam, I am glad you are here.' In that way, I have immortalized both Carolyn and Adam on that song. That is what music is all about, little moments like that. It also defines what Adam means to me – everything.

I always used to – and still do – try to get my family and mates in the videos. My brother Adam was in three videos in 2003–2004 alone: he was a backing singer in 'I'm Coming With You'; in 'Fly' he was just one of my mates hanging out in the studio; and in the remixed version of 'The Key' (released by underground dance act Minimum Chic) he was chilling on the side of a street. I think that is what music is about, having a laugh. Part of the impetus to be in entertainment and music has always been about people who didn't want to be an accountant, a lawyer, they wanted to be different. That's what it's about, you've got to have fun, don't over-think stuff. If you are in a band and you want to have your mate in the video, then do it. It's a laugh, it's a memory and it might be one of the things that you can have a drink over for the next ten years. Indeed, we do, often hanging out for England games with a great gang of mates including Stuart Roslyn, Adam Phillips, Simon Wharton and myself. I love my brothers and what I'd love is for the three of us to go out, it would mean the world to me, to walk down the street and go for a drink with them.

Adam has also played on stage with me in front of many thousands of people. We did a TV show at The Bercy in Paris for an awards ceremony. They ran a live vocal but the band were playing to a backing track, as often happens, so we put Adam on keyboards. There were 20,000 people in the audience and he loved it. In 2003 he joined me in a similar way for about five local radio performances (he bottled out of standing in front of 100,000 at Party in the Park!). My fans know him well and a few even have crushes on him – he loves it, but God forbid he should admit it!

Adam is my brother. He means the world to me. So does his wife, Samiri, a Pakistani he fell in love with. He sometimes visits me in LA where we play poker and go bowling and have a great time. He runs his own successful tiling company, The Tiling Guild, and I am very proud of him.

I will say that sometimes I miss the crazy side of Adam. He went through a stage when he changed his faith and was quite opinionated, dogmatic, too old for his years, and didn't seem able to let himself go. I didn't like that. I am pleased to see that this has mellowed somewhat. In the last few years he has become more interested in spiritualism and his wife Sam is fascinated by reiki healing, which definitely widens the sphere of conventional thinking. I really hope Adam encourages Sam with that, I think she would be great at it. He is becoming more interested in such things too – his mum Pauline always gives him stones such as amethyst (we've always got on with Pauline – she has never been anything other than supportive of Luke and me and is always so interested in what we are doing). With that in mind, I gave Adam a book called *The Bible of Stones* which contained every possible interpretation of a stone's meaning and significance. We sat for hours in a hotel room on my 2003 tour flicking through this book together. It is so good to be able to see Adam much more often now that I am effectively commuting between London and LA. I just wish we had each other's DNA.

I am so proud of Bros. Every day I have twenty or thirty people coming up to me and sharing their memories. I am inundated with people telling me about important moments in their life that Bros remind them of or actually helped create. Millions and millions of people bought our records, went to all those shows and shared all those memories with us. It is one of the luckiest things to be a creator of memories for people – and it happens all the time to me. In September 2004, when I played to 3000 people in the West Country, a guy asked me if I would help him propose to his girlfriend – a big fan – by signing a T-shirt and being there when he asked. What a brilliant privilege that is for me, I never take it for granted. For example, when I do a signing, I don't sign and move on, sign and move on, I prefer to think if it takes longer, maybe another two hours to connect with all these people, then so be it; it feels too contrived otherwise, too superficial. I love to be able to do that. I don't think there's a bigger honour, creating memories, how can you not feel good about that?

When the Bros *Greatest Hits* was reissued by Sony in 2004, it sold well, especially considering it wasn't advertised. People showed their own affectionate feelings for Bros. Part of that affection is *because* we were so decadent, the fast cars, the designer clothes, luxury apartments, jewellery, helicopters, private jets and stadium shows. In a way it is quite cool to be related to a band that was full of decadence but also delivered proper bona fide hits in the Eighties and early Nineties.

I hope this book allows Tom, Mick, Nicky, Luke and Craig to say, 'You know what? We've got a little piece of history here, we should embrace it.' It's very odd to me that Tom sometimes slags off Luke and me, not least because we've never gone after him. Not wishing to sound like a hippy, but I want this to be a book of healing in some ways because Bros was an amazing experience. It feels good to be really proud of that band and the fun we had.

A lot of misinformed people think my life is just one song: 'When Will I Be Famous?', but that's so wrong, it's just the most ridiculous misconception to me. That song was crucial, of course, but it was just one of hundreds of little moments in our lives. Besides, we had eleven Top Thirty hits with Bros, eight of which were in the Top Ten. It doesn't really matter to me any more what people think of Bros. We have our own little piece of history and that can never be taken away from

281

us. Knowing everything as I do now, the full picture, all the good and the bad, I wouldn't have missed it for a second.

Luke is now a very successful actor and Craig is a successful manager. However, I can't help thinking it would be such a laugh, such a great day to jump up on stage once more. We have been offered big, big money for a one-off reunion show. People were talking about a huge outdoor show which would make for a great summer's day. I've only felt like this since I came back to the UK in 2003; before that the prospect of a reunion was horrifying, too scary. But with the way that the British public *and* press have reacted to me and treated me, the idea of a reunion is now very tempting. I am only doing two or three Bros numbers in my shows out of a live set of twelve or so and the reaction is manic, so the thought of doing an entire set is very exciting.

I know Luke is probably more reserved about the idea; he has, after all, worked very hard carving himself out a very successful career as an actor. However, I meet a lot of drummers in my job and they say they can't understand how Luke cannot get on a kit and just smash away for a couple of hours – knowing he is a successful actor and he can go back to that life tomorrow.

The funny thing is, Luke and I had a mini-reunion all to ourselves in LA in 2001! The two of us, along with my friend Michael Guzman (who came to England with his wife and Daisy that time), were working out in a gym called Crunch in the city. Underneath this gym there is a music shop called Sam Ash, so after we'd freshened up we headed down there to check out a few instruments and generally browse around. Much to our delight, they had a soundproofed room with a drum kit set up ready to go. I looked at Luke and Luke looked at me, we exchanged a knowing nod and I went off to find a guitar.

We started jamming and it was magical. It felt really lovely, totally natural, a seamless fit. The hilarious thing is, I don't think Michael realized that this was the first time Luke and I had played together since Bros! He was sitting there tapping his feet, enjoying himself then suddenly he jumped up, grabbed the microphone and started screaming this absolutely awful rendition of a Prince rap over the music, he kept going, 'RRRReeally, RRRReeally!' It was just terrible. We were laughing so much, it was hard to continue playing – bloody awful he was.

Afterwards, Lukie and I gave each other a hug and it was a lovely, private little moment with each other. But it felt really powerful too: when Luke and I are together there is something really amazing going on. Although it very rarely happens any more, even walking down the street with my brother is an amazing experience, people react so positively to us. There is tremendous energy and this invincible vibe when we are together. I get a massive kick out of that.

I love being the Goss twins, it's brilliant. Fucking brilliant.

I have shared so much of my life with you over the course of this book. I've invited you deep into my psyche and have been as brutally honest as I can be, at times with painful consequences. You might think, looking at the difficulties I have had, that I could look back and wish I'd become a hair-dresser or vet after all.

No way.

I wouldn't have swapped all this for the world.

I adore making music, it is so vital to my well-being. On a more superficial level, I'll be honest with you, I also love fame. I don't like to hear celebrities complaining about fame being a burden. Of course, it has its negative moments, I can person-ally testify to that and probably more so than most famous

283

people, but being well-known is something to enjoy, to savour. Yes, occasionally you have to move to another restaurant because you are getting bothered but so what? Being famous helps. The good far, *far* outweighs the bad.

I have had a great time.

The press have been good to me for a while now. Yes, they built me up, I was in one of the biggest bands in the world, then they knocked me down, further than the ground, I was in a shallow-grave situation. I could barely breathe, genuinely. For two young men to have had that much wind knocked out of them and then to stand up and stay in the entertainment industry and not be beaten, through sheer will-power and the love of what we do, is a fantastic achievement. I am very proud of myself and I am very proud of Luke.

I'd love to be considered one of the quintessential British men who hasn't given up, has seen the world and is strong, healthy and with plenty of fight left in him. Maybe after reading my story, you might agree.

Afterword: Finished? . . . No, Work In Progress

I am sitting in the back of a blacked-out people-carrier which has pulled up at a service station. It is mid-September 2004 and the chill midnight air suggests that a hard winter is on its way. My driver Joe has filled up and comes back from the tills with a blanket to keep me warm in the back. I have just played to a sell-out crowd of 3000 people and am heading back to my apartment in Knightsbridge. I look across the forecourt and I see Tony and my mum sitting in their car, starting their engine having also filled up. They both look tired and travel-weary but enlivened by the night's show. Tony yawns. He has another four hours driving until he and Mum can lay their heads on their own pillow.

Sometimes I look at them and I ache. This is one of those moments. Over so many years, they have been there for me, done so many special things for me and I will never take that for granted. I know implicitly that they will do anything for Luke, Adam and me. They are the two most selfless people I've ever met. It is a privilege to be around them.

I look at them again and a surge of energy wells up in me. They are my main motivation in life, to make sure that I can create enough wealth and happiness so that they don't have to worry for the rest of their lives, to make them safe. I try to look after them as best I can and I think I do an okay job, as a son.

I am surrounded by people like this, people who care for me and want to see me do well. There have been times when I felt lonelier than any man on earth; God knows there have been the dark days. It is annoying how painful my life has been at times.

But I've hung in there.

I just don't know how to give in. I have pulled myself back from the abyss, when I was financially, emotionally and mentally bereft, and on more than one occasion. I went from having nothing to having nice things around me again, from being berated on a daily basis to being feted and lauded once more. I am very fortunate to still enjoy the luxury of being able to release records and sing them live to audiences who want to hear what I have to say. That anxiety before I came back to England has almost dissipated. I've started to feel so much optimism in my heart again and, dare I say it, the fear is slowly leaving my body.

It finally feels good to be Matt Goss. For the first time I really like being me. I have a good life, I feel comfortable in these shoes.

I can't retire, ever.

I *need* to keep working, not for financial gain, not for my ego to be massaged or to see the world. I've done that. I need to be immersed in music, always. This is what I do.

And I am only just beginning.

I am a blessed man.

Index

Index

Index

Index